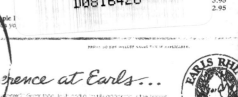

Menu

People keep asking "What is my secret?" Great food, fresh, and a no frills approach, is the honest answer. To keep prices low eat a little, eat a lot philosophy means you are eating the best for less. Garnishes, bread & butter & then omitted so that fresh, daily prepared meats, chicken, fish & vegetables are served deliciously at unbelievable prices.

That's the difference at Earls...

Eat a lot · Fun to Share

French Style Onion Rings	2.95
Thinly cut, crisp, lightly seasoned	
Fresh Herbed Italian Pan Bread	1.50
w/extra virgin olive oil	
Grilled Garlic Italian Pan Bread	1.95
Cheese Bread	2.95
Homecut Fries	1.95
– with gravy	2.25
– with peppercorn sauce	2.50
Fresh Herbed Crust Pizza	4.95

Fresh Made Soups & Salads

We Make Our Soups From Scratch

Earl's House Salad	3.95
Seasonal greens, romaine lettuce, tomato and cucumber tossed with Earl's personally selected balsamic vinegar and virgin olive oil	
Thai Chicken Salad	7.95
Thai dressing, chopped mint & cilantro over romaine, fresh steamed noodles & peanuts, with herbed lime chicken	
Acapulco Chicken Salad	6.95
w/sour cream & cilantro salsa	
Caesar Salad	3.95
w/Italian Grana Padano Parmesan	
Entree Size w/garlic bread	6.95
Hot Chicken Caesar	6.95
Blackened Chicken Caesar	6.95
Lots of Clams Chowder	3.50
Classic French Onion Soup	3.50

Fresh West Coast Salmon

Earl has this philosophy

Earl wanted to make Earl's different, so he built Earl's simple philosophy of great food, served fresh, without a lot of frills has never been compromised to this fast-pace time of short cuts, Earl has never changed his high standard of delicious, wholesome food prepared fresh daily.

That's the difference at Earl's

Eat a little Eat a lot

DRY RIBS	4.95
Fried until crispy and seasoned with coarse salt and pepper	
CHEDDAR AND BACON POTATO SKINS	4.95
Aged cheddar and hickory smoked bacon	
MONTEREY BAY CALAMARI	4.95
SALSA AND TORTILLA CHIPS	3.50
SALSA NACHOS	6.95
GUACAMOLE NACHOS	
GUACAMOLE & SALSA NACHOS	6.95
CHICKEN BURRITO	3.95
CHICKEN FINGERS	4.95
THUMBS UP	4.50
CHICKEN WINGS	3.50
FRENCH STYLE ONION RINGS	2.95
ITALIAN PAN BREAD	1.50
GARLIC BREAD	1.95
CHEESE BREAD	2.95
FRESH HOMECUT FRIES	1.75
with gravy	1.95

Soups and Salads

HOT CHICKEN CAESAR	6.95
BLACKENED CHICKEN CAESAR	6.95
THAI CHICKEN SALAD	7.95
ACAPULCO CHICKEN SALAD	6.95
CAESAR SALAD	3.95
EARL'S HOUSE SALAD	3.95

Entrées

Choice Grain Fed Lean, 28-day Aged Beef

	Market Price
Fresh West Coast Salmon w/garlic bread	9.95
Steak & Prawns	13.95
New York Steak	12.95
New York w/Madagascar peppercorn sauce	13.95
Blackened New York	13.95
Grilled Teriyaki Chicken Breast	9.95
Teriyaki Chicken & Prawns	13.95
Blackened Cajun Chicken	9.95
Charbroiled Chicken w/hickory B.B.Q. sauce	9.95
Rack of B.B.Q. Pork Ribs	14.95
1/2 Rack of B.B.Q. Pork Ribs	10.95
B.B.Q. Chicken & Ribs	14.95

Bigger, Better Burgers

Bigger Better Burger	5.95
w/ripe beefsteak tomato, lettuce, onion, mayonnaise, mustard & pickle	
Cheddar Burger	6.50
Bacon Cheddar Burger	6.95
Jack Burger	6.50
Bacon Jack Burger	6.95
Mushroom Burger	6.95
Cheddar Chicken Sandwich	6.50
Earl's Uniquely Great Clubhouse	6.95
B.C.L.T.	4.95
Chicken Quesadilla w/cheddar & jalapeno jack cheese (& salad)	6.95

Fresh Herbed Crust Pizza

Made Right Here With Pride

Earl uses ripe roma tomatoes, fresh basil, and aged Parmesan and Fontina Cheeses on his thin crispy herbed crust pizza. 4.95

Fresh Daily Desserts

Fresh Made From Our Own Kitchen

Fresh Baked Pecan Flan	3.50
Guittard Chocolate Pecan Flan	3.95
Frozen Yogurt Shakes	2.95
blackberry, raspberry, strawberry, chocolate, or vanilla	

Gourmet Blend Cappuccinos & Lattes

Menu

People keep asking "What is my secret?" Great food, fresh, and a no frills approach, is the honest answer. To eat a little, eat a lot philosophy means you are eating the best for less. Garnishes, bread & butter & then omitted so that fresh, daily prepared meats, chicken, fish & vegetables are served deliciously at unbelievable prices.

earls

THE COOKBOOK

EAT A LITTLE. EAT A LOT. 110 OF YOUR FAVOURITE RECIPES

appetite
by RANDOM HOUSE

Appetite by Random House® and colophon are registered trademarks of Penguin Random House LLC.

Library and Archives of Canada Cataloguing in Publication is available upon request.

ISBN: 9780147530073
eBook ISBN: 9780147530080

Photography by John Sherlock with additional images by David Strongman and Clinton Hussey
Photo on page 32 © Velychko/Shutterstock.com
Photo on page i: Jasper Avenue, Edmonton 2012
Recipe testing by Fay Duong
Project managed by Cate Simpson
Book design by Terri Nimmo
Printed and bound in China

Published in Canada by Appetite by Random House®, a division of Penguin Random House Canada Limited

www.penguinrandomhouse.ca

10 9 8 7 6 5 4 3 2

appetite
by RANDOM HOUSE

Penguin
Random
House

contents

list of recipes

EARL'S fresh food RESTAURANT

MAYBE NEXT TIME MERLOT
THE MISSING MALBEC
POSTPONED PINOT
MORE 2 COME MALBEC
PROBABLY NOT PINOT NOIR
COMING SOON

foreword

A cookbook, how about that? As the co-founders of Earls, we're delighted to be able to share all of these wonderful recipes with you. And we're happy to see so many stories from our first thirty-four years, as well as surprised that they're so interesting... we thought we ran a pretty tight ship!

It's clear how lucky we've been to be surrounded by so many remarkable people along the way, so if we regret anything, it's that between these covers there was room to feature so few. Every Earls is an intricate symphony of cleaners, dishwashers, bussers, cooks, hosts, servers, bartenders, chefs, managers and more, and the customer experience is entirely dependent on each of them. We have around seven thousand employees, and it's possible that as many as a hundred thousand people have worked with us since we started in 1982. Please know that if you are one of those people, your contribution is very much appreciated.

And then there's this book. Our thanks to the team behind it for the detailed recipes, the beautiful pictures, and the words, however fantastical. It's been a slice, and we think that's well reflected. Now, let's eat.

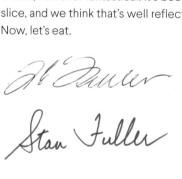

Bus and Stan Fuller
Vancouver, 2016

Left to right: Jeff Fuller, Stewart Fuller, Clay Fuller,
Leroy (Bus) Earl Fuller, Stanley Earl Fuller

our story

As this cookbook is being written, Leroy Earl "Bus" Fuller is eighty-seven, looks sixty-seven, and with his gnarly beard, high-tops and red pants, dresses twenty-seven. He's sitting on his back deck listening to some of the tall stories that others have been telling about him and dismissing them as lucky accidents of day-to-day existence. Bus is a born pragmatist who's so matter-of-fact about food, business and life that other people apparently feel compelled to embroider and philosophize on his behalf.

That's something to keep in mind as you read the story of Earls, the restaurant empire that Bus and his sons and colleagues have built over the last thirty-five years. Was there near-cosmic insight involved in seeking out family wineries and craft brewers back in the 1980s? Journeying to France and Italy to stuff suitcases full of sausage and cheese in the same decade? Recognizing around the same time that those Asian cultures are also on to something pretty delicious? Agreeing on the virtues of fresh, local and seasonal in the early 1990s? Seeking out farmers and ranchers who could supply the quality and freshness of meat and vegetables necessary to follow through? Hiring Iron Chefs, molecularists and farm-to-table enthusiasts alike in the 2000s?

Or alternatively, as Bus would have it—if he'll have it at all—maybe all of these things just happened because someone gave them a shot, and customers proved to like them, so they stuck.

In this book we've tried to keep to the middle ground, retelling those stories but also angling toward the Bus point of view, which we've taken as having something to do with the randomness of life and the natural inclination of people to try to do the right thing and to have fun and better themselves while doing it.

Which, roughly speaking, is how Bus landed in the restaurant business in the first place. Although born in Cincinnati, he grew up in Montana, and in 1954 was employed as a machinist at a refinery in tiny Sunburst, near the Alberta border, when he and his first wife decided to open a restaurant. Three years later, when he applied for an A&W franchise, the closest one available was in Edmonton, Alberta. Well, drive-ins did well in the 1950s, as maybe you've heard, especially in boom towns like Edmonton. Soon Bus was operating several A&Ws there, and before long he bought a territory in British Columbia, moving the family to Vancouver in 1968. Through the 1970s he continued to pick up territories and also branched out with a sit-down chain, known as Fuller's. By the early 1980s he'd converted his holdings into a public company called Controlled Foods that operated well over one hundred restaurants.

Alas, says Bus, Controlled Foods should have been called Confused Foods—the company was home to mostly run-of-the-mill restaurants; places where the servers only cared about their tips and the cooks were just counting the minutes to their smoke break. Just as bad, the early 1980s were dark days in western Canada,

George Piper and Stan Fuller

which was in recession. Bus had a failed Fuller's location in Edmonton that needed to be reopened, but how? Well, he reasoned, the times might be right for a new kind of place, one built around the simple and time-proven—and even more importantly, inexpensive—concept of burgers.

Bus's four boys had reached various levels of maturity, and the oldest, Stanley Earl, was also involved in the new business as co-founder. Between Leroy Earl and Stanley Earl, Earls seemed an apt name for the spot. Meanwhile, Bus couldn't help but notice that the four boys and their young friends all shared a taste for beer. He further reasoned that the legal drinking age had recently been dropped to 18; that dank beverage rooms and fancy restaurants shouldn't be the only place to get a drink; and that beer and wine might well be an important part of the Earls mix, along with the incredibly exotic concept of outdoor patios. And heck, why not furnish the inside with patio furniture, too? It would be way cheaper and would further the casual vibe.

And what do you know, the new restaurant proved to be pretty much an instant success—success being a

metric that to Bus is most accurately measured in dollars. Six months after it opened, our first location was bringing in lots of those, and the family would have rushed to open more except that they were strapped for cash. Fortunately, right about then, a buyer appeared for Controlled Foods, and a deal was happily transacted.

New Earls locations were quickly opened in Calgary and around Metro Vancouver, then throughout western Canada, a rapid expansion that was aided and abetted by a cast of characters led by Bus's four sons.

Stan is the quietest but also the oldest, and a classically responsible type who was washing dishes and bussing tables since the age of twelve. Naturally enough, he'd end up running us, stepping aside as president only in 2013 and remaining CEO today. (Bus, need we add, is chairman.) But when we launched in 1982, Stan was still in his twenties and just back from a sabbatical backpacking through South America, Europe and Asia. During that trip he developed a taste for spicy street food and smelly cheeses that would have a profound effect on our menus.

There is Clay, the son who in many ways is most like his dad. He has worked on lots of Earls projects, from Saskatoon to San Francisco, many of them with a design or wine connection.

Stewart is as comfortable in the kitchen as in the office, and while running an Earls location in San Francisco, he embraced the emerging Californian taste for light, simple preparations of the freshest and most local ingredients. Later he'd launch his own Alberta chainlet, Saltlik, but before that he served as our head development chef, making him one of only two Fullers with recipes in this book.

And there's Jeff, who quickly worked his way up through our ranks before leaving to become one of our fiercest competitors (backstopped by Bus, of course) with a chain of his own, now called Joey, that we have no opinion of whatsoever.

So those are the Fuller boys. The four are exceptionally competitive but get along just fine, swears Stan. That is, as long as none of them has to answer to another.

Equally high up on the playbill were our long-term chief development chefs, including two who were there from the earliest days. Between them, Vancouver-based Chuck Currie and Alberta-based Larry Stewart devised or perfected almost every dish that we served well into the 1990s.

Chuck was already with us at Controlled Foods in 1982 and was thrilled to take on the challenge of launching this new kind of restaurant, staying on long enough to see us into the new millennium. He is your basic force of nature, a multi-talented writer and musician (with a house painted in polka dots) who talked without pause, worked sixteen-hour stretches without flagging, chain-sipped bourbon without apparent effect, and brought to our kitchens both his intense creativity and an innate understanding of systems.

Larry, who joined in 1984 and was with us for a decade, came from the world of progressive fine dining and brought with him sophisticated techniques and a nuanced palate—attributes that contributed to our early ability to surprise our guests with an unexpected depth and range of flavours and that are still much in evidence in his long-standing Edmonton restaurant, the Hardware Grill.

After Larry left in 1994, Stew Fuller joined Chuck in the corporate kitchen. With fifty locations and some five hundred recipes, there was plenty of work for both of them, and for our new regional chefs too. That position—unique, we think, to the company—helped ensure a constant flow of information to individual locations, so that local head chefs and their kitchen staff always had a good idea of what was going on in Vancouver, and vice versa.

The years after the turn of the millennium were a lively time in Vancouver, where we're based, with an explosion of independent restaurants run by exciting young chefs (a bunch of whom got their start with us), together with an atmosphere of community and collaboration that was the very antithesis of the restaurant business as once carried on. We welcomed all of this and opened our kitchen doors to both the attitude and the exciting new food culture that came along with it. Come to think of it, we also invited in a lot of the chefs themselves. Local stars David Hawksworth, Rebecca Dawson, Scott Jaeger, Michael Noble (by then living in Calgary), Karen Lyons, Alberto Lemo, Adam Pegg, Alym Hirji and Reuben Major were just a few of those who have worked with or for us over the past decade or so, and most have recipes in this book.

The early 2000s also gave us a new head development chef, Mo Jessa. Mo had first seen the inside of an Earls kitchen in 1988 as a twenty-two-year-old, working a summer job alongside his twin brother, Al. The two caught the eye of Larry Stewart, who helped convince them that their futures might lie over a hot grill. In short order the two rose through the ranks almost exactly in tandem: as sous-chefs, chefs and then holding the new positions of regional chef. By the time Mo had taken over our top chef job, Al had shifted over to Joey, where he occupied the same post.

Mo moved out of the kitchen and became our president in 2013, and since then we've headed even further in the direction of collaboration, eliminating the post of chief development chef in favour of a group approach that we call the Chef Collective. At any given time, four to eight people split the duties in the test kitchen, which means more experience, more influences and more potential dishes for the menu. Chefs like Dawn Doucette (who happens to be Clay's daughter), Hamid Salimian, David Wong, Ryan Stone, Brian Skinner and the late Tina Fineza couldn't have more diverse approaches, and that goes double for their recipes. Between them, kitchen stops have included Noma and the Zuni Café and gold medals in a multitude of international chef competitions. Plus we still have the spiritual descendants of Chuck Currie, who have to balance creativity with figuring out how to get food out there correctly and quickly: people like executive chefs Phil Gallagher and Delane Diseko, as well as the brigade of regional chefs and kitchen stars from Whistler to Miami.

Obviously, our chefs have been crucial in devising and delivering the kind of food we're known for—but a huge chunk of the credit also has to go to our purchasing manager, George Piper, who is now semi-retired after almost forty years of working with Bus, but remains our director of wine experiences.

Food, no matter how it's prepared, is only as good as the ingredients that go into it, and that's where George came in. In an industry where suppliers and restaurants often treat each other as adversaries, he was the guy who kept thinking, "Why can't we all get along?" George liked to sign up suppliers for the long term and would move heaven and earth to find what the chefs were looking for. No surprise that we were among the first restaurants to develop supply lines for our vegetables in low-volume growing regions like the Okanagan, and

to contract with a single Alberta ranch—certified humane, no added hormones and antibiotic-free—for our beef. In recent years, we've been opening lots of restaurants in the US and following exactly the same strategy there.

George also developed our wine program, and alongside Andrew Wilton, our CFO at the time, spearheaded our shockingly early embrace of craft brews. Both were keen home brewers who believed that, like so many other things, beer is best fresh, as draft. That led to the debut of our Albino Rhino beer, now called Rhino Craft.

Over on the wine side, George found that our family-run business had a natural affinity with family-run wineries, which helps explain the long-term relationships we've enjoyed with the Perrins of France, the Kendall-Jacksons in California, Wolf Blass in Australia, and the Stewart family's Quail's Gate in British Columbia. Early on he shifted us to a system of listing our wine by flavour, intensity and food matches rather than country or varietal. And most recently, he gave us the grape equivalent of draft beer, with a unique new keg-like system that prevents oxygen from coming into contact

Bus Fuller

with wine like no other method. We're now a much bigger and more ambitious restaurant chain, but we have an even tighter focus on the ingredients that go onto the plate and into the glass.

There was another key contributor, David Vance, our chief designer and much more. When that first Earls opened in Edmonton, George got hold of a bunch of papier-mâché parrots to dress up what would otherwise have been a pretty plain room. When David came along a couple of years later, he might have rejected the birds as being a little jejune (designers, right?), but instead he recognized that they had become an important part of the brand, as they continued to be for the next twenty-five years. Moreover, they added a touch of youthful insouciance to his interiors, which were open, airy and always tailored to the space and location.

Quite a cast, and it's not hard to imagine what sometimes went on in the green room. Between the brothers' competitiveness, the chefs' desire to show off their culinary chops, George's command of wine, beer and food ingredients, and David's sophisticated eye, palate and sensibility . . . well, you can imagine. Add to that Bus's early recognition that the fatal problem with simple but profitable is that anyone can copy it, and it was almost instantly obvious that we had to push beyond those humble beginnings in burgers and beer.

During our first year the menu gradually expanded from the original sixteen items to a more standard twenty-three—even if, admittedly, ten of them were burger variations. Then, two or three years in, things really began to accelerate. Before our first decade was complete, the menu had increased to around sixty items, many of them cycling in and out from a roster that totalled about two hundred recipes. As well, a kind of mission statement emerged, one that was years ahead of its time: "Earl celebrates the seasons, the earth, the garden and the simple combinations that go together naturally. Earl selects unbelievably high quality ingredients and treats them with ultimate respect. Earl plates food with the natural wow appeal of its integral ingredients. He likes a no-frills approach. Everything on the plate has inherent value."

Of course, penning a highfalutin food philosophy is easy; following through on it at a burger joint, even one with aspirations, not so much. But follow through we tried very hard to do, as illustrated by the lengths that

Stan Fuller

Chuck Currie, George Piper and Stew Fuller went to in their quest to perfect the humble french fry. As Chuck explained in a summary of the odyssey that he later put to paper, you need a high-solids, high-starch, low-sugar potato to make a great french fry. Meanwhile, neither new potatoes nor potatoes that have been stored for a long time work well. So simply buying potatoes and chopping them up, as we did at first, wasn't optimal. You really need a committed supplier.

But finding someone to deliver the correct variety of potato, grown properly and used at the proper stage of maturity, didn't completely solve the problem either. The big potato suppliers strive for uniformity. They blanch out the natural sugars then spray with liquid sugar to add back sweetness and colour. To the guys, this did not represent "ultimate respect," nor did it produce the kind of french fry they wanted to serve. So they spent two years travelling down to Idaho potato country, eventually finding a supplier with the right kind of potatoes, then working with them to eliminate all of the industrial shenanigans. The company only agreed to supply the potatoes the way Chuck wanted them after he cooked up competing batches for Idaho's spud mavens to sample, then watched as the mottled-looking unprocessed ones were the first to be eaten. (Incidentally, from our inception till now, this type of side-by-side test where slightly different versions of the same dish are sampled by a large group of tasters has been the final arbiter of what goes on an Earls menu.)

So, let the record also show that we cared a lot—and that, come to think of it, we really did have a way with words. "Eat a little, eat a lot," was another early coinage, credited to Stan, and once again there was nothing empty about the phrase. In fact, it helped introduce the concept of grazing. It's hard to imagine now, but not so long ago a meal for most people came only in the form of sitting down with a big plate of food. Someone might have a between-meals "snack"—like a bag of chips or a candy bar—but not many people would pop into a restaurant to have a drink and share a plate of calamari, then have another drink, splitting another small plate or two, ultimately maybe skipping the old "meal" thing completely. This new way of dining was facilitated by a menu that quickly grew heavier on sides and appetizers— and represented yet another way that we helped invent the contemporary casual restaurant.

Then there was Stew's "Global Skillet," which captured our willingness to draw from food cultures all over the planet rather than concentrating on a single theme. The Mediterranean was our first focus, with the aforementioned calamari that showed up on one of our very first menus, while pastas soon followed. The Italian bent accelerated after we started installing forno ovens in all our locations later on in the 1980s. That meant thin-crust, wood-fired pizzas, of course, a startling departure from the cheesy pies available elsewhere. But those ovens were big and, with a cooking temperature of up to 600 degrees, very fast. What else were you going to put in them? Well, we certainly roasted vegetables à la the Med, but another of the many solutions was a surprisingly authentic chicken tandoori. Even before the 1980s were out, our menu was home to dishes from more than a dozen countries in Asia and Latin America, not to mention Europe. In the past couple of years, dishes like Korean bibimbap and a fattoush salad from the Middle East have been popular additions. In fact, on our current menus, maybe half of the items would have sparked the question, "What the hell is that?" when we first opened.

Now, a person might think that finding recipes originating in all those places would be a simple case of checking out cookbooks, visiting ethnic restaurants and so on. Because no restaurant chain would send teams numbering into the dozens to the four corners of the earth, and do this on a regular basis. That would be insanity, right?

Well, yes, sometimes insanity did ensue, but travelling like that is something we've always done. We call our seemingly obsessive journeying "inspiration trips," and they're yet another crucial part of the company culture. Maybe Stan's pre-launch travels had something to do with it, but in truth George and Stew have generally been the chief tour leaders. For George the impetus stemmed from his love of wine and beer and the need to find the right kind of suppliers. George started out by taking a handful of people along with him to spots like the Bordeaux region, and what do you know, his companions proved to really enjoy their visits to some of the great châteaux. Before long there were tours to slightly less heralded but equally interesting places, like Spain and Portugal, then Chile and Argentina. Sometimes there would be three or four people on the trip; sometimes dozens.

Stew, meanwhile, had his California experiences to draw from, and the US southwest was certainly a popular destination. But he and companions tracked down recipes and ingredients pretty much everywhere else too, because it's a big world out there, and we want to be a big part of it.

"Fresh Food Fresh" doesn't sound so radical today, but the claim couldn't have been made by any other chain in the early 1990s. From our earliest days we rejected the frozen portions that so much of the industry was moving toward, but Stew can take a lot of the credit for our dramatic shift toward fresh, local and seasonal right about the time that the most chef-driven restaurants also began to think along those lines.

Meanwhile, coming up with the phrase "Great food, Great people!" probably doesn't rank as the most ultra-creative moment in the company's history, but there's a surprising amount of meaning hidden within. Great food? Well, sure. That's why you're reading the cookbook. Great people? They're just as important.

Most obviously, right from that first location, Earls became a place where people liked to hang out, especially people in their twenties and thirties. Partly it was that western Canada didn't have a lot of great bars; partly it's that we came along at a time when not

Clay Fuller, Stan Fuller and Bus Fuller

everyone wanted to be in a bar; partly it's that we put out a pretty warm welcome. And maybe we're biased, but we think we've always attracted an interesting crowd. Many of the players on the great Edmonton Oilers dynasty teams of the 1980s were regulars at our Tin Palace location there, and the Great One even borrowed one of our phones to call Los Angeles and propose to Janet Jones!

But the other side of the people story revolves around the amazing folks who work with us. Back in 1982, one of our co-founders stipulated that Earls would never hire anyone older than he was. Fortunately, Stan wouldn't remain twenty-nine forever. But it's nevertheless true that our business has always been built on giving young people a chance to develop themselves, whether it's the eighteen-year-old in the kitchen who by week two is turning out dishes that would pass muster at a fine dining establishment, or the server who surprises with their understanding of the food and the glass of wine or beer that will make it taste even better.

Most of those young people will not stay with us forever, so they will need to be replaced by the next cohort, which is why we invest so much in training. Why too, the company philosophy is that all of our employees own their job, with support available when it's needed, but encouragement always to find their own way forward, within the context of a team. History shows that the training and experience picked up with us have stood those who've worked here in good stead, whatever they've moved on to doing.

Good memories are a good thing, of course, but at the same time we have a strong preference for promoting managers from within the company, which ensures there are opportunities for those who do want to stay, like the Jessas. Meanwhile, those inspiration trips may be crucial to developing the menu, but they're also aspiration trips for the dozens of employees who take part, and for their fellow employees back home who hear all about it later. Maybe we're getting a little corporate-speak here, but talk to Mo Jessa or one of the Fuller boys, and they'll insist that Earls is a people development company that happens to run a bunch of restaurants.

So there's still a cast of characters at Earls—a whole lot more of them, in fact, as befits a company that's grown so large, so quickly. We just keep adding locations, you see, especially in eastern Canada and the US, which have only recently begun to discover what western Canadians have known for more than three decades. As Bus might say—if he'll say anything at all—feed people well, give them a good time, and the rest will take care of itself.

Earls, Saskatoon

we are earls

Why an Earls cookbook?

Well, lots of reasons, but let's start with the day one of our guests sent us a copycat recipe. She was curious to know how close she was. (She actually missed only two ingredients.) We wondered if any of our other recipes had been copied, so we idly decided to google "Earls restaurant recipes."

Whoa! Thousands of hits, some of them from various chefs of ours, but lots of others concocted by home cooks and accompanied by disclaimers including:

Here's my version of . . .

I have absolutely no idea if this recipe is anywhere close to the actual recipe for . . .

While this isn't an exact copy of . . .

Now to figure out how to make . . .

There must have been thousands, more or less, of our not-quite-correct recipes online.

A lot of those kitchen sleuths did a really good job of duplicating our recipes, and they may even have had fun doing it, but it was nonetheless a bit of an eye opener for us. In the almost thirty-five years since Bus and Stan Fuller opened the first Earls, people wouldn't have kept coming back in, and one restaurant wouldn't have grown to sixty-seven (at last count), if they didn't love the food. So is it that much of a surprise that they would go home and try to replicate our dishes?

Well, no. What did surprise us, after we spent a moment thinking about it, is how difficult we'd been making it for them. There was a time when chefs jealously guarded their secrets, but we grew out of that

way of thinking a quarter century ago, and it's safe to say that, especially over the past decade, the rest of the industry has, too. Yet here we were, people who try hard to be the nice guys and gals of the restaurant world, neglecting to share.

So, two things. Sorry. And boy, did we try extra hard to make it up to you with this book.

Here are a few of the things you are going to find between these covers.

The epic tale of how the Fuller family and a core staff with names like Chuck, Larry, George and Mo launched a restaurant, and then a chain of restaurants that, no exaggeration, helped change the way people eat. And incidentally, when we use the word "epic," it's not in the way that it would have been used back then, to describe a momentous military battle. No, it's more in the contemporary "epic kegger" sense, in which a bunch of people run around doing often crazy things, and the next day no one can agree on what happened, but everyone's glad to have been a part of it.

And the recipes! After chief wrangler Cate Simpson, together with Mo Jessa and Stew Fuller, wrestled it down to four hundred recipes, we tested hundreds before we chose more than one hundred of them, carefully calibrated for the home kitchen. Earls test kitchen veteran Fay Duong spent months remaking them all in her own home to ensure that they will perform as well in your smallish kitchen as they do in our very large ones. Then another test kitchen vet, Dawn Doucette, remade most of them all over again to be photographed so beautifully by John Sherlock, who normally shoots just fancy food. These recipes work.

These recipes also span the decades. We knew from that googling thing, and also from the requests we get, that some of our very oldest recipes absolutely had to be included. Many of those have the additional virtue of being simple to make while using ingredients found in most cupboards and every supermarket. Those originals are joined by dishes from every decade of our existence, including a few very recent ones that might not be found anywhere except at our downtown Vancouver or Calgary flagship locations. The recipes are laid out in chapters that more or less follow our restaurant menu, beginning with Starters and ending with Desserts (with a few extras, like Brunch, and Pantry Items).

We think you'll find it fascinating to watch the parade of dishes go by, organized as they are by the decade they were introduced. Earls has never been the kind of restaurant chain that rests on its laurels, believing that if something appealed to people a generation ago, it still will today. None, we think that food trends are interesting, important and generally delicious. We've always kept a close eye on the culinary world, reasoning that although great chefs and tastemakers might stumble

now and then, they'll mostly come up with dishes that are worth checking out. So pretty much every major trend in the last four decades is represented: nouvelle cuisine, southwestern, pasta, California, West Coast, Asian fusion, Mexican, Middle Eastern, vegetarian, molecularist, locavore. We may have missed a few, but the point is, you could run down to the vintage store and buy some clothes and accoutrements, then go back home and throw a 1991 or 2006 dinner, seasonally appropriate even, just from this book. Moreover, the food will be terrific.

Being the kind of restaurant that wants to show people a good time, we also understand that some of you like a drink now and then, and since our beer, wine and cocktails have always been top-notch, those crucial subjects also generated a few words, many of them devoted to our classic recipes. Our advice is to find one of those first, then sip the result as you read all the others.

As perhaps you're beginning to see, in envisioning this cookbook we imagined it as being a lot like a great night out at Earls: the food, the drinks, the fun. True, it's only a book, so we had to start the conversation. But you can take it from here.

Earls, Washington, DC

EARLS WING WEDNESDAY REALLY FLIES

$2.99 FOR A POUND OF EARLS SCREAMIN' HOT WINGS EVERY WEDNESDAY ALL DAY.

earls

Great wing wednesdays. Great people.

starters, share plates and sides

We completely understand the virtue of humility, but gosh, it's hard to be modest when the conversation turns to the appetizers we've helped turn into restaurant staples— dishes such as, for example, dry ribs.

These can be found at all kinds of places nowadays, but the dish could have disappeared into the mists of gustatory history if not for Leroy Fuller himself. Bus is a long-time devotee of Vancouver's Chinatown, and during our early days he spoke longingly—and often—of a dish that he used to find in restaurants there but couldn't seem to anymore, a delicacy he knew as dry ribs. Development Chef Chuck Currie realized that it was his job to get such a creation onto the Earls menu, if for no other reason than that the boss wanted to eat them. And sure enough, he did eventually come up with a Chinese-inspired version using standard pork back ribs. Bus tolerated them, but stuck to his guns that they were nothing like the dry ribs of his memories . . . .

Then one day Chuck remembered an accidental encounter with a product called "button bones" or "tail section," which he'd received by mistake instead of the back ribs he'd asked for. Thinking he might be on to something, he hunted down a single box of the things, seasoned them with salt and pepper, threw them in the deep fryer, and then sprinkled them with pepper and coarse salt all over again. When he served them, Bus's eyes lit up. Dry ribs at last! The assembled crew consumed the entire box that night, along with plenty of beers. Leroy's Dry Ribs the dish quickly found its way onto our menu (and subsequently others) and this cut of pork, once all but impossible to find, is now widely available.

JACK STICKS

1980s 1990s 2000s 2010s

SERVES 4–6

1 lb (450 g) Jalapeño Jack cheese (whole block)

⅔ cup (160 mL) milk

½ cup (125 mL) all-purpose flour

¾ tsp (3.75 mL) baking powder

¼ tsp (1.25 mL) fine salt

2 cups (500 mL) Japanese bread crumbs (or panko)

Vegetable oil for frying

Salsa (page 241)

After Chuck perfected the intricate balance of cheese, panko breading and cooking technique that netted these specimens of gooey-good yet tidily eaten finger food, we wondered what to call them. They were similar to chicken fingers, we reasoned, so how about "cheese thumbs"? A cheese thumb—who wouldn't want one of those? Well, cheese thumbs sat on the menu all but unordered. A few weeks later someone slyly changed the name to "jack sticks," and a star was born.

1. Cut the block of Jalapeño Jack cheese into 3½- × ½- × ½-inch (9 × 1 × 1 cm) strips.
2. In a large shallow bowl, mix together the milk, flour, baking powder and salt. Place the Japanese bread crumbs into a pie plate or shallow container.
3. Dip the cheese strips into the batter, allow excess batter to drip away, then transfer into the bread crumbs. Knock off any excess crumbs, then return to the batter, then again into the bread crumbs. Transfer to a parchment-lined baking tray. Repeat with the remaining cheese strips. Place in the refrigerator to set for at least 2 hours.
4. Preheat a deep fryer or a large Dutch oven half full of vegetable oil to 375°F (190°C). Fry the Jack sticks for 45 seconds to 1 minute until light golden brown. Drain on clean paper towels. Serve immediately with salsa.

Any semi-hard cheese can be used in place of the Jalapeño Jack. Cheddar, Edam, fontina, havarti and Gouda are all cheeses that will melt very well after frying.

SPINACH ARTICHOKE DIP

Looking back through our early menus we're reminded how wonderful it was to not have a worry in the world—like, for example, about calories. But then there's this worthy Chuck Currie standard, which while not precisely spartan, does feature an actual vegetable, and one that's fairly good for a person, too. PS: Substitute kale for the spinach, serve with beet chips and hey, it's the twenty-first century.

1980s 1990s 2000s 2010s

SERVES 4–6

8 oz (225 g) cleaned spinach leaves

¼ cup (60 mL) finely diced white onion

Vegetable oil for frying

4 oz (115 g) cream cheese, room temperature

2 cups (500 mL) shredded mozzarella

1 cup (250 mL) finely diced canned artichokes (well drained)

½ cup (125 mL) finely diced water chestnuts

⅓ cup (80 mL) sour cream

⅓ cup (80 mL) mayonnaise

⅓ cup (80 mL) heavy cream

1 tbsp (15 mL) Frank's RedHot sauce

¾ tsp (3.75 mL) minced garlic

¾ tsp (3.75 mL) ground black pepper

¾ tsp (3.75 mL) Worcestershire sauce

½ tsp (2.5 mL) fine salt

½ tsp (2.5 mL) lemon juice

To serve

¼ cup (60 mL) salsa (optional, page 241)

Tortilla chips or grilled bread

1. Place the spinach in a lidded container and microwave for 3 minutes or until wilted. Or you can steam it for 3 to 5 minutes or until it's cooked. Spread out on a plate and allow to cool completely before squeezing the liquid from the spinach. Too much liquid will give you a watery dip. Finely chop the spinach and set aside.

2. Sauté the onions in the vegetable oil until translucent but not browned. Set aside to cool.

3. In a large bowl, mix the cream cheese, mozzarella, artichokes, water chestnuts, sour cream, mayonnaise, cream, Frank's hot sauce, garlic, black pepper, Worcestershire sauce, salt and lemon juice until well combined. Add the chopped spinach and sautéed onion to the mixture. Combine thoroughly. Can be stored in the fridge for up to 2 days.

4. When ready to serve, heat the spinach artichoke dip in a microwave-safe container for 1 minute. Stir well and heat for an additional minute. Top with salsa (if using) and serve immediately with a pile of tortilla chips or grilled bread.

Pre-washed spinach from the salad section of your local grocery store works well here. How finely you dice the ingredients depends on how chunky you like your dip.

GUACAMOLE

In the 1960s, when guacamole enjoyed its first minor American notoriety, it was publicized as a Hawaiian dish, and then in the 1970s it was said to come from Spain. By the 1980s, however, Tex-Mex had become fashionable, and guacamole could come out of the closet as a delicious thing the Aztecs had been making for half a millennium. We've switched up our guacamole recipe three times since introducing it shortly after we opened. This one from Chef Reuben Major is our current version.

1980s 1990s 2000s 2010s

SERVES 4–6

2 ripe avocados, peeled and seeded

½ cup (125 mL) finely diced tomatoes

2 tbsp (30 mL) minced pickled jalapeño slices, or 1 tbsp (15 mL) finely diced jalapeño, seeded

2 tbsp (30 mL) finely chopped green onion

3 tbsp (45 mL) freshly squeezed lime juice

1 tsp (5 mL) minced garlic

½ tsp (2.5 mL) ground cumin

½ tsp (2.5 mL) fine salt

Tortilla chips

1. Mash the avocados to desired consistency, depending on how smooth or chunky you like your guacamole. Fold in the tomatoes, diced jalapeño, green onion, lime juice, garlic, cumin and salt. Make sure all ingredients are well distributed. Serve immediately with fresh tortilla chips.

Hass avocados are a small green-black variety that is creamy and slightly sweet. To find a perfectly ripe avocado, look for thin, smoother skin (not as bumpy) and a stem that falls off easily.

GARLIC BREAD

We're Earls. What did you think? We wouldn't have garlic bread?

SERVES 4–6

4 focaccia pieces (page 24)

4 oz (115 g or ½ cup/125 mL) confit garlic butter, room temperature (page 243)

1. Preheat a nonstick pan over medium heat.
2. Cut the bread into rectangles, approximately 4 × 5 inches (10 × 12 cm). Slice each rectangle in half on a diagonal, creating two triangles. Butter all sides of the focaccia triangles with the confit garlic butter, evenly covering all surfaces.
3. Cook the focaccia on the preheated pan for approximately 1 minute per side until golden brown. Flip on all sides until the bread is warm and toasted and all the cut and buttered sides are golden brown. Serve immediately.

NACHOS

We're Earls. What did you think? We wouldn't have nachos?

1980s **1990s** 2000s 2010s

SERVES 4–6

1 package white corn tortilla chips (12 to 14 oz/350 to 400 g)

1 cup (250 mL) grated cheese (we use a combination of cheddar, jack, and mozzarella)

¼ cup (60 mL) sliced banana peppers

¼ cup (60 mL) finely diced tomatoes

¼ cup (60 mL) finely diced avocado

2 tbsp (30 mL) finely sliced green onions

2 tbsp (30 mL) finely diced red onion

2 tbsp (30 mL) thinly sliced jalapeño, seeded

2 tbsp (30 mL) roughly chopped cilantro leaves

2 tbsp (30 mL) sour cream

¼ cup (60 mL) salsa verde (page 42)

1. Preheat the oven to 400°F (200°C).
2. On a large ovenproof baking tray or 10-inch (25 cm) pizza pan, neatly arrange half the package of tortilla chips in a single layer. Sprinkle ½ cup (125 mL) of cheese evenly over the chips. Place in the oven and bake for 2 minutes, or until the cheese is slightly melted.
3. Top with remaining tortilla chips, evenly covering the first layer of chips and cheese. Drizzle with the remaining ½ cup (125 mL) of cheese over the second layer of chips. Return to the oven for 2 minutes or until the cheese is melted and the chips are slightly golden.
4. Garnish with the banana peppers, tomatoes, avocados, green onions, red onions, jalapeño and cilantro. Spoon the sour cream onto the centre of the nachos, creating a neat dollop. Serve immediately with the salsa verde on the side.

This is a vegetarian version of this dish. To make a heartier version of this shareable appetizer, layer some sautéed and seasoned ground beef, chopped quesadilla chicken or even pork tinga in with the cheese and chips.

POTATO SKINS

SERVES 6

3 medium-sized russet potatoes

Olive oil, for brushing on skins and baking sheet

Salt and pepper

5 slices bacon

1¼ cups (310 mL) grated sharp cheddar cheese

1¼ cups (310 mL) grated Monterey Jack cheese

½ cup (125 mL) sour cream

¼ cup (60 mL) finely sliced green onions

There is nothing like a plate full of crispy potato skins, filled with melty cheddar cheese and topped with bacon bits, sour cream and green onions. Oh, for the days of youth when one could eat potato skins with wild abandon. Remember when you could down a whole plate (along with a pitcher of beer) and feel none the worse the next morning? Sigh.

1. Preheat the oven to 425°F (220°C).
2. Scrub potatoes; pat dry. Rub skins with oil. Place potatoes on baking sheet. Bake until potatoes are tender, about 1 hour. Cool until potatoes can be handled. Keep oven at 425°F (220°C).
3. Cut each potato lengthwise into quarters. Scoop out centres, leaving ½-inch- (1 cm) thick layer of cooked potato on skins.
4. Oil a rimmed baking sheet and place potatoes, skin side down, on the sheet about 1 inch (2.5 cm) apart. Sprinkle with salt and pepper and bake until crisp and golden, approximately 10 minutes.
5. Cook bacon in a large heavy skillet over medium heat until brown and crisp. Drain and chop into ½-inch (1 cm) pieces.
6. Top the potatoes with cheeses and bacon and return to the oven for an additional 5 minutes, until cheese is melted and bubbly. Garnish with sour cream and green onions and serve immediately.

These potato skins are easy to make. Some approaches call for deep-frying, but that's not really necessary. You just want to bake the skins at a high enough heat so that they get crispy enough to hold the toppings.

FOCACCIA

Chuck came up with our first recipe for this Italian flatbread, but this is a later version from Chef Karen Lyons, one of our early culinary development chefs. We called this *fettunta* when we introduced it, as a tribute to the way we served it: toasted, rubbed with garlic, then drizzled with olive oil in the Tuscan style. (Literally, fettunta means "oily slice.") Focaccia is a winner any way you want to serve it, but oil and garlic provide added deliciousness—and slyly showing that you know what "fettunta" is all about can be pretty delicious too.

1980s **1990s** 2000s 2010s

MAKES ONE 13- x 18-INCH (33 x 45 CM) SLAB

3 cups (750 mL) all-purpose flour

3 cups (750 mL) bread flour

1 tbsp + 2¼ tsp (26.25 mL) dried instant yeast

2 tsp (10 mL) dried oregano

1½ tsp (7.5 mL) fine salt

1 tsp (5 mL) dried rosemary

1 tsp (5 mL) sugar

½ tsp (2.5 mL) dried thyme

2½ cups (600 mL) water (80°F/27°C)

¼ cup (60 mL) olive oil

1 tsp (5 mL) vegetable oil, for coating bowl

1 tbsp (15 mL) cornmeal (optional)

To garnish before baking

1 tbsp (15 mL) olive oil

1 tsp (5 mL) coarse salt (if desired)

1. Combine the all-purpose flour, bread flour, yeast, oregano, salt, rosemary, sugar and thyme in the bowl of a stand mixer. Using the paddle attachment, mix all ingredients well. Add the water and olive oil. Incorporate the wet ingredients on low speed until all the flour is moistened, approximately 3 minutes. Switch to the dough hook and knead on medium-high speed for 10 minutes. The dough should pull away cleanly from the bowl and form a smooth ball.
2. Remove bowl from the mixer and transfer the dough to a clean surface. Fold the dough over itself a few times and shape into a smooth oval, tucking the edges under itself.
3. Coat the bowl with a light coating of vegetable oil and return the dough back to the bowl. Cover with a damp towel and allow to rest for 15 to 20 minutes.
4. Meanwhile, coat a 13- × 18-inch (33 × 45 cm) baking pan with oil or cooking spray and line the bottom with parchment paper. Optionally, sprinkle with cornmeal—this will help release the focaccia and provide some texture to the bottom crust.
5. Stretch out the dough to fit into the pan; it should easily form a rectangular shape. Pat it gently or use a rolling pin to even out the surface. Allow to proof in a warm place for approximately 30 minutes or until the dough rises to just above the lip of the baking tray.
6. While the bread is proofing, preheat the oven to 500°F (260°C).
7. Once the bread is fully risen, drizzle with olive oil, and gently spread the oil with a brush to coat the entire surface. Bake on the lower rack of the oven for 15 minutes. The focaccia will sound hollow when tapped in the centre. The crust will be golden brown and crisp. Transfer to a wire rack to prevent a soggy bottom crust. Cool completely.

You can use 1 tablespoons (15 mL) of Italian seasoning in place of the dried herbs in the focaccia if that is what you have on hand.

LEROY'S DRY RIBS

For this recipe from Chuck, pork spareribs will be easier to find than pork rib tails or button bones, and will work almost as well—though, as you'll have read in the introduction to this section, Leroy himself would disagree.

1980s **1990s** 2000s 2010s

SERVES 4–6

2 lb (1 kg) pork spareribs cut into strips (sometimes called sweet and sour cut) or pork button bones (or pork rib tails), cut into 1-inch (2.5 cm) strips across the bone

Vegetable oil for frying

¼ cup (60 mL) coarse salt

¼ cup (60 mL) coarsely ground black pepper

1. If the strips are not already cut, prepare the ribs by cutting the strips between the bones to create individual bite-sized pieces. Preheat a deep fryer or a large Dutch oven half full of vegetable oil over medium-high heat.
2. Once the oil has reached 350°F (180°C), carefully fry a third of the pork ribs, loosening up the pieces in the hot oil to make sure no ribs are stuck together, as this may cause uneven cooking. Fry each batch of ribs for a total of 4 minutes or until golden brown and crispy. Drain from the oil and transfer to a metal bowl. Immediately sprinkle generously with salt and pepper as you toss the ribs in the bowl. The objective is to cover the ribs with an even coating of seasoning. Keep warm. Repeat with the remaining two-thirds of the ribs. Serve immediately.

To make sure the salt and pepper sticks to the dry rib pieces, season them immediately after deep-frying. Whichever cut you use, ask the butcher to cut the pieces into 1-inch (2.5 cm) strips across the bones, and then again between the bones to make 1- to 2-inch (2.5 to 5 cm) bite-sized pieces that cook up evenly.

HOT WINGS

Feel free to use your favourite hot sauce. At Earls we use Frank's RedHot for the perfect level of heat, and fresh, never frozen chicken.

1980s 1990s 2000s 2010s

SERVES 4 AS AN APPETIZER

2 lb (1 kg) chicken wings

Vegetable oil for frying

Frank's RedHot sauce, for coating wings

Parmesan dip (recipe follows)

Celery sticks

1. Prepare the wings by cutting through the joints and splitting the drumette from the wingette. If your chicken wings come with wing tips, cut through this joint as well and discard the tips (or save them for stock).
2. Preheat a deep fryer or a large Dutch oven half full of vegetable oil over medium-high heat.
3. Once the oil has reached 350°F (180°C), carefully fry half the batch of wings, loosening up the pieces in the hot oil to make sure no wings are stuck together, as this may cause uneven cooking. Fry each batch of wings for a total of 7 minutes or until golden brown and crispy. Drain from the oil and transfer to a metal bowl. Immediately toss the first half of wings with 2 tablespoons (30 mL) hot sauce. The objective is to coat the wings evenly with hot sauce. Keep warm. Repeat with the remaining half of the wings. Serve immediately with Parmesan dip and celery sticks.

PARMESAN DIP

1¼ cups (310 mL) mayonnaise

⅓ cup (80 mL) sour cream

¼ cup (60 mL) finely grated Parmesan cheese

3 tbsp (45 mL) malt vinegar

3 tbsp (45 mL) milk

1 tbsp (15 mL) sugar

½ tsp (2.5 mL) minced garlic

½ tsp (2.5 mL) dried basil

½ tsp (2.5 mL) dried oregano

1. Place all the ingredients in a mixing bowl and whisk until they are combined. Transfer to an airtight container and refrigerate. You can store this Parmesan dip for up to a week in the fridge.

CUSTOM SUSHI

Stew Fuller remembers being appalled the first time he ordered a salmon roll and discovered that the fish was raw. That was in the early 1980s, and Vancouver had only just begun the love affair with sushi that would ultimately see Japanese hole-in-the-walls chase short-order diners right out of town. We were early converts, but our first effort, a California roll made with imitation crab and guacamole, didn't impress Stew. A decade after his first sushi experience, he teamed up with an experienced sushi chef from one of our Vancouver locations to come up with a prawn dynamite roll that remains on our menu today. The next recipe takes you through making the sushi roll of your choice. Daunting, we know, but the second time around—with making it as with eating it—the process will seem pretty simple.

1980s **1990s** 2000s 2010s

SERVES 4-6

2 cups (500 mL) short-grain Japanese rice

2 cups (500 mL) cold water

¼ cup (60 mL) rice vinegar

¼ cup (60 mL) sugar

2 tbsp (30 mL) fine salt

6-7 nori sheets, depending on how many rolls you want to make

Sesame seeds, for sprinkling

Sushi fillings (page 34)

PERFECT SUSHI RICE

1. Place the rice in a medium-sized bowl and cover with cool water. Using your hands, swirl the rice in the water to agitate any starch around the rice. Drain.
2. Repeat this step 3 times or until the water runs clear when draining off the bowl.
3. Place the rice and 2 cups (500 mL) of water into a medium-sized saucepan with a lid. Place over high heat and allow to come to a boil, uncovered.
4. Once it has come to a boil, reduce heat to the lowest setting and cover. Allow to cook for 15 minutes, then remove from heat and allow to stand with the lid still on for another 10 minutes.
5. In a small microwave-safe bowl, combine the rice vinegar, sugar and salt. Stir until well combined. Microwave for 45 seconds or until the solids have completely dissolved into the vinegar. Reserve 2 tablespoons (30 mL) of the seasoned vinegar for sushi rolling. Add 2 additional tablespoons (30 mL) of water to dilute this mixture. Set aside for next steps.
6. Transfer the rice into a very large bowl. Drizzle the seasoned vinegar over the spatula while waving the spatula back and forth. This method will disperse the vinegar more evenly than if you just drizzle it directly over the rice. Using a slicing motion with the spatula, gently separate the grains of rice while allowing the seasoning to be absorbed. This will allow excess steam to be released quickly and help the individual rice grains dry out slightly.
7. Push any stray rice grains back into the centre of the bowl and mix well so that they are also seasoned properly.
8. Cover the rice with a damp towel to keep it from drying out.

SUSHI ROLLING TECHNIQUE

1. Wrap a bamboo sushi mat with plastic wrap and place on a clean cutting board. Place a sheet of nori on the centre of the mat. There are approximately 6 deep lines spaced approximately 1 inch (2.5 cm) apart running through the nori. Depending on the thickness of your sushi roll, you may have to trim the nori to avoid excess seaweed in your roll. If making thinner rolls with just one or two ingredients (e.g., cucumber or avocado rolls), then begin with half the square sheet of nori (the trimmed sheet should measure 7.5 × 4 inches [20 × 10 cm]). If thicker rolls are what you have planned, then trim 2 "sections" off the square sheet, resulting in an approximately 7- × 6-inch (18 × 15 cm) rectangle. Always cut parallel to the lines on the sheet of nori.

2. Lightly coat your fingers in some cold water. This will prevent the rice from sticking to your hands. Use approximately ½ cup to ¾ cup (125 to 180 mL) of rice per sushi roll, depending on the size of your nori. Gently spread the rice on the back left corner of the nori, pushing the rice with the fingers of your left hand while "pulling" the remaining rice gently with your right hand while you move the rice to the back right corner and all over the nori sheet.

3. Gently press the rice around the nori until an even layer of rice covers the entire trimmed sheet of nori. Try to keep the individual grains of rice loose; do not squish or press the rice too aggressively or you will end up with an overworked rice cake.

4. Sprinkle the rice evenly with sesame seeds. Flip over so that the rice is now on the bottom.

5. Arrange your desired sushi filling ingredients across the nori a third of the way toward the back. Try not to overfill your roll, otherwise it will not close or form properly.

6. Once the ingredients have been placed, tuck your thumbs underneath the bamboo mat and place your fingers over your sushi filling ingredients. Roll your mat and nori away from you, applying gentle pressure as you close the first part of the nori and rice over itself in a rolling motion. Like the curl of a wave, continue this motion until the front edge of the nori closes in on itself and secures the ingredients in place. Make sure to slide the bamboo mat out of your roll so that the mat eventually folds over itself with your roll in between.

7. Finish forming the roll by using the mat to apply gentle pressure using your thumb and fingers to tighten the roll. Remove the mat and place the roll in the centre of your cutting board.

8. Dip the tip of a sharp knife in some water and allow the water to run down the blade. Cut the roll briskly in half, and then place the two halves evenly together, re-wet the knife and cut each half into three. This should give you a total of eight evenly cut rolls.

9. Arrange carefully on a plate, placing the end pieces cut side up. Garnish with desired sauces and serve.

Sushi Filling Ideas

Vegetables
- julienned cucumber (seeded)
- julienned carrots
- julienned snow peas
- julienned jicama
- thinly sliced red peppers
- thinly sliced avocado
- thinly sliced mango
- thinly sliced pineapple
- julienned green onion
- whole and trimmed blanched asparagus
- whole and trimmed blanched green beans
- roasted sweet potato strips
- julienned roasted red peppers (page 243)
- tempura vegetables
- julienned shiso leaf

Seafood
- sushi-grade or sashimi-grade fish, such as salmon, tuna or hamachi/yellowtail
- smoked salmon
- cooked crab meat or artificial crab meat
- cooked lobster meat
- cooked shrimp
- scallops
- masago or tobiko (fish roe)
- unagi (grilled freshwater eel)
- tempura shrimp

Meat
- chicken teriyaki
- seared steak
- ham or Spam
- bacon
- tonkatsu (deep-fried breaded pork)
- braised pork belly
- thinly sliced omelette

Miscellaneous garnishes and sauces
- cream cheese
- togarashi
- pickled ginger
- Japanese mayo (Kewpie brand)
- Teriyaki marinade (page 163)
- Wasabi mayo (recipe follows)
- Sriracha mayo (recipe follows)

WASABI MAYO

MAKES 1 CUP (250 mL)

¼ cup (60 mL) rice vinegar

¼ cup (60 mL) sugar

2 tbsp (30 mL) water

1 tbsp (15 mL) wasabi powder

¾ cup (180 mL) mayonnaise

¼ tsp (1.25 mL) fine salt

1. Bring the rice vinegar and sugar to a simmer in a small saucepan. Reduce by half, and then allow to cool to room temperature.
2. Combine the water and wasabi powder. Drizzle in the cooled rice vinegar syrup and whisk very well to combine.
3. Add the mayonnaise and salt, mixing well.
4. Transfer to an airtight container and refrigerate. The wasabi mayo can be stored refrigerated for a week.

SRIRACHA MAYO

MAKES 1 CUP (250 mL)

¾ cup plus 1 tbsp (210 mL) mayonnaise

2½ tbsp (37.5 mL) Sriracha

2 tsp (10 mL) mirin (Japanese rice wine)

1. Place all the ingredients in a mixing bowl and whisk until combined.
2. Transfer to an airtight container and refrigerate. The Sriracha mayo can be stored refrigerated for a week.

SERVES 4–6

Vegetable oil for frying

1½ lb (680 g) chicken tenders

1 cup (250 mL) reserved chili chicken flour mixture (from the chili chicken batter recipe, page 37)

4 oz (115 g) wonton wrappers or lotus root

Chili chicken batter (recipe follows)

Gochujang sauce (recipe follows)

Szechuan lime glaze (recipe follows)

1 tbsp (15 mL) sesame seeds

Pickled cucumbers and red onions (recipe follows)

½ cup (125 mL) finely chopped green onions

Make sure you use wonton wrappers and not gyoza or dumpling wrappers, which are quite a bit thicker and won't come out as crisp after frying. The pickled onions are best held overnight before use to fully absorb all the flavours. Gochujang is a Korean hot sauce that literally means "hot pepper paste." It is made from fermented red chilies, glutinous rice, soybeans and salt and imparts a complex, savoury, pungent and spicy flavour to dishes.

CHILI CHICKEN

Our original chili chicken, devised by Chuck, was loosely based on Szechuan cooking. And damn, it's pretty good. Kids love it, and it's a go-to meal for staff looking for something quick and cheap. But time passes, and certain styles of food pass with them even as others rise to the fore. One of the cuisines that's been coming up in recent years is Korean, elements of which Chef Collective member David Wong brought in when he revised this dish a couple of years ago. In-house, we call his new version "KFC," for Korean Fried Chicken—and damn, it's even better: all fresh spices and citrus, a made-from-scratch marinade, and about a hundred more ingredients than its simpler predecessor—that's what you're getting with this recipe. But you know what? A lot of our customers loved the original recipe. New chili chicken? Old chili chicken? If we were in the cola business, we might have gone with one or the other, but we're not, so both remain on the menu. But the chili chicken is our little secret, so easy to make we're almost guilty about it, so we shared the more complicated "KFC" recipe.

1. Preheat a deep fryer or a large Dutch oven half full of vegetable oil over medium-high heat to 350°F (180°C). Cut the chicken tenders into ¾-inch (2 cm) pieces.
2. Place the reserved chili chicken flour mixture into a shallow bowl or pie plate. Toss the chicken tenders in the flour mixture, separating each piece carefully for maximum coverage. Shake off the excess. Refrigerate while you get the other ingredients ready.
3. Cut the wonton wrappers into ¾-inch (2 cm) strips (divide each wonton circle into 4 equal strips). You can cut through a stack at a time. Deep-fry wontons in small batches until light golden and crisp, approximately 50 seconds. Drain on a paper towel–lined baking tray.
4. If using lotus root, cut into 1⁄16-inch (2 mm) slices and pat dry. Fry for 30 seconds or until golden brown. Allow the oil to reheat to 350°F (180°C).
5. To fry the chicken, put half the floured tenders into the chili chicken batter, gently moving the chicken around with tongs to coat each piece completely. Once the oil has reached 350°F (180°C), carefully lower the tenders into the hot oil using a slotted spoon, separating the pieces with tongs after 5 seconds. Cook for 2 to 2½ minutes or until golden brown and just cooked through. Check the largest pieces of chicken to make sure they're cooked—the internal temperature should be 160°F (71°C). Remove from the fryer and drain on a paper towel–lined bowl. Allow the oil to return to 350°F (180°C), then repeat the process with the remaining half of the tenders.
6. Transfer the first batch of fried chicken into a large bowl. Add half the fried wonton strips and half the gochujang sauce. Toss together well to coat each ingredient. Pile high onto a serving platter. Repeat the procedure with the remaining half of the fried chicken. Doing this in smaller batches will ensure even distribution of the sauce. Transfer the sauced chicken to the same platter.
7. Drizzle 2 tablespoons (30 mL) of Szechuan lime glaze over the chicken and sprinkle with sesame seeds. Garnish with the pickled cucumbers and red onions, arranging them over and around the fried chicken pieces. Top with the chopped green onion. Serve immediately.

Top: Korean Fried Chicken

Bottom: Chili Chicken

CHILI CHICKEN BATTER

2 cups (500 mL) cornstarch

1 cup (250 mL) cake flour

1½ tsp (7.5 mL) fine salt

1 tsp (5 mL) ground black pepper

¾ tsp (3.75 mL) baking powder

¾ cup (180 mL) water

¼ cup (60 mL) vodka

1. In a large metal bowl, combine the cornstarch, cake flour, salt, black pepper and baking powder until well mixed. Set aside 1 cup (250 mL) of the mixture for dredging the tenders.
2. Combine the water and vodka in a separate bowl. Add to the remaining flour mixture and whisk to combine. There should be some lumps left in the batter: do not overmix or you will be left with a doughy fried coating on your chicken instead of a light, crisp shell. Use immediately.

GOCHUJANG SAUCE

½ cup (125 mL) gochujang paste

⅓ cup (80 mL) brown sugar

3 tbsp (45 mL) soy sauce

1 tbsp (15 mL) water

2 tsp (10 mL) rice vinegar

1 tsp (5 mL) minced ginger

1 tsp (5 mL) minced garlic

1. Combine all ingredients together with a whisk until fully incorporated. Transfer to an airtight container. Can be stored refrigerated for up to 5 days. Mix well before using.

SZECHUAN LIME GLAZE

1 cup (250 mL) white wine vinegar

⅔ cup (160 mL) sugar

¼ cup (60 mL) lime juice

1 tsp (5 mL) Szechuan peppercorns (common in the Asian section of your local market)

½ tsp (2.5 mL) coriander seeds

1. In a medium-sized saucepan, combine all ingredients and bring to a simmer. Reduce heat to low and continue simmering until the liquid reduces to ½ cup (125 mL) after straining.
2. Strain out the solids and transfer to a clean airtight container. Discard the solids.
3. Can be stored refrigerated for up to 9 days. Mix well before using.

PICKLED CUCUMBERS AND RED ONIONS

1¼ cups (310 mL) water

⅔ cup (160 mL) white wine vinegar

½ cup (125 mL) ⅛-inch (3 mm) sliced red onion rings

½ cup (125 mL) ⅛-inch (3 mm) sliced cucumbers

1. Bring the water and white wine vinegar to a boil.
2. Place the red onion rings in an appropriately sized container. Place the cucumbers in a separate container. Pour half of the pickling liquid into the onion container and the remaining half into the cucumber container. Push the vegetables into the liquid if necessary to make sure they are fully submerged.
3. Allow to cool to room temperature before lidding and transferring to the refrigerator. Allow to pickle for 24 hours before using. Can be stored refrigerated for up to 14 days.

PRAWN TACONES

The first decade of the new millennium will go down in history for the spectacular rise of the internet, the sad decline of rainforests—and the total global triumph of seafood tacos. Alym Hirji spent four years as our executive chef. If you like the fish tacos on the next page (and you do), you'll also like his prawn variation here, which is utterly distinct yet wonderfully similar.

1980s 1990s 2000s **2010s**

SERVES 4–6

4 flour tortillas or corn tortillas

1 tbsp (15 mL) melted salted butter

2 cups (500 mL) shredded green cabbage

Avocado lime crema (recipe follows)

Prawn filling (recipe follows)

½ cup (125 mL) shredded white cheddar

2 oz (57 g) pea shoots

1. Brush each side of the tortilla with butter. Heat over a medium-hot grill or grill pan until puffy but still pliable, approximately 10 seconds per side. There should be visible grill markings on the tortilla.
2. Meanwhile, toss the green cabbage with ⅔ cup (160 mL) of avocado lime crema. Set aside.
3. Cut the grilled tortilla in half. With the cut side on the bottom closest to you, spread out a scant ¼ cup (60 mL) of prawn filling in the centre of the tortilla. Top with 1 tablespoon (15 mL) of white cheddar. Portion out ¼ cup (60 mL) of dressed green cabbage and 4 pea shoots over the prawn and white cheddar. Roll into cones by folding the semicircles in half and then rolling to close. Repeat with the remaining cones. Serve immediately.

Small corn tortillas can also be used in place of the flour tortillas to make this a gluten-free dish—fold them up as tacos instead of rolling them into tacones.

AVOCADO LIME CREMA

1 cup (250 mL) sour cream

½ cup (125 mL) avocado pulp (about 1 small avocado, peeled and seeded)

2 tbsp (30 mL) lime juice

1 tbsp (15 mL) lime zest (about 1 whole lime)

1 tbsp (15 mL) finely chopped cilantro

½ tsp (2.5 mL) fine salt

1. Using an immersion blender or food processor, purée all ingredients together until completely smooth. The resulting sauce will be light green and have a silky texture. Refrigerate until ready to use.

PRAWN FILLING

1 lb (450 g) 21 to 30 count prawns, peeled and deveined

2 tsp (10 mL) quesadilla spice (page 238)

1 tbsp (15 mL) vegetable oil

1 tbsp (15 mL) minced garlic

1 tbsp (15 mL) tomato paste

1 tbsp (15 mL) lime juice

1 tbsp (15 mL) coarsely chopped cilantro

1. Dice the prawns into ½-inch (1 cm) pieces. Toss with the quesadilla spice until evenly coated.
2. Heat the vegetable oil in a nonstick pan and sauté the garlic until fragrant. Add the prawns and cook until the prawns begin to turn pink, approximately 2 to 3 minutes. Add the tomato paste, lime juice and cilantro. Stir well until heated through. Remove from heat and transfer to a serving dish.

FISH TACOS

1980s 1990s 2000s **2010s**

SERVES 4–6

1½ lb (680 g) Ocean Wise™ cod fillet

Fish taco marinade (recipe follows)

½ tsp (2.5 mL) fine salt

12 each 6-inch (15 cm) flour tortillas

1 tsp (5 mL) vegetable oil

Buttermilk Valentina crema (recipe
  follows)

2 cups (500 mL) finely shaved green
  cabbage

Pineapple chili salsa (recipe follows)

Salsa verde (recipe follows)

1 cup (250 mL) roughly chopped cilantro

1 lime

Valentina hot sauce (optional)

Somewhat surprisingly, the fish taco appears to be a twentieth-century innovation, probably originating on the Pacific Coast side of the Baja Peninsula in the fishing towns south of Tijuana and owing some of its flavours to the local Japanese population. In the classic Baja version, the fish is deep fried, but we've opted for pan-frying in the recipe below. (Chef Tim Pennington from Earls Boston points out that barbecuing is another delicious way to cook both the fish and the taco shells at home. Cut the marinated fish into good-sized chunks or squares and skewer them before placing them on the grill.) Chef Collective member David Wong finished the dish with a suave buttermilk crema in addition to a rollicking assortment of the usual trimmings.

1. Cut the cod fillets into 1- × 5-inch (2.5 × 12 cm) rectangular pieces. If the pieces are too short, you can use several small pieces per taco as opposed to one long piece. Coat in the fish taco marinade and refrigerate for 24 hours.
2. After 24 hours, remove from the marinade and season lightly with salt. Preheat a nonstick pan over medium heat.
3. Cook the cod until golden, approximately 1 to 2 minutes per side. The cod should be flaky and very tender once cooked. Transfer to a plate.
4. Wipe down the pan. Heat over medium-low heat for the flour tortillas. Brush both sides of the flour tortillas with vegetable oil and toast on the nonstick pan until pliable, approximately 15 to 20 seconds per side.
5. Spoon approximately 1 tablespoon (15 mL) of buttermilk Valentina crema down the centre of 1 flour tortilla. Top the crema with some shredded cabbage, followed by some cod, pineapple chili salsa, salsa verde and chopped cilantro. Repeat with the remaining tortillas until all the cod is used up.
6. Cut the lime into wedges and serve with the tacos along with additional hot sauce if desired.

FISH TACO MARINADE

1 cup (250 mL) confit garlic oil
   (page 242)

2 tbsp (30 mL) finely chopped cilantro

1 tbsp (15 mL) lime zest

2 tsp (10 mL) ground cumin

2 tsp (10 mL) ground coriander

2 tsp (10 mL) fine salt

1. Combine all ingredients together
    with a whisk until fully incorpo-
    rated. If made ahead, transfer to
    an airtight container and
    refrigerate for 3 days maximum.

BUTTERMILK VALENTINA CREMA

¼ cup (60 mL) sour cream

¼ cup (60 mL) mayonnaise

3 tbsp (45 mL) Valentina hot sauce or
   your favourite Mexican-style hot
   sauce

1 tbsp (15 mL) buttermilk

1. Combine all ingredients with a
    whisk until fully incorporated. If
    made ahead, transfer to an
    airtight container and refrigerate
    for 5 days maximum.

PINEAPPLE CHILI SALSA

1 small pineapple

2 tbsp (30 mL) finely sliced Fresno
   chilies, seeded

2 tbsp (30 mL) finely diced red onion

1 tbsp (15 mL) lime juice

1 tbsp (15 mL) finely chopped cilantro

Pinch fine salt

1. Peel and core the pineapple and
    cut it into ¼-inch (½ cm) dice.
    You should have around 2 cups
    (500 mL) of diced pineapple.
    Add the Fresno chilies, red onion,
    lime juice, cilantro and salt.
    Combine all ingredients very
    well. Serve immediately.

SALSA VERDE

1 lb (450 g) tomatillos

3 medium-sized garlic cloves

1 stemmed jalapeño pepper

1 tbsp (15 mL) vegetable oil

1 tbsp (15 mL) roughly chopped cilantro

1 tbsp (15 mL) lime juice

½ tsp (2.5 mL) fine salt

1½ tbsp (22.5 mL) finely diced red onion

1. Preheat the oven to 450°F (230°C). Remove the outer
    husks from the tomatillos.
2. Toss the tomatillos, garlic and jalapeño with the
    vegetable oil until they are well coated. Arrange on a
    parchment-lined rimmed baking tray and bake in the
    oven for 8 minutes or until the tomatillos are slightly
    charred. Remove from the oven and allow to cool to
    room temperature.
3. Once cooled, transfer to a food processor and add
    the cilantro, lime juice and salt. Pulse until all ingredi-
    ents are finely chopped, approximately ⅛-inch to
    $\frac{1}{16}$-inch (2 to 3 mm) pieces. Add the red onion and mix
    well. Serve immediately or transfer to an airtight
    container and refrigerate for 4 days maximum.

CRISPY THAI PRAWNS

In 2014 we unveiled a dazzling new test kitchen that a lucky few guests are able to sit inside at our downtown Vancouver location. Not only is the kitchen open to the public but guests throughout the restaurant can order dishes being tested and are encouraged to offer feedback. Around the same time we unveiled a new Chef Collective, featuring a rotating cast of up to a half-dozen chefs, including Hamid Salimian, who arrived from Diva at the Met, which has long been one of Vancouver's leading fine dining spots. Hamid gave us this dish, and what a knockout, if we may be so bold! Sweet, hot, sour, salty, savoury—even on a continent saturated with Thai restaurants, few other dishes are this serious in intent.

1980s 1990s 2000s **2010s**

SERVES 4–6

Vegetable oil for frying

½ cup (125 mL) reserved tempura flour mixture (from the tempura batter recipe, page 44)

1 lb (450 g) 26 to 30 count prawns, peeled and deveined

Tempura batter (recipe follows)

Cilantro paint (recipe follows)

1 cup (250 mL) 1-inch (2.5 cm) chopped napa cabbage

½ cup (125 mL) finely sliced daikon radish

¼ cup (60 mL) 1-inch (2.5 cm) diagonal cut green onion

¼ cup (60 mL) roughly chopped mint leaves

¼ cup (60 mL) roughly chopped cilantro

2 tbsp (30 mL) roughly chopped Thai basil leaves

Lemongrass vinaigrette (recipe follows)

Sweet and sour glaze (recipe follows)

¼ cup (60 mL) roasted peanuts

2 tbsp (30 mL) crispy fried onions (common in the Asian food section of your grocery store)

1 serrano pepper, thinly sliced into rings

1 lime, cut into 4 wedges

1. Preheat a deep fryer or a large Dutch oven half full of vegetable oil over medium-high heat.
2. Place the reserved tempura flour mixture into a shallow bowl or pie plate. Toss the prawns into the reserved flour mixture to give each piece a light coating of flour. Shake off the excess.
3. Take half the floured prawns and put them into the tempura batter, gently folding with a fork to fully coat each prawn.
4. Once oil has reached 350°F (180°C), carefully place each prawn, one at a time, into the hot oil and cook for 2 minutes or until golden brown and just cooked through. Remove from the fryer and drain on a paper towel lined bowl. Repeat the process with the remaining half of the prawns.
5. Meanwhile, using the back of a spoon, spread a thin layer of cilantro paint on the centre of the bottom of your serving bowl or platter.
6. Toss together the napa cabbage, daikon, green onion, mint, cilantro and Thai basil leaves. Drizzle with some of the lemongrass vinaigrette and toss again until well coated. Arrange the salad in the centre of your serving platter or bowl, on top of the cilantro paint.
7. Neatly pile the deep-fried prawns over the salad. Drizzle with 2 tablespoons (30 mL) of the sweet and sour glaze. Garnish with the peanuts, crispy onions and serrano pepper rings. Serve with lime wedges.

This recipe has lots of steps and unusual ingredients, but it's worth the trouble. The resulting dish is very complex and authentic. The lemongrass vinaigrette and sweet and sour glaze can be made several days ahead.

TEMPURA BATTER

¾ cup (180 mL) rice flour or cornstarch

¾ cup (180 mL) cake flour

1 tsp (5 mL) fine salt

¾ cup (180 mL) lager (ice cold)

1 tbsp (15 mL) vodka (ice cold)

1. In a large metal bowl, combine the rice flour, cake flour and salt until well mixed. Set aside ½ cup (125 mL) of the mixture for dredging the prawns.
2. Combine the lager and vodka in a separate bowl. Add to the remaining flour mixture and whisk to combine. There should be some lumps left in the batter; do not overmix or you will be left with a doughy fried coating on your prawns instead of a light, crisp shell. Use immediately.

CILANTRO PAINT

2 tbsp (30 mL) minced peeled ginger

1 tsp (5 mL) minced garlic

1 bird's-eye chili

2 tbsp (30 mL) vegetable oil

½ cup (125 mL) chopped cilantro

1. Combine all ingredients in a small food processor. Purée until very smooth. You may need to stir the ingredients several times to get the mixture to purée completely. Use immediately.

LEMONGRASS VINAIGRETTE

½ cup (125 mL) fish sauce

¼ cup (60 mL) brown sugar

¼ cup (60 mL) lime juice

¼ cup (60 mL) lemon juice

2 tbsp (30 mL) finely minced lemongrass

2 tbsp (30 mL) finely chopped cilantro

2 tbsp (30 mL) vegetable oil

1 tbsp (15 mL) minced peeled ginger

1 tsp (5 mL) minced garlic

1 bird's-eye chili

1. Combine all ingredients in a deep container. Using a food processor or hand-held blender, purée all ingredients until they are emulsified and the herbs are finely chopped.
2. Strain the mixture through a sieve, pressing down with a spatula to maximize extraction. Discard the solids. Transfer to an airtight container and refrigerate. The vinaigrette can be stored refrigerated for 5 days. Mix well before use.

SWEET AND SOUR GLAZE

½ cup (125 mL) dark corn syrup

¼ cup (60 mL) fish sauce

2 tbsp (30 mL) lime juice

2 tbsp (30 mL) lemon juice

2 tbsp (30 mL) brown sugar

2-inch (5 cm) piece of lemongrass, cut into ½-inch (1 cm) pieces

1-inch (2.5 cm) piece of ginger, cut into ½-inch (1 cm) slices

3 pieces lime leaves

1 bird's-eye chili

1. Combine all ingredients into a large pot and bring to a simmer over medium heat (the mixture will foam as it heats up). Reduce heat to low and continue to simmer until the liquid is reduced to ½ cup (125 mL) and coats the back of a spoon. This process will take approximately 2 hours. Allow to cool to room temperature.
2. Strain the liquid and discard the solids. Transfer to an airtight container and refrigerate. The glaze can be stored refrigerated for 5 days.

Crispy Thai Prawns

SICILIAN CALAMARI

1980s 1990s 2000s **2010s**

SERVES 4–6

Vegetable oil for frying

1 lb (450 g) small calamari tubes, cleaned

1 cup (250 mL) gluten-free breading or flour and bread crumb mixture (see note)

Greek citrus yogurt (recipe follows)

Oven-dried grape tomatoes (recipe follows)

Salted cucumber (recipe follows)

¼ cup (60 mL) quartered red radishes

¼ cup (60 mL) halved Sicilian olives

1 jalapeño, thinly sliced and seeded

8 mint leaves, torn in half

8 basil leaves, torn in half

8 parsley leaves

It's a western Canadian oddity that a large proportion of restaurants are operated by Greeks, and many have had calamari on the menu since the 1970s, when local palates might have found such a dish quite challenging. The first Earls menu also sported a Greek-style calamari—probably the first on a non-Greek menu—but the Chef Collective recently updated this classic squid dish, giving it more of a Sicilian slant, with brighter flavours and colours that make it look as good on the table as it tastes in the mouth.

1. Preheat a deep fryer or a large Dutch oven half full of vegetable oil over medium-high heat to 400°F (200°C).
2. Cut calamari into ¼-inch (½ cm) rings.
3. Place the breading mixture into a shallow bowl or pie plate. Toss the calamari in the flour mixture, separating each piece carefully to ensure maximum coverage. Shake off the excess.
4. Once oil has reached 400°F (200°C), carefully lower the calamari using a slotted spoon into the hot oil, breaking up the clumps of calamari with tongs after 5 seconds. Cook for 45 seconds to 1 minute or until calamari is a light golden brown. Remove from the fryer and drain in a paper towel–lined bowl.
5. Dollop ¼ cup (60 mL) of the Greek citrus yogurt onto one side of the serving plate. Using a small offset spatula or the back of a spoon, spread the yogurt in a thin layer over half the serving platter in a neat, attractive swipe.
6. Carefully pile the calamari on the side of the plate opposite the Greek yogurt. Randomly scatter the oven-dried tomatoes, salted cucumber, radishes, olives and jalapeño over and around the calamari. Garnish with the mint, basil and parsley. Serve with extra Greek citrus yogurt on the side.

Use your favourite gluten-free breading for this recipe, or if you prefer, you can use equal parts all-purpose flour and fine bread crumbs. At Earls, we use Nextjen Gluten-Free Fried Chicken Mix for our gluten-free calamari.

GREEK CITRUS YOGURT

3 medium garlic cloves, whole

1 tbsp (15 mL) lemon juice

1 tsp (5 mL) lemon zest

¼ tsp (1.25 mL) fine salt

½ cup (125 mL) plain Greek yogurt

1. Blanch the garlic cloves for 7 minutes in boiling water. Immediately cool down in ice water to halt cooking. Place the garlic, lemon juice, lemon zest and fine salt into a mini food processor or chopper and pulse until the garlic is minced. Add to the yogurt and mix well. Set aside for serving with the calamari or transfer to a clean airtight container. Can be stored refrigerated for up to 3 days.

OVEN-DRIED GRAPE TOMATOES

1 dry pint (1½ cups/375 mL) grape tomatoes

2 tbsp (30 mL) confit garlic oil (page 242)

1 sprig thyme

¼ tsp (1.25 mL) fine salt

¼ tsp (1.25 mL) ground black pepper

1. Preheat the oven to 200°F (95°C).
2. Halve the grape tomatoes lengthwise and place in a bowl along with the rest of the ingredients. Toss together well to evenly coat the tomatoes with the seasonings. Transfer to a parchment-lined rimmed baking tray, making sure all the tomatoes have their cut sides facing up and are not crowded or stacked.
3. Place in the preheated oven and bake for 2 to 2½ hours. The tomatoes will begin to wilt, shrink and dry out. Remove from the oven and discard the thyme. Leave the tomatoes spread out on the baking sheet until completely cool. If making ahead, wrap with plastic wrap and use within 3 days.

SALTED CUCUMBER

½ English cucumber

1 cup (250 mL) water

1 tsp (5 mL) fine salt

1. Peel, seed and quarter the cucumber lengthwise. Cut ½-inch (1 cm) diagonal slices at a 45-degree angle to get about 1½ cups (375 mL) of cucumber slices. Place in a clean container.
2. Mix the water and salt until well dissolved. Pour into the container, pressing the cucumber slices down to make sure they're covered by the salted water. Refrigerate for 24 hours before draining and using.

TUNA TOSTADA

Dawn Doucette has Earls in her blood even though she grew up in Saskatoon as the daughter of a heavy equipment salesman—it's just that the sales guy happened to be Clay Fuller. She worked as a server at our location there before making her own circuitous way toward our Vancouver base. She arrived with a résumé that included cooking at San Francisco's Zuni Café, and founding her own little bistro in the countryside near Burlington, Ontario. A long-time test kitchen mainstay, a sometime Chef Collective member and a key contributor to this book, she also whipped up this dish—more evidence for the archaeologists of the future that this was the Taco Age.

1. Heat a pot of oil to 350°F (180°C). Cut the tortillas into quarters.
2. Using a slotted spoon or a sieve, lower the tortilla quarters into the oil and fry for 45 seconds or until crisp. Drain immediately on a paper towel–lined tray or plate. Season with fine salt.
3. Cut the avocado in half lengthwise and remove the seed and peel. Thinly slice each half lengthwise into 8 slices for a total of 16 slices.
4. Place a dollop of jalapeño cilantro aioli on each tortilla chip. Top with a slice of avocado, a slice of chili-rubbed tuna and a pinch of fine salt.
5. Toss the jicama with the lime juice and season lightly with fine salt. Divide evenly among the 16 tostadas.
6. Garnish each tostada with 1 piece of radish, 3 cilantro leaves and 1 piece of pickled Fresno chili.
7. Space some dollops of cilantro aioli evenly on the bottom of your platter and arrange the tostadas over each dollop. This will keep the tostadas from sliding around on the plate. The tostadas should all face the same direction. Add the lime wedges.

1980s 1990s 2000s **2010s**

SERVES 4–6

4 white corn tortillas, 6 inches (15 cm)

1 avocado

Jalapeño cilantro aioli (recipe follows)

Chili-rubbed tuna loin (recipe follows)

1 tsp (5 mL) fine salt

½ cup (125 mL) finely julienned jicama

1 tbsp (15 mL) lime juice

¼ cup (60 mL) thinly shaved radish

¼ cup (60 mL) cilantro leaves or micro cilantro

1 tbsp (15 mL) pickled Fresno chilies, ⅛-inch sliced rings

4–6 lime wedges for serving

JALAPEÑO CILANTRO AIOLI

⅓ cup (80 mL) garlic cloves

1 poblano pepper, halved and seeded

1 jalapeño pepper, halved and seeded

¼ cup (60 mL) finely chopped cilantro

½ tsp (2.5 mL) fine salt

2 tbsp (30 mL) olive oil

1 cup (250 mL) mayonnaise

1. In a medium-sized pot of boiling salted water, blanch the garlic for 15 minutes until soft throughout. Immediately shock in an ice bath until completely cool, then drain well.
2. Place the poblano and jalapeño peppers on a rimmed baking tray, cut side down, pressing firmly to flatten the peppers. Broil under medium-high heat until the skin is fully charred and the peppers are soft, approximately 10 minutes. Cool to room temperature.
3. Combine the peppers, blanched garlic, cilantro, salt and olive oil in a food processor and purée until very smooth. Pass through a sieve, discarding any bits of skin or solids. Combine the purée with the mayonnaise and mix very well. If made ahead, transfer to an airtight container and refrigerate. The aioli can be stored refrigerated for 5 days maximum.

CHILI-RUBBED TUNA LOIN

1½ lb (680 g) ahi or albacore tuna loin, 1½ to 2½ inches (4 to 6 cm) in diameter

1 tbsp (15 mL) ground coriander

1 tbsp (15 mL) chipotle powder

1 tbsp (15 mL) ancho chili powder

1 tbsp (15 mL) chili powder

2 tsp (10 mL) fine salt

1. Bring a large pot of water to a boil and simultaneously prepare an ice bath.
2. Using a pair of tongs or slotted spatula, gently lower the tuna into the boiling water. Cook until it is white and barely cooked, approximately 5 seconds. Remove from the boiling water and transfer immediately to the ice bath to stop the fish from cooking further. Remove after 1 minute. Blot gently with paper towel.
3. Mix the coriander, chipotle powder, ancho chili powder, chili powder and salt together. Spread the mix on a shallow plate. Roll the tuna around in the spice blend to get even coverage.
4. Place the tuna on a small baking tray or in a container and freeze for approximately 2 hours, long enough to firm it up and make it easier to slice into 16 slices.
5. Slice into ¼-inch (½ cm) slices crosswise. Use immediately.

Tuna Tostada

SERVES 4-6

3 cups (750 mL) roasted pork, shredded (recipe follows)

Sticky bun sauce (recipe follows)

Steamed buns (recipe follows)

½ cup (125 mL) coarsely chopped roasted peanuts

½ cup (125 mL) coarsely chopped cilantro

½ cup (125 mL) diagonally cut green onions

Lime wedges if desired

ROASTED PORK DRY RUB

1½ tbsp (22.5 mL) paprika

1½ tbsp (22.5 mL) granulated onion

1 tbsp (15 mL) cayenne powder

1 tbsp (15 mL) garlic powder

1½ tsp (7.5 mL) fine salt

1 tsp (5 mL) ground black pepper

1. Combine all ingredients together with a whisk until fully incorporated. If made ahead, transfer to an airtight container.

STICKY PORK BUNS

Pork shoulder is a great cut of meat, and a bit of an unsung hero. It's not a pricey cut, easy to work with and has tons of flavour. It's the secret behind many of the bars and barbecue joints we love but we wanted to challenge ourselves to come up with a completely different way to cook it. Chef Collective member Jeff McInnis of *Top Chef* and Yardbird Miami fame works with us while at the same time running his New York City restaurant Root & Bone. He put together these Chinese sticky pork buns cooked and served in a classic dim-sum steamer but folded taco-style and garnished in the fashion of Southeast Asia.

1. Reheat the shredded roasted pork if necessary. Toss with half the bun sauce until well coated.
2. Split each steamed bun slightly, keeping the folded side intact. Top each bun with some shredded roasted pork, peanuts, cilantro and green onion. Drizzle with extra sticky bun sauce if desired. Serve immediately with lime wedges.

ROASTED PORK

4 lb (1.8 kg) boneless pork shoulder roast

Roasted pork dry rub (recipe follows)

1½ cups (375 mL) chicken broth

1. Preheat the oven to 325°F (165°C).
2. Blot the pork shoulder dry with paper towels and place on a clean cutting board.
3. Using a paring knife, make 4 to 5 random cuts, about 2 to 3 inches (5 to 8 cm) deep and 1 inch (2.5 cm) long, into the top (fat) side of the pork shoulder. Season the entire shoulder with the dry rub, filling the cuts with the rub and making sure all surfaces have an even coating.
4. Place in a Dutch oven or a metal pan with a tight-fitting lid. Add the chicken broth and bring to a simmer over medium-high heat. Cover with a lid. Transfer to the oven and cook for 3 hours. Test to see if the meat is fork-tender: the meat should be easily pierced with a fork and fall apart with a little pressure. If the meat is still a little firm, keep cooking and check it every 20 minutes until it is tender enough.
5. Remove from the oven and transfer the pork to a platter or bowl. Using two forks, shred the meat into 1- to 2-inch (2.5 to 5 cm) chunks. Add the cooking liquid and mix to moisten the meat. Set the meat aside for filling the buns or transfer to a clean airtight container. Can be stored refrigerated for up to 5 days or frozen for 2 weeks.

STICKY BUN SAUCE

1 cup (250 mL) hoisin sauce

1 tbsp (15 mL) red wine vinegar

1½ tsp (7.5 mL) Sriracha

1. Combine all ingredients together with a whisk until fully incorporated. If made ahead, transfer to an airtight container and refrigerate for 9 days maximum.

STEAMED BUNS

MAKES 12–14 BUNS

1 cup (250 mL) warm water

1 tbsp (15 mL) vegetable oil, plus
    additional 1 tsp (5 mL) for brushing

1½ tsp (7.5 mL) instant yeast

3 tbsp (45 mL) sugar

3 cups (750 mL) all-purpose flour, plus
    additional 2 tbsp (30 mL) for dusting

1 tbsp (15 mL) dried milk powder

¼ tsp (1.25 mL) fine salt

½ tsp (2.5 mL) baking powder

This is a great party food—
let guests put together their own
mini-buns and top with whatever
garnishes they want. Making a big
batch of roasted pork shoulder will
pay off for future meals. Simply
freeze the leftovers for making
pastas, sandwiches or even tacos!

1. For this recipe you will need a bamboo steamer to cook the dough. Fill your wok with at least 2 inches (5 cm) of water. Place your bamboo baskets on top. Setting this up will allow for an easier process once your dough is ready to go. You will also need to cut out 4- × 4-inch (10 × 10 cm) parchment squares.
2. Combine the warm water, oil, yeast and sugar into the bowl of a stand mixer.
3. Combine the flour, milk powder, salt and baking powder in a separate bowl.
4. Using the paddle attachment, mix the liquids for 1 minute until well combined. Add the dry ingredients and mix for 2 minutes. If the dough sticks to the sides of the bowl, add 1 additional tablespoon of flour. Knead for 2 more minutes. Switch to a dough hook and knead for 4 minutes on medium speed until dough is smooth, clears the sides of the bowl and forms a ball.
5. Turn out the dough onto a lightly floured surface. Knead for 2 minutes by hand, then shape into a smooth ball. Cover with a damp towel and allow to rise for 1½ hours or until double in size.
6. Punch down the dough lightly to break any large air bubbles. Cut the dough in half and gently roll out into a log shape, about 1½ inches (4 cm) in diameter. Cut each log into 1½-inch (4 cm) pieces and using the palm of your hand against the counter, roll each piece of dough into a ball. Repeat with the remaining pieces, covering the already shaped balls with the damp towel to avoid drying out.
7. Take the first ball, and using a rolling pin, shape into an oval about 2 × 4 inches (5 × 10 cm). Brush the front half of each oval with a light coating of vegetable oil, then fold in half, patting together gently. Transfer to a 4- × 4-inch (10 × 10 cm) square of parchment paper and place in the bamboo steamer basket, then cover. Do not turn the heat on yet.
8. Repeat the rolling and shaping procedure with the remaining dough balls, filling the steamer as you make them. Make sure you leave ample space between buns, as they will expand while steaming. After the last bun is made and placed into the steamer, set a timer for 10 minutes. When the timer sounds, turn the heat on high. As soon as you begin seeing steam rise from the top of the bamboo steamer, turn the heat down to medium and continue steaming for 5 minutes. After 5 minutes, turn off the heat but do not remove the lid. Allow the residual heat to finish cooking the buns for 2 minutes. This gentle heat will make softer, fluffier buns that do not collapse. Allow to cool slightly before serving. Use immediately.

SUNFLOWER MUSHROOM PÂTÉ

1980s 1990s 2000s **2010s**

SERVES 4–6

½ cup (125 mL) toasted sunflower seeds

2 tbsp (30 mL) olive oil

¼ cup (60 mL) thinly sliced shallots

¼ cup (60 mL) thinly sliced leeks
  (washed very well to remove grit)

1 tsp (5 mL) minced garlic

1½ cups (375 mL) thinly sliced portobello
  mushrooms (gills removed)

½ tsp (2.5 mL) thyme leaves

¼ cup (60 mL) white wine

1 cup (250 mL) water

1½ tsp (7.5 mL) fine salt

2 tbsp (30 mL) water

1 tsp (5 mL) sherry vinegar

2 tsp (10 mL) cornstarch

¾ tsp (3.75 mL) agar

Pinch ground pepper

Pinch nutmeg

Herb aioli (recipe follows)

Dill oil (recipe follows)

Pickled red pearl onions (page 158)

Toasted sunflower seeds

Maldon salt

Freshly ground black pepper

Taro chips (recipe follows)

Pâté is one of the most luxurious foods, but with liver as its primary ingredient, it's not for everyone—it's not even for every carnivore. Enter this alternative from Chef Collective member Brian Skinner, former owner of Vancouver vegetarian mecca, the Acorn. In it, mushrooms replace the liver, and sunflower seeds provide some extra structure. With pâtés, people have been programmed to accept a brown blob, but here the herb aioli even adds a little unexpected colour. Indulgent yet nutritious, this delicious dip complements a pâté.

1. Place the sunflower seeds into a deep bowl and cover with at least 2 inches (5 cm) of hot water. Set aside to soak for a minimum of 2 hours and a maximum of 24 hours. Place in a strainer and rinse off with cold water. Drain well and set aside.

2. Heat the olive oil in a pot over medium heat until it ripples. Sauté the shallot, leeks, garlic, mushrooms and thyme leaves until shallots are translucent, approximately 15 minutes. Deglaze with the white wine and reduce until almost dry. Stir in 1 cup (250 mL) of water, salt and reserved soaked sunflower seeds. Reduce heat to low and simmer until approximately half of the liquid has evaporated, approximately 15 minutes.

3. In a small bowl, whisk together 2 tablespoons (30 mL) of water, vinegar, cornstarch, agar, ground black pepper and nutmeg. Stir into the simmering mushroom sunflower seed mixture and bring back to a simmer for 1 minute. The texture will be thick at this point.

4. Place in a blender and purée until completely smooth. Transfer to a serving bowl and refrigerate until fully cooled and set.

5. Garnish the mushroom pâté with some herb aioli, dill oil, a few pieces of pickled pearl onion and some toasted sunflower seeds. Season with some Maldon salt and fresh ground black pepper. Serve with taro chips or crackers.

Agar is a seaweed-based thickener similar to gelatin.
If you serve this dish without the herb aioli (which has egg yolk),
this recipe is completely vegetarian and gluten-free.

HERB AIOLI

1 egg yolk

½ cup (125 mL) watercress leaves (loosely packed)

¼ cup (60 mL) basil leaves (loosely packed)

¼ cup (60 mL) chives (loosely packed)

2 tsp (10 mL) Dijon mustard

2 tsp (10 mL) sugar

1 tsp (5 mL) lemon zest

1 tbsp (15 mL) tarragon leaves

1 tbsp (15 mL) thyme leaves

1 tsp (5 mL) lemon juice

½ tsp (2.5 mL) fine salt

1 ice cube

½ cup (125 mL) vegetable oil

1. Combine all ingredients except for the vegetable oil into a blender. Purée until completely smooth, approximately 30 seconds. Don't blend too long or the herbs will overheat and turn dark instead of being a vibrant green.
2. With the blender running, stream in the vegetable oil until it emulsifies into a mayonnaise-like consistency. If made ahead, transfer to an airtight container and refrigerate. The aioli can be stored refrigerated for 5 days maximum.

DILL OIL

¼ cup (60 mL) dill sprigs (tightly packed)

¼ cup (60 mL) vegetable oil

1. Blanch the dill in a small pot of boiling water for 4 minutes. Strain and immediately place in an ice bath until fully cooled. Chop roughly into 1-inch (2.5 cm) pieces.
2. Combine the vegetable oil and blanched dill in a blender and purée on high for 1 minute.
3. Place in a small pot and simmer for 12 minutes over the lowest heat. Allow to cool to room temperature. Strain slowly through 3 layers of cheesecloth or a coffee filter, allowing the oil to seep through. Give the filter a light squeeze to extract any remaining oil before discarding the solids. If made ahead, transfer to an airtight container and refrigerate. The oil can be stored refrigerated for 1 week maximum.

TARO CHIPS

MAKES ABOUT 3 CUPS

Vegetable oil (for deep-frying)

1 large taro root (peeled and ends trimmed off)

2 tsp (10 mL) fine salt

2 tsp (10 mL) sugar

1 tsp (5 mL) ground caraway seed

¼ tsp (1.25 mL) ground fennel seed

¼ tsp (1.25 mL) ground cumin seed

Pinch ground black pepper

1. Preheat a deep fryer or a large Dutch oven half full of vegetable oil over medium-high heat.
2. Halve the taro root lengthwise and using a mandoline, slice into 1⁄16-inch (2 mm) thick half moons.
3. Combine the salt, sugar, ground caraway, ground fennel, ground cumin, and black pepper. Set aside.
4. Once the oil has reached 300°F (150°C), carefully fry half the sliced taro root until golden brown, approximately 4 to 5 minutes. Stir several times to make sure the pieces do not stick together. Drain from the oil and spread out over a paper towel–lined baking tray. Immediately season with the caraway salt. Repeat with the rest of the taro slices. Serve immediately with the mushroom pâté.

Sunflower Mushroom Pâté with Taro Chips

CRISPY TUNA SUSHI CONE

The *Washington Post* says that Hidekazu Tojo's Vancouver restaurant Tojo's "is grander and more enticing than a geisha's dance." We don't know what that means either, but we do know that it's one of the best Japanese spots on the continent, so when we needed a little help to complete the development of this dish, we called Tojo over to tweak it. The flavour and textural effects of so many elements combined so adroitly are difficult to describe, but let's give it a shot:

It's all in a cone.
Ginger meets Sriracha meets
tuna. Kapow!

1980s 1990s 2000s **2010s**

SERVES 4

4 sheets soy paper (common in the Asian food section of your grocery store)

Sushi rice (page 31)

Tempura crunch (recipe follows)

¼ cup (60 mL) Thai basil (about 12 leaves)

1 whole avocado (peeled, seeded and cut into ¼-inch/½ cm lengthwise slices)

Sriracha mayo (page 34)

2 tbsp (30 mL) pickled ginger (about 8 slices)

1 cup (250 mL) julienned cucumber

½ cup (125 mL) julienned carrots

Marinated tuna (recipe follows)

2 tbsp (30 mL) tobiko

2 sprigs cilantro

1. Cut 1 sheet of soy paper in half lengthwise. Place one half-sheet of soy paper horizontally on a completely dry surface. Using damp fingers, gently spread 2 tablespoons (30 mL) of sushi rice over the left half of the soy paper, resulting in a 4-inch (10 cm) square of rice. Sprinkle evenly with 2 teaspoons (10 mL) of tempura crunch. Press the tempura crunch gently to make it stick to the rice.

2. In this order, spread the following over the right side of the square of rice (the centre of the soy paper): 3 leaves of Thai basil, 1 slice of avocado, 1 teaspoon (5 mL) Sriracha mayo, 2 slices pickled ginger, ¼ cup (60 mL) julienned cucumber, 2 tablespoons (30 mL) julienned carrots, 1 piece marinated tuna and 1 teaspoon (5 mL) tobiko. Ensure all ingredients are distributed evenly from top to bottom with the carrots and cucumbers sticking out slightly over the top of the soy paper.

3. Gently take the bottom left corner of the soy paper and fold it toward the top right corner of the rice (or the centre of the soy paper), forming a triangle on the left half of the soy paper. At this time, you will have formed the beginnings of a cone, with the bottom end closed and the top end wide open displaying the ingredients. Continue rolling tightly, following an arc pattern, heading toward the bottom right corner of the soy paper. Roll tightly until just a small corner of the soy paper remains. Use 2 to 3 kernels of rice to stick the soy paper together by smearing the rice kernels and using it as a "glue" to keep the cone together. Hold the cone upright and garnish with ¼ teaspoon (1.25 mL) of Sriracha mayo, ¼ teaspoon (1.25 mL) tempura crunch, ¼ teaspoon (1.25 mL) tobiko and 1 leaf cilantro. Repeat with the remaining cones. Serve immediately.

Although this recipe uses soy paper, you can also use nori with equally good results. Try both and see which you prefer!

TEMPURA CRUNCH

Tempura Batter (page 44)

1. Preheat a deep fryer or a large Dutch oven half full of vegetable oil over medium-high heat.
2. Once the oil has reached 400°F (200°C), use a slotted spoon to drizzle tempura batter into the hot oil. Remove the cooked batter with a slotted spoon and drain immediately on paper towels once fully crisp and golden. Allow to cool to room temperature. Break up the fried batter into ¼-inch (½ cm) pieces. Use immediately.

MARINATED TUNA

8 oz (225 g) Ahi tuna loin (sushi grade)

½ cup (125 mL) mirin

⅓ cup (80 mL) soy sauce

1 tbsp (15 mL) Sriracha

1 tsp (5 mL) dashi powder

½ tsp (2.5 mL) fine salt

1. Cut the tuna loin into 4- × ½-inch (10 × 1 cm) rectangular pieces. Combine the mirin, soy sauce, Sriracha, dashi powder and salt.
2. Marinate the tuna in the soy mixture for 2 hours, refrigerated. Remove from the marinade after 2 hours. Discard marinade. Use the tuna immediately.

LOS CABOS CHICKEN TACOS

Reuben Major now runs his own restaurant in Vancouver, Belgard Kitchen, but before that, when he was head development chef, he couldn't help but notice two things: one, the global taco frenzy; two, that the tortilla soup we'd been serving for a decade was about as good as Mexican food gets. Inspired by that soup, he used its taste profile to create this dish. Note his solution to the universal problem of keeping chicken tender. Fancy methods like *sous vide* and other kinds of slow cooking are one way to avoid toughness, but so is poaching. And not only is the chicken seriously moist, the meat is permeated by the seasonings.

1. Preheat a nonstick pan or griddle over medium-low heat.
2. Brush both sides of the tortillas with vegetable oil and toast on the nonstick pan until pliable, approximately 15 to 20 seconds per side. Immediately sprinkle some nacho cheese over the heated tortillas until the cheese begins to melt. Transfer to a platter. Top the cheese with some tomato poached chicken followed by some avocado corn salsa.
3. Toss together the cabbage, lettuce, cilantro, lime juice, honey and salt.
4. Top each taco with some of the cabbage mixture. Drizzle with some hot sauce and top with jalapeño rings. Cut the lime into wedges and serve with the tacos along with additional hot sauce if desired.

SERVES 4–6

12 6-inch (15 cm) white corn tortillas

1 tsp (5 mL) vegetable oil

1 cup (250 mL) nacho cheese

Avocado corn salsa (recipe follows)

Tomato poached chicken (recipe follows)

1 cup (250 mL) finely shaved green cabbage

1 cup (250 mL) finely shaved green leaf lettuce

¼ cup (60 mL) finely chopped cilantro

1 tbsp (15 mL) lime juice

1 tsp (5 mL) honey

¼ tsp (1.25 mL) fine salt

2 tbsp (30 mL) Valentina hot sauce or your favourite hot sauce

1 peeled and seeded jalapeño, sliced into ⅛-inch (3 mm) rings

1 lime

AVOCADO CORN SALSA

2 pitted and peeled avocados, cut into medium dice

½ cup (125 mL) corn kernels

2 tbsp (30 mL) finely chopped green onion

2 tbsp (30 mL) finely chopped cilantro

1½ tbsp (22.5 mL) lime juice

1 tsp (5 mL) honey

½ tsp (2.5 mL) fine salt

¼ tsp (1.25 mL) ground cumin

¼ tsp (1.25 mL) ground coriander

1. Combine all the ingredients in a large bowl and mix well. The avocado should break up slightly as you are incorporating all the ingredients.
2. Serve immediately, as the avocado will turn brown if made ahead.

TOMATO POACHED CHICKEN

1 lb (450 g) boneless skinless chicken breasts or thighs

3 tbsp (45 mL) quesadilla spice (page 238)

1 28 oz can (approximately 3½ cups/800 mL) crushed tomatoes

1½ cups (375 mL) water

1 peeled and quartered red onion

¼ cup (60 mL) smashed garlic cloves

1 quartered lime

1 serrano pepper

1 tbsp (15 mL) fine salt

1 tsp (5 mL) ground black pepper

1 tbsp (15 mL) Valentina hot sauce

1. In a large bowl, toss together the chicken and 1 tablespoon (15 mL) of quesadilla spice, covering the chicken evenly. Allow to marinate for at least 20 minutes so that the flavours can permeate the chicken.
2. In a large pot, bring the crushed tomatoes, water, onion, garlic, lime, serrano pepper, 2 tablespoons (30 mL) of quesadilla spice, salt, and black pepper to a simmer. Add the chicken and submerge into the simmering sauce. Return to a simmer and cook, uncovered, for 20 minutes. Check the largest and thickest piece of chicken for doneness. The chicken should register 160°F (71°C). Once it has reached temperature, remove the chicken from the heat and transfer it to a clean platter to cool slightly. Cut the chicken into thin slices, approximately ¼ inch (½ cm). Toss evenly with some of the tomato simmering liquid and Valentina hot sauce so that the meat is moist and flavourful.

HONEY CAJUN POPCORN

Unlike almost everyone else these days, we make no claim to be a sports bar, and in fact our televisions are often turned off. That said, who doesn't want to watch the big game for the local team? This little treat from Chef Ryan Stone is something we sometimes bring out on game nights.

1980s 1990s 2000s **2010s**

MAKES 2½ QUARTS OR 10 CUPS (2.5 L)

1 tbsp (15 mL) vegetable oil

1 tbsp (15 mL) melted salted butter

½ cup (125 mL) popping corn

1 tbsp (15 mL) honey

2 tsp (10 mL) Cajun blackening spice (page 239)

¾ tsp (3.75 mL) fine salt

1. Heat the vegetable oil and butter in a large pot with 3 kernels of popping corn until all 3 pop. Remove the 3 pieces of popped corn. Add the popping corn to the pot, and stir until each kernel is coated with oil. Add the honey, stir again, then cover with a lid and leave on high heat. Once popping begins, start shaking the pot and continue until the popping accelerates. Then turn off the heat and continue to shake until popping stops. Remove the lid and allow the popped corn to release steam and become crispy.
2. Transfer to a large mixing bowl and toss with the Cajun blackening spice and salt. Serve immediately.

PATIO DINING

In 1982, when we opened our first location in Edmonton, the only other way to find al fresco dining would have been to check the white pages for Mr. Fresco's address and then head over at dinnertime to watch him eat. Maybe we exaggerate, but even in Vancouver there were darned few places with patios.

Bus and Stan don't claim to have been deliberately trailblazing with their emphasis on patio dining right from the start. True, Stan was just back from southern Europe, where outdoor dining is a fundamental part of life, but honestly, it was easy to move some tables and chairs outside the Edmonton restaurant because they'd furnished the entire place with patio furniture to save money. But as the 1980s progressed, outdoor dining caught on, and we were happy to lead the way down a trail that we'd been among the first to blaze.

Of course, it didn't hurt to have David Vance, our designer and patio master, on side. We were among the first to design our locations with pleasant enclosed seating areas where precious parking spots might otherwise have been located. Soon enough, the patio furniture was purpose-built to fit the space, and entire walls of glass were designed to roll away. Some of our most recent locations have inside/outside bars extending on either side of an exterior wall.

Then there was the food. How long have we been in the patio business? Long enough to go through three different guacamole recipes (one of which you'll find in the Starters, Share Plates and Sides section.

And maybe this will come as a surprise, but people seem to enjoy having a drink outside. You could even say that sitting on a patio or deck with a glass in hand became a thing. Beer and wine, of course, but also cocktails. Especially cocktails. We'll admit that our mixed drinks were standard issue during our first, oh, quarter century, but that certainly hasn't been the case since Cameron Bogue came on board. A ski bum who originally took up bartending so he could spend his days on the slopes, Cameron soon found perfecting drinks as interesting as tackling fresh powder and joined the founding generation of creative, competitive bartenders who have been transforming cocktail culture since the turn of the millennium. He joined us after a stint running the cocktail programs at Daniel Boulud's five New York City locations, took careful stock of what we were serving, and ultimately switched up every drink, taking care to avoid the three p's: packaged mixes, processed ingredients and pasteurized products. We could have filled this entire book with his inventive craft cocktails had there been this space, instead we stuck to a couple of Earls classics, revamped of course by Cam.

Today, at a minimum, a drink served at Earls involves house-squeezed citrus juices and the assurance that no commercially prepared powders are involved. Some of Cameron's drinks became much more elaborate (check the Brunch chapter for his very complex Caesar), but others became simpler. In fact, the recipes for making margaritas and Bellinis seen here are only slightly more complicated than opening a beer, just one of the qualities that makes them ideal patio sippers.

MARGARITA

In the trade, a sour that's been sweetened with an orange liqueur such as Triple Sec is called a daisy. And what's the Spanish word for "daisy" but "margarita"? Now you know where the name came from. Incidentally, we sell 700,000 of these a year, and squeeze 700 limes a day at our restaurants.

MAKES 1 MARGARITA

Margarita salt

1 fl oz (30 mL) simple syrup (equal parts sugar and water, stirred until dissolved)

1 fl oz (30 mL) fresh lime juice

1 fl oz (30 mL) cold water

.75 fl oz (22.5 mL) El Jimador Blanco

.25 fl oz (7.5 mL) Triple Sec

1 wide strip lime zest

1. Rim a double rocks glass with a ½ rim of margarita salt and fill with ice cubes.
2. In a martini shaker, combine the simple syrup, lime juice, water, El Jimador Blanco and Triple Sec. Pack the shaker with ice and top with the lid. Shake vigorously 12 times to mix ingredients. Strain over fresh ice into the glass. Garnish with the lime zest. Add a 6-inch (15 cm) straw.

BELLINI

The classic Italian Bellini is quite a different thing, with not much more than Prosecco, peach purée and a few drops of berry juice for colour. Instead of going that route for our patios, Cameron Bogue came up with what he thinks is an equally authentic take, but this time on the classic Canadian Bellini. Because why not, eh?

MAKES 1 BELLINI

2 fl oz (60 mL) white peach purée

1 fl oz (30 mL) white peach syrup

1.25 fl oz (37.5 mL) amber rum

1 fl oz (30 mL) white wine

1 fl oz (30 mL) soda

1 fl oz (30 mL) sangria, either your favourite store-bought brand or using your favourite recipe

1. Fill a martini glass with ice.
2. In a martini shaker, combine the white peach purée, peach syrup, amber rum and white wine. Fill the shaker with ice, top with a lid and shake vigorously 10 times. Strain into the glass. Top with soda and float the sangria on top. Serve with a straw.

soups and salads

It's said that soups are a barometer of quality, and, what do you know, we did well with ours right from the start. That might seem odd for a hamburger joint, except that we had Chefs Chuck Currie and Larry Stewart, and they always insisted that ours be made from scratch.

Ah, but salads... When we first opened it was really tough to sell them, even though we knew, and our guests knew, they should be eating some greens. And then along came the Caesar. We introduced the Caesar salad when we first started opening fancier versions of the first Earls, called Tin Palaces at the time. We haven't included the recipe here, because we have to keep some secrets, but in the years since, and especially recently, we've introduced some spectacular salads, so we know you'll be able to find one you love.

MUSHROOM SOUP

Chuck, our longest-serving chief development chef, is also a musician and writer, and this is a soup that really gets him going. It's a classic, of course, but one that lends itself to infinite variation. How about dried porcini with Madeira, he suggests. Or shiitakes with sake? Garnish it with, well, what have you got? Sure, it will serve six to eight, but it will also serve just you, for a couple of days or more.

1980s 1990s 2000s 2010s

SERVES 6-8

1 tbsp olive oil

1 cup (250 mL) finely diced onion

3 cups (750 mL) or 8 oz (225 g) ½-inch (1 cm) sliced button mushrooms

1 tsp (5 mL) fine salt

½ tsp (2.5 mL) ground black pepper

2.67 oz (75 g or ⅓ cup/80 mL) salted butter

½ cup (125 mL) all-purpose flour

4 cups (1 L) chicken stock

1 cup (250 mL) heavy cream

¾ cup (180 mL) sherry

¼ cup (60 mL) finely chopped green onions

1. Heat the olive oil in a heavy-bottomed stockpot or Dutch oven until it ripples. Sweat the onions until translucent, approximately 3 minutes.
2. Add the mushrooms, salt and pepper and sauté until mushrooms are just soft.
3. In a separate small pot, melt the butter over medium heat. Add the flour and cook, stirring often, until the roux (flour/butter mixture) is blond and smells slightly toasty.
4. Add the roux to the mushrooms and onions, stirring well to break up any lumps.
5. Add the chicken stock, cream and sherry to the roux mixture, whisking well to avoid any lumps. Bring to a simmer while stirring the bottom well.
6. Garnish each bowl with a sprinkle of green onions and serve immediately.

Button mushrooms are called for in the recipe,
but feel free to substitute cremini, portabello,
or even a mixture of different varieties.

FRENCH ONION SOUP

What's the most soul-stirring aroma in the culinary world? It might occur during the act of deglazing, when sherry hits a hot pan in which onions have just been caramelized, as occurs while preparing this recipe from Chef Larry Stewart.

1980s **1990s** 2000s 2010s

SERVES 4–6

3 oz (85 g or ⅓ cup + 1 tbsp/95 mL) butter

2½ lb (1.15 kg) thinly sliced onions

1 tsp (5 mL) ground black pepper

1 tsp (5 mL) fine salt

1 tsp (5 mL) finely chopped fresh thyme

½ tsp (2.5 mL) sugar

½ tsp (2.5 mL) dried oregano

Pinch dried tarragon

1 bay leaf

⅓ cup (80 mL) sherry

10 cups (2.5 L) beef stock

3 cups (750 mL) shredded Swiss cheese (Gruyère or Emmenthal)

¼ cup (60 mL) finely grated Parmesan cheese

4 to 6 slices French bread (1 inch/2.5 cm thick)

2 tbsp (30 mL) olive oil

1. Melt the butter over medium heat in a heavy-bottomed pot or Dutch oven. Add the onions, black pepper, salt, thyme, sugar, oregano, tarragon and bay leaf to the pot. Stir well so that all ingredients get a light coating of butter.
2. Turn the heat to low and cover, allowing the onions to soften completely, approximately 15 to 20 minutes.
3. Remove the lid and cook over low heat for approximately 2 hours, stirring frequently. The onions should be the colour and consistency of molasses.
4. Deglaze the pot with sherry, scraping up all the onions from the bottom of the pot.
5. Add the beef stock and bring to a boil. Simmer for a further 30 minutes or until the stock has reduced by a third and is slightly thickened. Remove the bay leaf.
6. Preheat the oven to 350°F (180°C).
7. Combine the shredded Swiss cheese and Parmesan cheese in a bowl until evenly distributed.
8. Brush each side of the French bread with some olive oil, and then place it on a rimmed baking tray. Toast for 10 minutes in the preheated oven. Flip over to the other side and toast for a further 5 minutes until golden brown. Remove from the oven.
9. Ladle the soup into oven-safe serving bowls. Place 1 slice of toast over each serving of soup.
10. Top the toast with a thick layer of cheese, distributing it right to the edges of the soup bowls.
11. Place in the oven for 15 minutes, then broil for approximately 1 to 2 minutes until the cheese turns golden brown. Watch this step closely as the strength of each broiler varies. As soon as the cheese begins to turn golden, remove it from the heat.
12. Allow the cheese to cool slightly. Serve.

Use any combination of cheese you like for the topping. Toasting the bread really well allows maximum absorption once placed on the soup. A mushroom-heavy vegetable stock can be used to make this a vegetarian dish. Be sure to cut the onions on the north–south axis so that they retain a little structure.

THAI CHICKEN SALAD

When Chuck came up with this salad a quarter century ago, Thai food was a foreign concept to most of us. The dressing combines sweet, spicy and salty elements as many a Thai sauce would, and the salad nourishes and refreshes with its generous sprinkling of fresh chopped cilantro and mint. The dish became an instant hit, and imitations quickly found their way onto other restaurant menus.

1. Bring a pot of salted water to a full boil. Blanch the noodles for 2 minutes, stirring well to loosen up the clumps of noodles.
2. Drain immediately and flush with cold water to stop cooking. Allow to drain and cool completely. Coat lightly with vegetable oil to prevent sticking.
3. Combine the romaine, red and yellow peppers, red onion, cucumber and drained noodles. Drizzle with the Thai dressing and toss very well, allowing the dressing to be fully absorbed by the noodles.
4. Divide into individual salad bowls and garnish evenly with the mint, cilantro, grape tomatoes and roasted peanuts.

SERVES 4-5

1 lb (450 g) Chinese fresh steamed egg noodles

2 tsp (10 mL) vegetable oil

1 lb (450 g) chopped romaine hearts

½ cup (125 mL) julienned red peppers

½ cup (125 mL) julienned yellow peppers

½ cup (125 mL) thinly sliced red onion (sliced lengthwise)

½ cup (125 mL) thinly sliced 3-inch (8 cm) cucumber sticks (seeds removed)

Thai dressing (recipe follows)

½ cup (125 mL) whole or torn mint leaves

½ cup (125 mL) loosely packed cilantro leaves

1 dry pint (1½ cups/375 mL) grape tomatoes

¼ cup (60 mL) roasted peanuts

Try to cut the herbs at the last minute as they tend to wilt and discolour if made ahead too early.

THAI DRESSING

1 cup (250 mL) ketjap manis (Indonesian sweet soy sauce, found in the Asian food section of your grocery store)

1 cup (250 mL) freshly squeezed lime juice

1 tbsp (15 mL) sambal oelek (a chili and garlic paste found in the Asian food section of your grocery store)

1 tbsp (15 mL) finely minced garlic

1. Combine all ingredients together until fully incorporated. Transfer to an airtight container.
2. Can be stored refrigerated for up to 5 days.

SANTA FE CHICKEN SALAD

Chris Remington worked with us for almost a decade, first as a prep chef and later in the test kitchen. It was during an inspiration trip to Scottsdale, Arizona, that he and a gang of fellow chefs discovered a salad dressing that would be ideal for a salad he had been working on. The restaurant wouldn't share the recipe, so back they went to order another bunch of salads, this time with dressing on the side. In keeping with standard corporate protocol, the precious elixir was then smuggled back to Vancouver in someone's luggage. A few days of experimentation—and voila!

1980s **1990s** 2000s 2010s

SERVES 4–6

4 brined half chicken breasts (page 239)

¼ cup (60 mL) Cajun blackening spice (page 239)

8 oz (225 g) mixed greens

8 oz (225 g) chopped romaine hearts

1 15 oz can (approximately 1¾ cups/ 435 mL) black beans, rinsed and drained

1 cup (250 mL) thawed frozen corn

½ cup (125 mL) ½-inch (1 cm) chopped dried dates

1 cup (250 mL) peanut lime vinaigrette (recipe follows)

½ cup (125 mL) crumbled feta cheese

1 cup (250 mL) tortilla strips (page 83)

1 avocado

1 lime, cut into 6 wedges

1. Remove skin from the chicken breasts. Dredge the chicken in the Cajun blackening spice until lightly coated on all surfaces.
2. Place on a preheated grill or pan-fry in a heated skillet with some vegetable oil, flipping the chicken after 4 minutes to ensure even cooking. Cook for a further 4 minutes, and check for doneness on the thickest part of the breast. The meat should register 160°F (71°C) on an instant-read thermometer.
3. While the chicken is cooking, assemble the salad by combining the mixed greens, romaine, black beans, corn, dates and peanut lime vinaigrette in a large salad bowl. Toss together with tongs until all ingredients are coated lightly with the vinaigrette.
4. Divide evenly into bowls and top with feta cheese and tortilla strips.
5. Cut the avocado in half and remove the seed. Slice longthwise into ¼-inch (¼ cm) slices and scoop out using a spoon. Garnish each bowl of salad with a quarter of an avocado, approximately 4 slices, and top with the sliced blackened chicken.
6. Add a lime wedge and serve immediately.

The best dates to use are the Medjool dates, but any variety of dried dates will do. Instead of using a knife, use a pair of kitchen shears to cut the dates into pieces. Dip the shears in water whenever the stickiness starts to build up.

PEANUT LIME VINAIGRETTE

3 tbsp (45 mL) roasted peanuts

1 tbsp (15 mL) minced garlic

¼ tsp (1.25 mL) ground cumin

4½ tbsp (67.5 mL) freshly squeezed lime juice, divided

1 tbsp (15 mL) olive oil

1 tsp (5 mL) sherry vinegar

2 tbsp (30 mL) chopped cilantro (tightly packed)

½ tsp (2.5 mL) fine salt

¼ tsp (1.25 mL) ground black pepper

½ cup (125 mL) vegetable oil

1. Using a food processor or hand-held blender, purée the peanuts, minced garlic, cumin, 2 tbsp (30 mL) of lime juice, olive oil and sherry vinegar until extremely smooth, almost like peanut butter.
2. Add the cilantro, remaining lime juice, salt and pepper. Continue to purée until the cilantro is finely incorporated into the dressing and chopped into pieces no greater than ⅛ inch (3 mm).
3. With the machine running, continue to purée the vinaigrette while pouring the vegetable oil in a slow stream. This will create a strong emulsion so the oil does not separate.
4. Transfer to an airtight container and refrigerate. The peanut lime vinaigrette can be stored refrigerated for 5 days.

SANTA FE BLACK BEAN SOUP

Larry remembered eating a soup like this at a restaurant in New Mexico and was inspired to try his own version. He seems to have done pretty well, because almost three decades later, this southwestern-flavoured soup is one of our longest-standing and most frequently ordered dishes. The name? There is no actual Santa Fe connection, but around 1990 this New Mexico mountain town was just the hippest place—Berlin and Brooklyn rolled into one, except with everyone dressed in pastels.

1980s **1990s** 2000s 2010s

SERVES 4-6

1⅓ cups (330 mL) dried black turtle beans

7 cups (1.7 L) chicken stock

½ cup (125 mL) roughly chopped bacon

½ cup (125 mL) roughly chopped carrots

½ cup (125 mL) roughly chopped celery

½ cup (125 mL) roughly chopped onion

1 tbsp (15 mL) roughly chopped garlic

1½ tbsp (22.5 mL) Mexican chili powder

2 tsp (10 mL) fine salt

½ tsp (2.5 mL) ground black pepper

½ tsp (2.5 mL) ground cumin

½ tsp (2.5 mL) ground cayenne pepper

½ cup (125 mL) sour cream garnish (recipe follows)

¼ cup (60 mL) finely chopped cilantro

1. In a large Dutch oven or heavy stockpot, bring all ingredients except for the sour cream garnish and cilantro to a simmer over medium-high heat.
2. Turn heat to low and continue to simmer, covered, for 3 hours. This long simmering time will allow the flavours to develop in the soup.
3. After three hours, remove from the heat and purée until smooth using a hand-held immersion blender. Alternatively, you could also use a stand blender and purée the soup in batches.
4. Ladle into individual bowls and top with 2 tablespoons (30 mL) of sour cream garnish and some cilantro. Serve immediately.

SOUR CREAM GARNISH

⅓ cup plus 1 tbsp (95 mL) sour cream

2 tbsp (30 mL) milk

1. Place all the ingredients in a mixing bowl and whisk until all ingredients are combined.
2. Transfer to an airtight container and refrigerate. The sour cream garnish can be stored refrigerated for 3 days.

Since this soup is puréed in the final step, the cuts on the vegetables and bacon don't have to be exact. You can add extra chili powder or cayenne if you like a spicier soup.

ORGANIC GREEN SALAD

Development chef Reuben Major helped us push our salad offerings along a little with this lovely little side salad, where crisp romaine and apple slices add a little crunch, feta cheese a little savoury sourness, candied pecans some nutty sweetness and baby greens the prospect of rosy good health.

1980s 1990s **2000s** 2010s

SERVES 4-6

8 oz (225 g) romaine hearts

8 oz (225 g) mixed greens

½ green apple

½ cup (125 mL) apple cider vinaigrette
   (recipe follows)

½ cup (125 mL) crumbled feta

¼ cup (60 mL) candied pecans (page 89)

1. Cut the romaine hearts into 1½-inch (4 cm) crosswise pieces. Transfer to a large salad bowl.
2. Add the mixed greens. Combine thoroughly so that the lettuces are evenly distributed.
3. Core the apple and slice into ⅛-inch (3 mm) julienne. Add to the salad bowl.
4. Drizzle the apple cider vinaigrette over the lettuce and toss gently until all the leaves are fully coated.
5. Evenly distribute the salad to individual servings. Garnish each serving with feta cheese and candied pecans. Serve immediately.

APPLE CIDER VINAIGRETTE

3½ tbsp (52 mL) apple cider vinegar

1½ tsp (7.5 mL) lemon juice

1 tbsp (15 mL) minced shallots

1 tsp (5 mL) peeled minced ginger

1 tsp (5 mL) lemon zest

¼ tsp (1.25 mL) fine salt

¼ tsp (1.25 mL) ground black pepper

2½ tbsp (37.5 mL) olive oil

1. Combine all ingredients with a whisk until fully incorporated. Transfer to an airtight container. Can be stored refrigerated for up to 5 days. Mix well before using.

Cut the apples at the very last minute to avoid oxidization.
Otherwise you can prep ahead and toss the apples in some lemon juice
and water to avoid browning.

TORTILLA SOUP

By the turn of the century we had the happy habit of calling on guest chefs who could lend us particular types of expertise. In the case of Mexican celebrity chef Susanna Palazuelos, though, we made ourselves the guests, with Stew and one of our culinary development chefs, Alberto Lemo, heading down to Acapulco to work in her kitchen. Every Thursday was *pozole* day there, and they'd join the crowd at a little hole in the wall where everyone ordered the traditional Mexican soup. Stew and Alberto came back with recipes for both pozole and tortilla soups, and this is the one that stuck. We've come to think of it as a delicious enchilada in a bowl.

1980s 1990s **2000s** 2010s

SERVES 4–6

2 tbsp (30 mL) vegetable oil, divided

¼ cup (60 mL) finely diced shallot

1 lb (450 g) halved Roma tomatoes

½ cup (125 mL) finely diced white onion

⅔ cup (160 mL) canned crushed tomatoes

2 tsp (10 mL) minced garlic

4 cups (1 L) vegetable stock

2½ tsp (12.5 mL) fine salt

¼ tsp (1.25 mL) ground black pepper

1 tbsp (15 mL) fresh oregano leaves

1 avocado, peeled and pitted

¼ cup (60 mL) sour cream

¼ cup (60 mL) shredded Jalapeño Jack
   and cheddar blend

Tortilla strips and fried pasilla chilis
   (recipe follows)

chili oil (optional)

1. Heat 1 teaspoon (5 mL) of vegetable oil in a heavy-bottomed pot or Dutch oven until it ripples. Add the shallot and sauté until translucent and fragrant, approximately 1 minute. Transfer to a medium-sized bowl.
2. To the same bowl, add the Roma tomatoes, white onion, crushed tomatoes and garlic. Purée with a hand-held immersion blender or a food processor until no solids remain.
3. In the same heavy pot or Dutch oven, heat the remaining vegetable oil until it ripples. Add the tomato purée and bring to a slow simmer. Cook for 8 minutes, stirring occasionally.
4. Add the vegetable stock, salt, pepper and oregano leaves. Return to a simmer then remove from the heat.
5. Slice the peeled and pitted avocado lengthwise into ¼-inch (½ cm) slices.
6. To garnish the soup, ladle the soup into individual bowls until two-thirds full. Add the garnishes in the following order: a quarter of the sliced avocado, 1 tablespoon (15 mL) sour cream, 1 tablespoon (15 mL) cheese, 1 tablespoon (15 mL) fried pasilla chilies, 1 tablespoon (15 mL) fried tortilla strips. Drizzle with chili oil if desired.
7. Serve immediately.

TORTILLA STRIPS AND FRIED PASILLA CHILIS

1 dried pasilla chili (available in the
   Mexican section of your local market)

2 yellow, red, or blue corn tortillas
   (6 inches/15 cm)

¼ tsp (1.25 mL) fine salt

Vegetable oil for frying

1. Put on gloves before handling pasilla chilies, as they can cause irritation to people with sensitive skin. Remove the stem and slice the dried pasilla chili in half lengthwise. Remove all the seeds and discard. Slice the chili into ⅛- × 2-inch (3 mm × 5 cm) strips and set aside.
2. Cut the corn tortillas in half, then cut across the halves to make ⅛- × 2-inch (3 mm × 5 cm) strips.
3. Heat a pot of oil to 350°F (180°C). Using a slotted spoon or a sieve, lower the pasilla strips into the oil and fry for 5 seconds. Drain immediately and pat dry.
4. Using the same slotted spoon or sieve, fry the tortilla strips for 45 seconds or until crisp. Drain immediately on a paper towel-lined tray or plate. Season with fine salt.

If you like your soup very hot, make sure the soup is piping hot before garnishing it, as the additional ingredients will cool it down quite quickly.

WINTER SPINACH SALAD

1980s 1990s **2000s** 2010s

SERVES 4–6

1 lb (450 g) baby spinach leaves

¾ cup (180 mL) crispy onions, divided

½ cup (125 mL) chopped sun-dried tomatoes, rehydrated if not oil-packed

Balsamic vinaigrette (recipe follows)

½ cup (125 mL) candied pecans (page 89)

4 oz (115 g or ½ cup/125 mL) goat cheese

16 to 20 pitted kalamata olives

Balsamic reduction (store-bought)

During our first decade we had a menu. Full stop. But some time in the 1990s we came to the realization that ingredients are cheapest and at their best when they're in season. Accordingly, we began to perplex our guests with menu items that came and went on a seasonal basis, such as this one from Rebecca Dawson, one of Vancouver's original locavore chefs, which takes advantage of spinach's ability to keep right on growing when temperatures dip down toward freezing. The quality is shared with chard, kale and many other delicious greens, should you wish to substitute.

1. In a large mixing bowl, toss together the spinach, ¼ cup (60 mL) of crispy onions, the sun-dried tomatoes and the balsamic vinaigrette.
2. Evenly distribute between serving plates. Top each salad with the remaining crispy onions, candied pecans, goat cheese and olives, dividing equally between each serving.
3. Drizzle 2 teaspoons (10 mL) balsamic reduction over each salad.
4. Serve immediately.

BALSAMIC VINAIGRETTE

¼ cup (60 mL) balsamic vinegar

2 tsp (10 mL) Dijon mustard

2 tsp (10 mL) minced shallots

½ tsp (2.5 mL) minced garlic

½ tsp (2.5 mL) fine salt

¼ tsp (1.25 mL) ground black pepper

¼ tsp (1.25 mL) fresh thyme leaves

½ cup (125 mL) vegetable oil

1. Combine the balsamic vinegar, mustard, shallots, garlic, salt, black pepper, thyme and oil in a small bowl. Using a food processor or hand-held blender, slowly add the oil and purée all ingredients until emulsified and the shallots are finely chopped.
2. Transfer to an airtight container and refrigerate. The vinaigrette can be stored refrigerated for 5 days. Mix well before use.

You can find balsamic reduction in the vinegar section of most grocery stores. Or you can easily make your own by reducing two parts balsamic vinegar to one part sugar until thick and syrupy.

WEST COAST SALAD

When Reuben Major first cooked this up in our test kitchen, he says there were some probing questions—mostly along the lines of, "What is this kwin-o-a stuff anyway?" Blended with the quinoa are greens, avocado, nuts, feta, berries and, a little unusually for us, carrots, adding colour, sweetness and crunch.

1980s 1990s **2000s** 2010s

SERVES 4

1 oz (28 g or 2 tbsp/30 mL) room-temperature salted butter

1 lb (450 g) 21 to 30 count prawns, peeled and deveined

1 tsp (5 mL) fine salt, divided

1 tsp (5 mL) ground black pepper, divided

4 oz (115 g) spinach

4 oz (115 g) mixed greens

1 cup (250 mL) quartered strawberries or whole blueberries

½ cup (125 mL) julienned carrots

¼ cup (60 mL) finely chopped cilantro

White quinoa (page 101)

Citrus honey vinaigrette (recipe follows)

1 medium-sized avocado, diced within the peel

½ cup (125 mL) crumbled feta cheese

½ cup (125 mL) candied pecans (page 89)

1. Heat the butter in a nonstick skillet over medium heat. Once the butter begins to foam, add the prawns and cook until they begin to turn pink, approximately 3 to 4 minutes.
2. Season with ½ teaspoon (2.5 mL) each salt and black pepper. Transfer to a plate and keep warm.
3. In a large bowl, dress the spinach, mixed greens, strawberries or blueberries, carrots, cilantro and quinoa lightly with the citrus honey vinaigrette. Season lightly with the remaining salt and pepper. Divide between 4 salad bowls.
4. Scoop out the diced avocado and divide between each salad, ensuring the diced avocado pieces are not clumped together.
5. Garnish each salad with 2 tablespoons (30 mL) of feta cheese and 2 tablespoons (30 mL) of candied pecans.
6. Serve immediately.

CITRUS HONEY VINAIGRETTE

1 tbsp (15 mL) mayonnaise

1 tbsp (15 mL) honey

1 tbsp (15 mL) lemon juice

2 tsp (10 mL) red wine vinegar

1 tsp (5 mL) grainy mustard

1 tsp (5 mL) Dijon mustard

1 tsp (5 mL) lemon zest

¼ tsp (1.25 mL) fine salt

3 tbsp (45 mL) olive oil

3 tbsp (45 mL) grapeseed or vegetable oil

1. Using a food processor or hand-held blender, purée all ingredients until they are emulsified.
2. Transfer to an airtight container and refrigerate. The vinaigrette can be stored refrigerated for 5 days. Mix well before use.

ROCKET, PEAR AND BEET SALAD

A British Columbia native who decamped to Europe for kitchen time in several Michelin-starred establishments, David Hawksworth cheffed for many years at Vancouver's landmark West, one of Canada's leading fine dining spots, before leaving to develop Hawksworth, which instantly became even more of a destination. In between he spent a little time helping us out, leaving behind this delicious variation of a classic salad.

1980s 1990s 2000s **2010s**

SERVES 4

1½ lb (680 g) trimmed beets

2 pears (any variety)

2 tbsp (30 mL) lemon juice

1 tbsp (15 mL) olive oil

4 oz (115 g) arugula

½ tsp (2.5 mL) fine salt

½ tsp (2.5 mL) ground black pepper

1 cup (250 mL) goat cheese coulis (recipe follows)

½ cup (125 mL) finely shaved Parmesan cheese

½ cup (125 mL) candied pecans (recipe follows)

1. Place the beets in a large pot of salted water and bring to a boil. Lower the heat to a simmer and cook until a paring knife easily pierces the largest beet, approximately 45 minutes. Immediately cool in an ice bath to stop the cooking and to help loosen the peels. Use your hands to rub the peels off the flesh; it should slip off easily. Allow the beets to cool completely, then cut into ¾-inch (2 cm) wedges.
2. Quarter and core the pears and slice each quarter into 4 lengthwise. You will have ½-inch (1 cm) thick wedges. Toss with 1 tablespoon (15 mL) of lemon juice to avoid discoloration.
3. Mix the remaining 1 tablespoon (15 mL) of lemon juice with the olive oil. Drizzle over the arugula and toss until evenly coated. Season with the salt and pepper.
4. Dollop ¼ cup (60 mL) of goat cheese coulis on each plate and use a spoon to spread it evenly on one edge of the plate. This is where you will lay out the beets and pears.
5. Arrange the beets and pears over the goat cheese coulis, dividing them evenly between each plate. Top with the dressed arugula.
6. Garnish with the shaved Parmesan cheese and candied pecans. Serve immediately.

Bosc, Bartlett, Anjou, Comice or Concorde:
use whichever pear is in season. Anjou and Concorde pears
do not brown as easily as other varieties, so they are
best for salads. Make a double batch of the candied pecans—
they're a great way to add crunch to any salad.

GOAT CHEESE COULIS

4 oz (115 g) goat cheese

¼ cup (60 mL) sour cream

2 tbsp (30 mL) heavy cream

2 tbsp (30 mL) vegetable oil

1½ tbsp (22.5 mL) white wine vinegar

⅔ tsp (3.5 mL) lemon juice

¼ tsp (1.25 mL) fine salt

1. Using a food processor or hand-held blender, purée all ingredients until homogeneous. The mixture should be smooth, and no lumps should remain from the goat cheese.
2. Transfer to an airtight container and refrigerate. The goat cheese coulis can be stored refrigerated for 5 days.

CANDIED PECANS

1 cup (250 mL) pecan halves or pieces

1 tbsp (15 mL) maple syrup

1 tbsp (15 mL) brown sugar

1 tsp (5 mL) vegetable oil

¼ tsp (1.25 mL) fine salt

1. Preheat the oven to 350°F (180°C).
2. Mix together all the ingredients in a small mixing bowl until well combined.
3. Spread onto a parchment paper–lined rimmed baking tray and use a spatula to ensure all the remaining syrup gets drizzled onto the pecans.
4. Bake for approximately 12 to 15 minutes or until dark golden brown. Stir every 5 minutes for even caramelization.
5. Remove from the oven and allow to cool completely. Break apart into bite-sized clusters before transferring to an airtight container.
6. Can be made ahead and stored at room temperature for 1 week.

JERUSALEM SALAD WITH MOROCCAN SPICED CHICKEN

1980s 1990s 2000s **2010s**

SERVES 4

4 brined half chicken breasts (page 239)

Moroccan spice (recipe follows)

Sumac yogurt (recipe follows)

2 cups (500 mL) baby arugula

½ cup (125 mL) thinly sliced radishes

½ cup (125 mL) parsley leaves

½ cup (125 mL) mint leaves, torn in half crosswise if longer than 2 inches (5 cm)

¼ cup (60 mL) pickled red onions (page 37)

½ cup (125 mL) halved grape tomatoes

¼ cup (60 mL) salted cucumber (page 48)

¼ cup (60 mL) medium-diced roasted red peppers (page 243)

¼ cup (60 mL) halved grapes

Preserved lemon dressing (page 222)

Baked pita croutons (recipe follows)

This dish from Chef Collective member Ryan Stone combines flavours from opposite ends of the Sahara and sub-Sahara for a rocking version of this Middle Eastern salad staple.

1. Preheat the oven to 500°F (260°C).
2. Coat the brined chicken breasts with an even layer of the Moroccan spice. All surfaces should be well coated with the spice mixture. Transfer to an oiled rimmed baking tray.
3. Bake in the oven for approximately 4 minutes, then flip and continue cooking for 3 minutes. The internal temperature of the chicken should register 160°F (71°C).
4. Allow to rest for 1 minute before cutting each breast into 8 pieces. Keep warm.
5. Dollop 2 tablespoons (30 mL) of sumac yogurt onto each plate. Using the back of a spoon, spread the yogurt in a circular fashion until it forms a 6-inch (15 cm) circle. Repeat with all the other plates.
6. In a large mixing bowl, combine the arugula, radishes, parsley, mint, pickled red onions, grape tomatoes, cucumber, red peppers and grapes. Toss well. Drizzle with about ½ cup (120 mL) of the preserved lemon dressing and toss again to coat each component.
7. Add the baked pita croutons and toss one last time. Adding the pita at the last minute will keep the pita crisp. If you prefer softer croutons, then add them with all the other vegetable components and toss everything together with the dressing.
8. Plate the salad over the sumac yogurt, evenly distributing all the ingredients between the four servings.
9. Arrange the chicken breast pieces in and around the salad. Serve immediately.

MOROCCAN SPICE

¼ cup (60 mL) pecan pieces

½ cup (125 mL) za'atar spice (homemade or store-bought; can be found in the Mediterranean section of your local market)

1. Pulse the pecan pieces in a small food processor until the pecans are roughly ⅛ inch (3 mm) across.
2. Combine with the za'atar and toss until fully incorporated.
3. Transfer to an airtight container and store at room temperature. Use within a month.

SUMAC YOGURT

2 tbsp (30 mL) olive oil

1 tbsp (15 mL) minced garlic

1 tbsp (15 mL) sumac

½ tsp (2.5 mL) ground black pepper

¾ cup (180 mL) yogurt

1 tbsp (15 mL) cold water

1 tsp (5 mL) fine salt

1. Heat the olive oil, garlic, sumac and black pepper in a small pot over medium heat until the spices are sizzling and the garlic is fragrant, approximately 1 to 2 minutes. Immediately remove from heat and allow to cool to room temperature.
2. Combine the yogurt, water, salt and the cooled garlic oil. Whisk until fully incorporated. Transfer to an airtight container and refrigerate. The yogurt can be stored refrigerated for 5 days. Mix well before use.

BAKED PITA CROUTONS

6 pieces pita bread

⅓ cup (80 mL) olive oil

½ tsp (2.5 mL) fine salt

½ tsp (2.5 mL) ground black pepper

1. Preheat the oven to 375°F (190°C).
2. Split each pita into two rounds. Brush the pita with the olive oil and sprinkle with the salt and pepper.
3. Arrange the halves in a single layer on two parchment-lined rimmed baking trays. Bake until crisp, approximately 10 to 12 minutes. The pita halves should be completely crispy and a deep golden brown. Remove from the oven.
4. Season immediately with the salt and pepper.
5. Allow to cool completely before breaking each half into 4 or 5 pieces.

CHICKEN AVOCADO SALAD

In the 1970s and 1980s a generation of chefs rebelled (to the extent that chefs, you know, rebel) against sauce-driven haute cuisine. This dish by Hamid Salimian may not have been directly inspired by Paul Bocuse or one of his contemporaries, but when we eat it we like to imagine the year is 1977 and we're celebrating at the best *nouvelle cuisine* place in town because we just got a songwriting credit we didn't really deserve and it happens to have been on Fleetwood Mac's new album, *Rumours*. But that's just us. Maybe your 1970s fantasies have more to do with Cheryl Tiegs or Burt Reynolds.

1980s 1990s 2000s **2010s**

SERVES 4

4 brined boneless chicken half breasts (page 239)

6 slices bacon

1 large head iceberg lettuce (approximately 1 lb/450 g)

¼ cup (60 mL) truffle mayonnaise (recipe follows)

1 cup (250 mL) oven-dried grape tomatoes (page 18)

1 diced avocado

Lemon grapeseed vinaigrette (recipe follows)

California dressing (recipe follows)

¼ tsp (1.25 mL) fine salt

¼ cup (60 mL) chervil leaves

¼ cup (60 mL) tarragon leaves

½ cup (125 mL) finely sliced radish coins

1 cup (250 mL) croutons

½ cup (125 mL) thinly shaved curls of aged Gouda cheese

1. Using a preheated grill or cast iron grill pan, grill each breast over medium-high heat for 5 minutes. Flip the breasts and continue cooking for 3 minutes more. Check for doneness on the thickest part of the breast. The internal temperature of the meat should register 160°F (71°C) on an instant-read thermometer. Remove from heat immediately. Set aside while you prepare the rest of the salad.
2. Cook the bacon to desired doneness and chop into 1-inch (2.5 cm) lengths. Allow to drain on paper towels.
3. Halve the iceberg lettuce and then slice each half into 4 even wedges. Slice each wedge in half crosswise.
4. Spread 2 tablespoons (30 mL) of truffle mayonnaise on the bottom of each salad plate. Neatly but randomly arrange the equivalent of 2 wedges of iceberg lettuce over the truffle mayonnaise (each portion will be a quarter of the head of iceberg lettuce).
5. Randomly scatter a quarter of the oven-dried tomatoes over each plate of iceberg lettuce, followed by a quarter of the diced avocado.
6. Drizzle with 2 tablespoons (30 mL) of lemon grapeseed vinaigrette and 2 tablespoons (30 mL) of California dressing. Season with a pinch of fine salt. Repeat with the remaining salads.
7. Garnish each salad evenly with chervil, tarragon, radish and croutons.
8. Using a vegetable peeler, shave thin curls of Gouda over the salad.
9. Cut each grilled chicken breast into thirds and arrange in and around the iceberg lettuce. Serve immediately.

TRUFFLE MAYONNAISE

3 tbsp (45 mL) mayonnaise

2 tsp (10 mL) confit garlic oil (page 242)

1 tsp (5 mL) truffle oil

1. Combine all ingredients well using a whisk.
2. If made ahead, transfer to an airtight container and refrigerate. The mayonnaise can be stored refrigerated for 5 days maximum.

LEMON GRAPESEED VINAIGRETTE

3 tbsp (45 mL) lemon juice

2 tbsp (30 mL) grapeseed oil

1 tbsp (15 mL) olive oil

2 tsp (10 mL) honey

1. Combine all ingredients well using a whisk.
2. If made ahead, transfer to an airtight container and refrigerate. The vinaigrette can be stored refrigerated for 5 days maximum.

CALIFORNIA DRESSING

3 tbsp (45 mL) grapeseed oil

2 tbsp (30 mL) champagne vinegar

2 tsp (10 mL) grainy Dijon mustard

2 tsp (10 mL) minced shallots

1 tsp (5 mL) minced anchovies

1 tsp (5 mL) minced capers

1 tsp (5 mL) honey

1 tsp (5 mL) tarragon

Pinch fine salt

1. Combine all ingredients in a food processor and blend into a paste.
2. If made ahead, transfer to an airtight container and refrigerate. The dressing can be stored refrigerated for 5 days maximum.

Chicken Avocado Salad

MAPLE-GLAZED SALMON AND BUTTERNUT SQUASH SALAD

1980s 1990s 2000s **2010s**

SERVES 4

1 tbsp (15 mL) fine salt

1 cup (250 mL) trimmed green beans

1 cup (250 mL) farro

1 small butternut squash (approximately 1½ lb/680 g)

2 tsp (10 mL) olive oil

1 tsp (5 mL) fine salt

½ tsp (2.5 mL) ground black pepper

1 lb (450 g) salmon fillet, divided into 4 portions

2 tbsp (30 mL) maple butter, melted (recipe follows)

Additional salt and pepper to taste

6 oz (170 g) mixed greens

6 oz (170 g) baby spinach

⅓ cup (80 mL) lemon honey vinaigrette (recipe follows)

3 oz (85 g or ⅓ cup/80 mL) goat cheese

¼ cup (60 mL) salted pumpkin seeds

¼ cup (60 mL) dried cranberries

With its farro and salmon, its spinach and goat cheese, its green beans and pumpkin seeds, this dish from Dawn Doucette covers all the food groups, while also spanning farm, field and ocean. It couldn't shout "Canada" any louder if it had vocal cords.

1. Preheat the oven to 450°F (230°C).
2. Bring a pot of water to a rolling boil. Add the salt and blanch the green beans for 3 to 4 minutes depending on the thickness of your beans. Taste and cook according to your preference. Reserve the salted cooking water. Submerge the beans in ice water to stop cooking.
3. Add the farro to the boiling water and return to a boil. Lower heat to medium-low and simmer for 30 minutes, uncovered. The farro will remain quite chewy even when completely cooked. Once cooked through, drain and allow to cool to room temperature.
4. Peel the butternut squash and remove the seeds. Cut into 1-inch (2.5 cm) dice. Toss with the olive oil, salt and pepper. Roast in the preheated oven for 20 to 25 minutes, turning once halfway through cooking so that both sides are caramelized. The squash is cooked once a fork pierces it without any resistance. Remove from the oven and allow to cool to room temperature.
5. Cut the salmon fillet into 4 even pieces. Place the salmon on a foil-lined rimmed baking tray. Drizzle with half the melted maple butter. Season lightly with salt and pepper. Roast in the 450°F (230°C) oven for 6 to 8 minutes or until the internal temperature of the salmon registers 130°F (54°C) on an instant-read thermometer. Immediately remove from the oven and drizzle with the remaining maple butter.
6. Combine the mixed greens and spinach in a large bowl. Add the cooked farro, roasted butternut squash and lemon honey vinaigrette. Toss well so that each ingredient is coated lightly in the dressing.
7. Divide among the plates. Cut or crumble the goat cheese into ½-inch (1 cm) pieces and divide evenly over each salad. Garnish with the pumpkin seeds and dried cranberries.
8. Serve each salad with 1 piece of the maple-glazed salmon.

MAPLE BUTTER

1 tbsp (15 mL) maple syrup

1 tbsp (15 mL) melted butter

1. Combine both ingredients until well mixed. Use immediately.

LEMON HONEY VINAIGRETTE

½ cup (125 mL) vegetable oil

2 tbsp (30 mL) rough chopped shallot

2 tbsp (30 mL) lemon juice

1 tbsp (15 mL) lime juice

1 tbsp (15 mL) white wine vinegar

1 tbsp (15 mL) honey

2 tsp (10 mL) grainy dijon mustard

1 tsp (5 mL) confit garlic (page 242)

1 tsp (5 mL) fine salt

1 tsp (5 mL) ground black pepper

⅛ tsp (0.63 mL) red pepper flakes

1. Using a food processor or hand-held blender, purée all ingredients until emulsified and the shallots are finely chopped.
2. Transfer to an airtight container and refrigerate. The vinaigrette can be stored refrigerated for 5 days. Mix well before use.

CREAM OF TOMATO SOUP

1980s 1990s 2000s **2010s**

SERVES 4-6

1 tbsp (15 mL) vegetable oil

½ cup (125 mL) roughly chopped onion

½ cup (125 mL) roughly chopped carrots

½ cup (125 mL) roughly chopped celery

½ cup (125 mL) roughly chopped red
pepper

1 cup (250 mL) roughly chopped peeled
russet or Yukon gold potatoes

1 tsp (5 mL) minced garlic

1 tsp (5 mL) fine salt

1 tsp (5 mL) dried oregano

½ tsp (2.5 mL) ground black pepper

2¾ cups (660 mL) vegetable stock

1 tsp (5 mL) Worcestershire sauce

4½ cups (1.125 mL) canned San Marzano
tomatoes

⅔ cup (160 mL) heavy cream

¼ cup (60 mL) finely chopped parsley
(optional)

½ cup (125 mL) croutons (optional)

With a tomato soup, the goal is sumptuous depth of complicated flavour brightened by a brilliant pop of colour and acid energy, right? Thanks to soup master Larry, our version of this lunchtime stalwart has always had that, but something it also had was a roux, or flour, base. A few years ago, we decided to switch all our soups and sauces over to vegetarian stocks, and Dawn Doucette reformulated Larry's original recipe as seen here. Adding the tomatoes with the cream just before serving brings this soup alive in a way that just isn't possible otherwise.

1. Heat the vegetable oil in a deep heavy stockpot or Dutch oven until it ripples. Add the onions, carrots, celery and red peppers, sautéeing until the onions are translucent and the carrots are tender, approximately 10 minutes.

2. Add the potatoes, garlic, salt, oregano, black pepper, vegetable stock and Worcestershire sauce. Bring to a boil and then simmer, covered, until potatoes are soft, approximately 15 minutes. Remove from heat. Using a hand-held or a stand blender, purée until the soup is extremely smooth and no chunks remain.

3. Break up the canned San Marzano tomatoes using your hands until the pieces are no greater than ½ inch (1 cm) across. Add to the pot along with the cream.

4. Return to a simmer and then immediately remove from the heat.

5. Serve with parsley and some croutons if desired.

PRAWN, MELON AND QUINOA SALAD

1980s 1990s 2000s **2010s**

SERVES 4

1 oz (28 g or 2 tbsp/30 mL) room-temperature salted butter

1 lb (450 g) 21 to 30 count prawns, peeled and deveined

1 tsp (5 mL) fine salt, divided

1 tsp (5 mL) ground black pepper, divided

10 oz (285 g) arugula

White quinoa (recipe follows)

Basil vinaigrette (recipe follows)

1 cup (250 mL) thinly sliced honeydew melon

1 cup (250 mL) seasonal berries (quartered strawberries, blueberries, raspberries)

1 cup (250 mL) thinly sliced cucumber half moons

2 tsp (10 mL) olive oil

½ cup (125 mL) crumbled feta cheese

1 cup (250 mL) mint leaves

Freshly cracked black pepper

Brian Skinner says that the first dish he ever presented as part of the Chef Collective is exactly the sort of thing he makes for himself and his family, so he was doubly pleased when it was added to the menu. Ideal for spring and summer, it combines the crunchy sweetness of melon, the acidity of feta and the tartness of berries. With the food groups covered, it's a meal in itself, but imagine it also as one of two or three salads at a barbecue.

1. Heat the butter in a nonstick skillet over medium heat. Once the butter begins to foam, add the prawns and cook until they begin to turn pink, approximately 3 to 4 minutes.
2. Season with ½ teaspoon (2.5 mL) each salt and black pepper. Transfer to a plate and keep warm.
3. In a large bowl, dress the arugula and quinoa lightly with the basil vinaigrette. Season lightly with the remaining salt and pepper. Divide between 4 salad bowls.
4. Neatly arrange the melon and berries among the 4 salads, trying not to weigh down the greens.
5. Toss the cucumber and olive oil and place on and around the salad greens. Divide equally between the 4 bowls.
6. Garnish each salad with 2 tablespoons (30 mL) of feta, ¼ of the mint leaves and 3 twists of freshly cracked black pepper.
7. Drizzle 1 tablespoon (15 mL) of basil vinaigrette over each salad and top with the sautéed prawns. Serve immediately.

WHITE QUINOA

1 cup (250 mL) white (regular) quinoa

2 cups (500 mL) water

½ tsp (2.5 mL) fine salt

1. Rinse the white quinoa under running water. Drain well.
2. Bring the water and salt to a boil and immediately add the drained quinoa.
3. Lower the heat to medium and stir occasionally to prevent sticking.
4. Simmer until all the water has been absorbed and quinoa has doubled in size, approximately 15 to 20 minutes.
5. Test for doneness. The quinoa should still retain a slight chew. If the quinoa is still undercooked, cover with a lid and allow the residual steam to continue cooking the quinoa.
6. Spread out the cooked quinoa onto a parchment-lined baking tray and allow to cool completely.
7. Use in the salad recipe or transfer to an airtight container and refrigerate. The quinoa can be stored refrigerated for 5 days.

BASIL VINAIGRETTE

3 tbsp (45 mL) ice-cold water

2 tbsp (30 mL) white balsamic vinegar

¼ cup (60 mL) roughly chopped basil leaves

1 tbsp (15 mL) minced shallots

2 tsp (10 mL) Dijon mustard

1 tsp (5 mL) minced ginger

½ tsp (2.5 mL) minced garlic

½ tsp (2.5 mL) lemon zest

¼ tsp (1.25 mL) fine salt

⅓ cup (80 mL) olive oil

1. Using a food processor or hand-held blender, purée all ingredients until emulsified and the basil, shallots and ginger are finely chopped.
2. Transfer to an airtight container and refrigerate. The vinaigrette can be stored refrigerated for 5 days. Mix well before use.

WARM POTATO SALAD

This classic side salad by Reuben Major is awfully good any time of the year, but to elevate it a little further during summer and early fall, buy fresh corn on the cob, grill it on the barbecue and slice the kernels off the cob.

1980s 1990s 2000s **2010s**

SERVES 4–6 AS AN ACCOMPANIMENT

2 lb (1 kg) baby red potatoes

2 tbsp (30 mL) olive oil

1 tbsp (15 mL) confit garlic oil (page 242)

½ cup (125 mL) corn kernels (thawed if frozen)

½ cup (125 mL) ½-inch (1 cm) chopped cooked bacon

Potato salad dressing (recipe follows)

2 tbsp (30 mL) finely chopped chives

1. Preheat the oven to 425°F (220°C).
2. Halve the red potatoes and toss with the olive oil until thoroughly coated. Transfer to a parchment-lined rimmed baking tray, arranging the pieces cut side down in a single layer.
3. Bake for 35 to 40 minutes or until potatoes are tender when pierced with a fork.
4. Transfer to a large mixing bowl and drizzle with the confit garlic oil. Allow to cool slightly.
5. Using the same baking tray and oven setting, heat the corn and bacon in the oven for 5 minutes or until slightly roasted. The objective is to give the corn some colour and heat the ingredients thoroughly. Remove from the oven.
6. Toss the potatoes, corn, bacon and dressing until well coated and all ingredients are mixed evenly.
7. Garnish with the chives and serve immediately.

POTATO SALAD DRESSING

⅔ cup (160 mL) mayonnaise

⅓ cup (80 mL) sour cream

¾ tsp (3.75 mL) lemon juice

¾ tsp (3.75 mL) finely chopped chives

¼ tsp (1.25 mL) fine salt

1. Combine ingredients with a whisk until fully incorporated. If made ahead, transfer to an airtight container and refrigerate for 9 days maximum.

CLAM CHOWDER

Don't worry too much about following this recipe to the letter—we don't. In fact, Larry Stewart's original recipe is regarded as something of a test of skill by our younger chefs, who are encouraged to cook the bacon by sight, the vegetables by feel, and the roux by aroma. Traditionally, New England clam chowder is creamy, while Manhattan is tomato based, so ours, we guess, should be called Connecticut clam chowder. Whichever shoreline gets the credit, this is a dish that speaks loudly of the seaside and that our guests would never allow us to drop from the menu.

1980s 1990s 2000s 2010s

SERVES 6–8

1 51 oz can (1.44 kg) chopped sea clams in juice

4 slices (½ inch/1 cm) bacon

3 oz (85 g or ⅓ cup + 1 tbsp/95 mL) butter

⅓ cup (80 mL) all-purpose flour

¼ cup (60 mL) clam base

1 cup (250 mL) ½-inch (1 cm) diced onion

1½ tsp (7.5 mL) ground black pepper

1½ tsp (7.5 mL) dried thyme

½ tsp (2.5 mL) dried tarragon

1 bay leaf

1½ cups (375 mL) 2% milk

1½ cups (375 mL) heavy cream

1 cup (250 mL) ½-inch (1 cm) diced carrots

1 cup (250 mL) ½-inch (1 cm) diced celery

1 cup (250 mL) ½-inch (1 cm) diced red potatoes

2 cups (500 mL) ½-inch (1 cm) diced tomatoes

1. Separate the clams from the clam juice by straining the liquid from the can of clams into a bowl lined with 2 layers of cheesecloth. Rinse the chopped clams under cold running water to remove any sand or grit. Strain the clam juice by lifting the cheesecloth out of the clam juice to capture any sediment. Set the clams and juice aside.
2. In a large Dutch oven or heavy stockpot, cook the bacon over medium-low heat until almost crispy.
3. Simultaneously, in a separate pot, melt the butter until foaming. Add the flour to the butter and whisk well until the roux is blond and the flour smells slightly nutty. At this point, the flour should be a very light beige.
4. Whisk in the clam base and cook for 30 seconds. Remove from heat.
5. Add the onion, black pepper, thyme, tarragon and bay leaf to the crisped bacon and allow to cook until onions are softened and translucent, approximately 10 minutes.
6. Add the roux/clam base mixture and the reserved strained clam juice to the onion/bacon pot, and mix well. Slowly add the milk and heavy cream, stirring constantly while the mixture returns to a simmer.
7. Add the carrots, celery and potatoes and allow to boil for 1 minute. Reduce heat to a simmer and cook until the vegetables are just soft, approximately 15 to 20 minutes.
8. Remove the pot from the heat and add the rinsed clams. Remove the bay leaf and stir in the chopped tomatoes.
9. Serve immediately.

sandwiches

When you have 67 (and counting) restaurants, you don't want to be talking about favourites very loudly, but that said, it's hard not to love our location in Saskatoon. Before we came along it was a big industrial bakery, and on top of it was the city's most iconic sign, which read "Don't Say Bread, Say McGavin's." Now, nothing lends itself to a great restaurant location like a big old factory, but what are you going to do with a sign that, while beloved, also happens to advertise a type of bread that you would never serve? Our solution: change the big sign's wording to "Don't Say Bread, Say Earls." Turn to page 8 to see a photo of this magnificent sign.

We really do bake all of our own bread products, in some cases from dough made on-site, in others with dough made off-site to our specifications. Our first hamburger buns helped differentiate us from the competition when we opened back in 1982, and continue to do so, especially our most current version from Chef Fay Duong, which is formulated in a buttery style reminiscent of brioches and Chinese buns. But we're probably equally well known for our sourdough, a recent introduction, and our focaccia, which seemed a startling innovation when we introduced it back in the 1980s. And don't even get us started on our own pan bread.

Feel free to sub in different wrappers for the sandwiches in this section: the key lies in their quality, not the subspecies of the bread family that they happen to belong to.

CHICKEN QUESADILLA

The quesadilla is an old Mexican dish, of course, but it's fair to say that Chuck's version was inspired by the interpretation common in the southwestern US, where it's more of a deluxe grilled cheese sandwich. Taking it one step further, we imagined it as the kind of deluxe grilled cheese sandwich that children of all ages might want to share while happily gathered together over drinks.

1980s 1990s 2000s 2010s

SERVES 4–6

1½ lb (680 g) chicken tenders or boneless skinless breasts

2 tbsp (30 mL) quesadilla spice (page 238)

2 tbsp (30 mL) melted confit garlic butter (page 243)

8 oz (225 g) shredded Jalapeño Jack and cheddar blend

1 cup (250 mL) canned diced green chilies

4 to 6 flour tortillas (10 inches/25 cm)

Salsa, for garnish (page 241)

Sour cream, for garnish

1. Preheat the oven to 350°F (180°C).
2. If using chicken breasts, cut each half breast into 4 lengthwise strips. This will help the chicken cook evenly as well as increase the surface area for the quesadilla spices to stick to. Toss the chicken with the quesadilla spice, mixing well to make sure each piece has an even coating.
3. Arrange on a rimmed parchment-lined baking tray. The chicken pieces should be in one layer, largely oriented in the same direction, touching edge to edge to prevent overcooking.
4. Drizzle the melted garlic butter all over the chicken. Lightly cover the tray with foil and bake for 18 to 20 minutes. Check for doneness by testing the biggest piece– the internal temperature should reach 160°F (71°C).
5. Immediately take out of the oven and remove the foil. Allow to cool to room temperature before proceeding to the next step.
6. Once the chicken is cool, cut into ¼-inch (½ cm) diagonal slices. Mix with the cheese and diced chilies. Make sure all ingredients are well combined.
7. Divide evenly between the tortillas and fold each tortilla into a half-moon shape, spreading the chicken filling evenly to within ½ inch (1 cm) of the edges.
8. Cook on a hot griddle or in a nonstick pan until the filling is hot throughout and the cheese is melted. The tortilla should be a light golden brown and slightly crispy.
9. Cut each quesadilla into 4 wedges. Serve with salsa and sour cream.

CHICKEN, FIG AND BRIE SANDWICH

1980s **1990s** 2000s 2010s

MAKES 4 SANDWICHES

4 brined half chicken breasts (page 239)

½ tsp (2.5 mL) ground black pepper

4 ciabatta buns, split

¼ cup (60 mL) confit garlic mayo (recipe follows)

½ cup (125 mL) fig jam (recipe follows)

1 cup (250 mL) spinach leaves

1 cup (250 mL) roasted apples (page 207)

6 oz (170 g) triple cream brie

Chris Remington ticked off most of the food groups with this sandwich, which makes for a pretty sweet lunch. In August and again in late fall, figs do their amazing ripening thing, swelling up to double their size in a matter of hours. Pick some up at a farmers' market or greengrocer, slice them thinly and sub in for the fig jam, because why not?

1. Butterfly each half breast by making a horizontal cut along the curved edge of the half breast. Try to slice as parallel to the cutting board as possible so that the breast cooks evenly. The resulting half breast will have a "heart" shape once opened up. Season evenly with black pepper.
2. Grill each breast over medium-high heat, skin side up, for 4 minutes. Flip skin side down for 2 minutes more. Check for doneness in the thickest part of the breast. The meat should register 160°F (71°C) on an instant-read thermometer. Remove from heat immediately. Set aside while you prepare the rest of the sandwich.
3. Toast the split ciabattas until crusty on the outside but still soft on the inside. Spread 1 tablespoon (15 mL) of garlic confit mayo on each crown and 2 tablespoons (30 mL) of fig jam on each heel.
4. Arrange 9 or 10 spinach leaves over the garlic confit mayo side and ¼ cup (60 mL) of roasted apples over the fig jam side.
5. Slice the brie into ¼-inch (½ cm) slices and arrange over the spinach leaves, trying to attain maximum coverage for each crown.
6. Place the cooked chicken over the roasted apples on the heel of each ciabatta. Close the sandwiches.
7. Secure each sandwich with toothpicks before cutting on the diagonal. Serve immediately.

To get clean slices of brie, freeze the whole round of brie for 30 to 40 minutes. Spray your knife with cooking spray before each slice.

CONFIT GARLIC MAYO

¾ cup (180 mL) mayonnaise

¼ cup (60 mL) confit garlic (page 242)

¼ tsp (1.25 mL) fine salt

¼ tsp (1.25 mL) ground black pepper

1. Place all the ingredients in a mixing bowl and whisk until all ingredients are combined.
2. Transfer to an airtight container and refrigerate. The confit garlic mayo can be stored refrigerated for a week.

FIG JAM

4 oz (115 g or about 15 whole) dried Mission figs

½ cup (125 mL) cold water

2 tbsp (30 mL) apple juice

2 tbsp (30 mL) sugar

1 tsp (5 mL) lemon juice

½ tsp (2.5 mL) ground cinnamon

1. Remove the stem end of each dried fig using a paring knife.
2. Combine all the ingredients in a medium-sized saucepan and bring to a boil. Reduce heat to a simmer and cook until the liquid has reduced slightly and the figs are soft, approximately 8 minutes. Remove from heat and allow to cool for approximately 15 minutes.
3. Transfer to a food processor or use a hand-held immersion blender and purée until smooth.
4. Transfer to an airtight container and refrigerate. The fig jam can be stored refrigerated for 2 weeks.

CLUBHOUSE ON FOCACCIA SANDWICH

1980s **1990s** 2000s 2010s

MAKES 4 SANDWICHES

4 brined half chicken breasts (page 239)

½ tsp (2.5 mL) ground black pepper

8 slices dry-cured bacon

4 focaccia pieces (4 × 6 inches/
   10 × 15 cm), split

¼ cup (60 mL) mayo

4 green leaf lettuce leaves

8 slices beefsteak tomato

There was a time when a restaurant without a clubhouse sandwich was like a car without a vinyl roof. Still, us being us, we wanted to switch things up a little. Stew had that focaccia bread of ours, and reasoned that a clubhouse is pretty good to begin with, so perfecting it was mostly a case of paying close attention to ingredient quality. If vinyl roofs looked as good and made as much sense as his recipe, they'd still be with us.

1. Butterfly each half breast by making a horizontal cut along the curved edge of the half breast. Try to slice as parallel to the cutting board as possible so that the breast cooks evenly. The resulting half breast will have a "heart" shape once opened up. Season with black pepper.

2. Grill each breast over medium-high heat, skin side up, for 4 minutes. Flip to skin side down for 2 minutes more. Check for doneness on the thickest part of the breast. The meat should register 160°F (71°C) on an instant-read thermometer. Remove from heat immediately. Set aside while you prepare the rest of the sandwich.

3. Cook the bacon over medium-high heat until it reaches your desired doneness. Drain on paper towels.

4. Toast the split focaccias until crusty on the outside but still soft on the inside. Spread 1 tablespoon (15 mL) of mayo on each crown.

5. Arrange 1 green lettuce leaf over the mayo side and top the lettuce with 2 slices of tomato.

6. Place the bacon on the heel of each focaccia and top with the grilled chicken.

7. Close each sandwich and secure it with toothpicks before cutting on the diagonal. Serve immediately.

Dry-cured bacon is far superior to regular cured bacon. It has less moisture so that you get a crispier rasher. Also, the flavour is much more intense as the bacon flavour is more concentrated in the dry-cured product. Try it and see the difference!

CUBANO SANDWICH

1980s 1990s 2000s **2010s**

MAKES 4 SANDWICHES

8 oz (225 g) thinly sliced Virginia ham

8 oz (225 g) thinly sliced porchetta ham

1 oz (28 g or 2 tbsp/30 mL) butter

8 slices sourdough bread

¼ cup (60 mL) mayonnaise

2 tbsp (30 mL) Dijon mustard

4 oz (115 g) thinly sliced Swiss cheese

8 slices dill pickle

Within the Italian-based slow food movement, porchetta occupies a special place as one of the most classic and delicious yet labour-intensive dishes. A deboned pork loin is arranged with layers of herb stuffing, fat and skin, and then rolled and spit-roasted, traditionally over wood. The porchetta ham called for here is a lightly cured version (for which someone else has already done the work) that can be found in Italian markets and delis. As for the name, Cuban sandwiches combining pork and cheese are common in places like Miami, and time spent there opening our Dadeland location gave Dawn Doucette the inspiration for this sandwich. She countered the sweetness of the porchetta with our sourdough bread, which balances the dish and distances our version from the Florida norm.

1. Heat the Virginia and porchetta ham in the microwave for 45 seconds or until just warm. This will ensure a thoroughly hot sandwich and cheese that melts nicely.
2. Spread the butter over one side of the sourdough bread. Flip the bread so that the buttered side is facing down.
3. Arrange the bread so that you have crowns on the top row and heels on the bottom row.
4. Spread 1 tablespoon (15 mL) of mayonnaise on each crown and ½ tablespoon (7.5 mL) of mustard on each heel.
5. Evenly distribute the sliced cheese over the heels and top with the heated ham, making sure there is even coverage.
6. Place two pickles over each crown and close the sandwiches.
7. Place the sandwiches on a preheated griddle or nonstick pan. Cook until golden brown on the first side, approximately 3 minutes.
8. Flip and continue cooking until the second side is also golden brown and the cheese is fully melted.
9. Transfer each sandwich to a plate and serve immediately.

LOBSTER AND PRAWN ROLL

Those inspiration trips of ours aren't always to crazily exotic locales. During a trip to Los Angeles, Dawn Doucette kept noticing an East Coast mainstay sandwich on restaurant menus, tried a couple of versions, and thought, "Hmmm." She came back to Vancouver, added some prawns to make it really West Coast, some diced celery to give it a little crunch and sprinkled in some other things that she thought would work. Then she took the dough we use to make our brioche-style hamburger buns and fashioned it into more of a hoagie-bun shape, because in this case, that's how we roll.

1980s 1990s 2000s **2010s**

MAKES 4 ROLLS

4 lobster roll buns (page 123)

1.5 oz (42 g or 3 tbsp/45 mL) room-temperature butter

8 oz (225 g) cooked lobster meat

4 oz (115 g) poached prawns, shelled and deveined

¼ cup (60 mL) finely diced celery

2 tbsp (30 mL) finely chopped capers

1 tbsp (15 mL) finely chopped parsley

⅓ cup (80 mL) mayonnaise

2 tsp (10 mL) lemon juice

½ tsp (2.5 mL) Worcestershire sauce

½ tsp (2.5 mL) tabasco sauce

Pinch fine salt and ground black pepper

1. Preheat a nonstick pan on medium heat. Cut the lobster roll buns in half and spread the cut sides with a light coating of butter.
2. Cook on the hot pan on both sides until golden brown and toasted. Transfer to a serving platter.
3. Roughly chop the lobster meat and prawns into approximately ½-inch to ¾-inch (1 to 2 cm) chunks.
4. Transfer to a large bowl and add the celery, capers, parsley, mayonnaise, lemon juice, Worcestershire, tabasco, salt and ground pepper.
5. Toss all the ingredients very well.
6. Fill each toasted lobster roll with the dressed lobster and prawn salad, evenly dividing between the 4 rolls.
7. Serve immediately.

BURGERS & STEAKS, BEER & WINE

Back in 1982, there were sixteen items on our menu. Not bad for such a new place!

Oh, did we mention that ten of them were hamburgers? No? Then we probably also neglected to specify that a single burger accounted for about two-thirds of our food sales. At the future home of Prawn, Melon and Quinoa salad and Beef Bibimbap, two out of every three people pretended to carefully peruse the menu and then said, "I'll have the bacon cheddar burger."

But then, this was a bacon cheddar burger like no one had ever seen. The bun was freshly baked, the beef patty was hand-formed ground chuck and huge. There was copious lettuce, and a tomato slice half an inch thick. There were four slices of bacon, and the cheese wasn't some processed slice, like everywhere else's, but a luscious chunk of medium cheddar. Before we opened that first place in Edmonton, Bus called in a bunch of people and asked them what they thought. Delicious, everyone said, but it will never sell—too big and messy. Thank you, said Bus, who then completely ignored them, because Bus is never wrong. Well, almost never. A few months later he convinced Chuck to add a 32-ounce porterhouse steak to the menu. That one really was too big, and no one ever ordered it.

Still, it's hard to overstate the role that our burgers and steaks have played, certainly during the early years, but also today. Likewise, the beer and wine that make for such perfect pairings. All of which means it's time to introduce, once again, our purchasing manager, George Piper, who elevated the buying of beef, beer and wine to levels never previously imagined. Early on George found a small supplier called Intercity Packers, then showed up every Tuesday to work with his favourite cutter to ensure that our steaks were exactly as he specced them.

Before long, George became equally concerned about our beef's provenance and how it was raised. During the 1990s we switched over to Certified Angus Beef, with its heightened assurance of texture, flavour and overall quality. Later we discovered a new Alberta enterprise called Spring Creek Ranch that guarantees their animals' diet and treatment, and ensures that the meat is free of added hormones and has never been treated with steroids or antibiotics. (We also love that Spring Creek is biodynamic and that they power over 2,500 homes in the town near the ranch on electricity derived from the methane gas the cows produce. Yup, powered by poop.) Today we split our beef supply between Canadian and American beef suppliers who provide us with 100 percent Black Angus beef that is humanely treated, some who even get to chow down on the spent grains from the brewery down the way, raised without antibiotics, steroids and added growth hormones, making us the first chain restaurant in North America to not only consciously source 100 percent of our chicken, eggs, seafood and vegetables, but also to serve 100 percent certified ethical beef.

So, yes, the beef is very, very good, and getting it to where it is now definitely involved a lot of work, and not just from George: our meat guy Dave Bursey did some heavy lifting. But if you really want to get George going, ask him about the beer and wine.

Back in the day, he was the guy who had to build himself an elaborate home brewery because otherwise he couldn't drink beer of a quality that suited him. Okay, he was one of the two guys, the other being Andrew Wilton, who was our CFO and as mad for British ales as George was for Czech Pilsners. When we got our first set of taps, George and Andrew worked with our supplier to ensure that our Albino Rhino (now Rhino Craft) was a notch or two better than anything else around.

But it was after 1989, with a switch to newly established Whistler Brewing, that things really began to get interesting. For one thing, Whistler Brewing was home to Gary Lohin who would go on to figure large in West Coast and Canadian craft beer scenes, when, several years later, those scenes would begin to exist. Today Gary's Central City Brewing is known for its Red Racer label (Red Betty in the US) and has twice been named Canadian brewery of the year. More importantly, at least to us, it now supplies most of our taps, under the Rhino

label—although we continue to work with small craft brewers in individual markets to make sure our beers are always fresh, local and interesting.

Then there is George's wine program, which has provided him the opportunity to travel in five-star comfort to the four corners of the grape-growing earth. Hey, we're not bitter, because George is always George, with that stealthy eye for value. So, just as we've long had our proprietary Rhino draft, we've also had our Rascal of the Vineyard wines, as reasonably priced as they are delicious.

Of course, some of that deliciousness is due to the way they're shipped, in giant casks instead of bottles. George is a bit of a nut about freshness, as maybe you've guessed, and with wine, freshness has little to do with age and much to do with oxidation, which can deaden flavours or render them off-tasting. There's a touch of oxidation going on in every bottle, just from the half-inch of air sitting in the neck. Not in any Rascal of the Vineyard wine, though, or any of our wines by the glass for that matter: George and Clay Fuller worked with a supplier to develop our in-house wine keg system, which shields the precious elixir from oxygen contact of any kind.

So that's our wine, beer and beef. Let us close by saying that too much of any of those is never a good thing. But the right amount is always an excellent one.

FORAGER BURGER

As a place that started out as a burger joint and remains very proud of its meat, you might not expect us to be devotees of food writer Michael Pollan, known for his criticism of the industrial food chain and his advice to "Eat food. Mostly plants. Not too much." But we try very hard to source our ingredients from producers with integrity, and we try equally hard to ensure that the "plants" component of our menu is top-notch and even predominant, with lots of salads and terrific vegetarian and vegan options. We challenged the same guy who did our Royale Burger, David Wong, to bring a similar level of excellence to its vegetarian equivalent, the Forager Burger. Eat plants? Done. Not too much? That's going to be tougher.

1980s 1990s 2000s 2010s

MAKES 7 PATTIES

¼ cup (60 mL) olive oil

1½ lb (680 g) button mushrooms, ¾-inch (2 cm) chopped

½ cup (60 mL) diced white onions

2 tsp (10 mL) minced garlic

2 tsp (10 mL) fine salt

2 tsp (10 mL) smoked paprika

2 tsp (10 mL) dried oregano

2 tsp (10 mL) ground black pepper

½ cup (60 mL) dry bread crumbs

¼ cup (60 mL) finely grated Parmesan cheese

¼ cup (60 mL) rolled oats

2 eggs

1. Heat the olive oil in a large Dutch oven or heavy-bottomed pot until it ripples. Sauté the mushrooms until completely caramelized and golden and all excess water has evaporated, about 12 to 15 minutes.
2. Add the onions and cook until caramelized. Add the garlic and cook until fragrant.
3. Add the salt, smoked paprika, oregano and black pepper. Continue cooking, stirring frequently, until the spices release their aromatics, about 2 minutes.
4. Remove from heat and transfer to a baking tray, spreading out in a thin layer. Allow to completely cool before the next step.
5. Combine the cooled mushroom mixture with the bread crumbs, Parmesan cheese, oats and eggs. Mix very well.
6. Scoop ¾-cup (180 mL) portions of the mixture onto separate sheets of parchment or waxed paper, spraying cooking spray between the paper and the patty.
7. Refrigerate for 2 hours to allow the patties to set. Pan-fry or grill for 3½ minutes per side until golden brown.

Bronx Burger

OUR ROYALE WITH CHEESE BURGER

What lies behind the enduring appeal of a well-constructed burger like our Royale with Cheese? Well, there's that bun, which takes its cues not from any American source but from egg-rich pastries like French brioches and Chinese pork buns. Plus: "It's an umami bomb," explains Chef Collective member David Wong, who has recently been fiddling with our burgers. Umami is one of the five basic tastes (along with sweetness, sourness, bitterness and saltiness), and, in essence, it's what makes a food savoury. The portobello mushroom and relished tomato inside are among the most umami-rich ingredients, while the smoked cheddar slice, which we make ourselves by melting cheese and beer together, has a strong mouth-coating feel, which is another cherished umami characteristic. And then there's that ground 100 percent Black Angus chuck. If we may be forgiven, ooh, mommy!

BURGER BUNS

Fay Duong's brioche-style buns are the secret weapon in the burger wars.

MAKES 10 BUNS

1¼ cups (310 mL) lukewarm water

2½ tbsp (37.5 mL) melted salted butter

3 large eggs, divided

4⅓ cups (1.02 L) all-purpose flour

⅓ cup (80 mL) sugar

1½ tsp (7.5 mL) fine salt

1 tbsp + 1 tsp (20 mL) instant yeast

2 tbsp (30 mL) sesame seeds

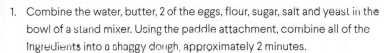

1. Combine the water, butter, 2 of the eggs, flour, sugar, salt and yeast in the bowl of a stand mixer. Using the paddle attachment, combine all of the ingredients into a shaggy dough, approximately 2 minutes.
2. Switch to a dough hook and continue kneading until the dough is soft and smooth. It should not stick to the sides of the bowl and should form a ball around the hook. This will take 5 to 6 minutes on medium speed.
3. Remove the dough from the bowl and spray the bowl with cooking spray. Return the dough to the bowl and cover with a damp towel. Allow to rise for 1½ hours or until doubled in size. The temperature of your home will determine how long this process takes.
4. Gently deflate the dough as you remove it from the bowl. Form it into a long log and divide it into 10 evenly sized pieces.
5. On a clean counter, using your hands, shape the balls into smooth rounds using a cupping and turning motion. Place the balls on a parchment-lined rimmed baking tray.
6. Flatten slightly to about 3 inches (8 cm) across. Allow space between each bun, as they will double in size again.
7. Cover with a damp towel and allow to rise a second time for approximately 1 hour. The buns should be noticeably light and airy on the inside. While the buns are on their second rise, preheat the oven to 375°F (190°C).
8. Beat the remaining egg with 2 tablespoons (30 mL) water. Carefully and gently brush the buns with the beaten egg and drizzle lightly with sesame seeds.
9. Bake in the preheated oven for 15 to 18 minutes or until golden brown. Allow to cool before slicing.

Note: For the lobster roll buns, simply shape each dough ball from step 5 into a longer cylindrical shape, approximately 3 inches (8 cm) long and 1½ inches (4 cm) wide. Continue with the remaining steps.

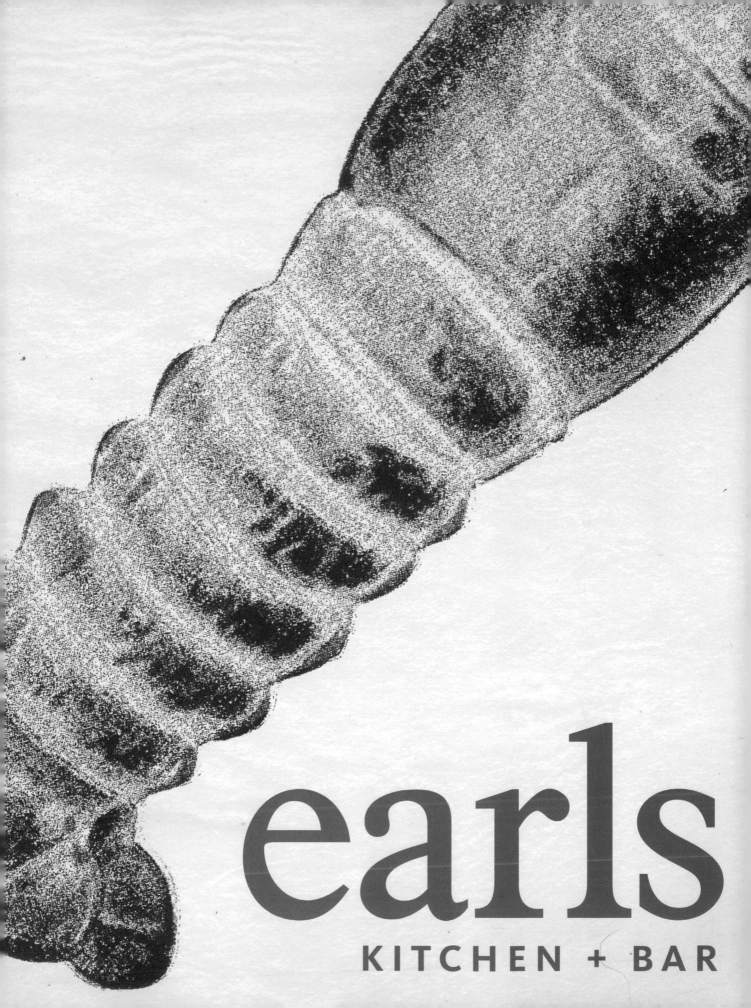

earls
KITCHEN + BAR

pizza

When we first began installing forno ovens at most locations beginning in the late 1980s, there was widespread popular reaction—usually along the lines of "What's a forno oven?"

Wood-fired, brick-lined ovens just weren't a thing back then, so it was lucky indeed that George Piper and Chuck happened to get invited for dinner to the North Vancouver home of a food importer who had one of the few backyard ovens in the city at that time. The fellow had paid a contractor to build the thing from scratch, and it didn't even work all that well—but the potential!

Forno ovens are an Italian thing, of course, but upon looking into it, our guys discovered that restaurants in the American Southwest were just then beginning to introduce them, with great success. They found a supplier, and within months we had our own ovens up and running.

Coming up with our own pizza was another thing. Back then there were a few, ever so slightly different styles of pizza around, but all of them involved a lot of dough and globs of inexpensive cheese, and none of those gooey pies was of the quality we wanted to serve. Fortunately, our sister chain, Joey, known at the time as Joey Tomato's Kitchen, was Mediterranean in style with very respectable pizza, so we borrowed their recipe to begin with. That was fine for a while, but around 2005 we were ready to move on, and it fell to Fay Duong to test fourteen different doughs before coming up with the recipe we use today, which is allowed to rise, then is pounded down, and then ferments in the fridge for thirty-six hours before it's ready for the oven.

Our thin-crust, rough-edged pizza wouldn't be unfamiliar to a resident of Naples, where pizza is believed to have originated. Nor, come to think of it, to someone accustomed to the artisanal pizza spots that have sprouted up in recent years, a quarter century after we lit our first fires.

MARINARA PIZZA

It's 1990 and you call up the local pizza place. "Got anything on a wood-fired, thin crust with maybe just some artichokes, shallots and roasted peppers?" Larry knew exactly what the answer to that question would have been when he set out to make a pizza for us that would have seemed at home in Naples itself.

1980s **1990s** 2000s 2010s

MAKES 2 PIZZAS

2 portions pizza dough (page 135)

Cornmeal (optional)

¾ cup (180 mL) San Marzano tomato
   sauce (page 240)

1½ cups (375 mL) shredded mozzarella or
   provolone cheese

½ cup (125 mL) coarsely chopped
   sun-dried tomatoes, rehydrated if not
   oil-packed

½ cup (125 mL) sliced roasted shallots

½ cup (125 mL) sliced roasted red
   peppers (page 243)

3 pieces canned artichoke hearts,
   quartered

¼ cup (60 mL) finely grated Parmesan
   cheese

1 bunch basil leaves or 2 tsp (10 mL)
   finely chopped parsley

1. Preheat the oven to 500°F (260°C). If you have a pizza stone, preheat on the rack in the middle position of the oven.
2. Stretch out the pizza dough to a 12-inch (30 cm) circle, trying to achieve an even thickness throughout. Place on a floured baking tray or use cornmeal if you have some on hand. Repeat with the second portion of dough.
3. Spread half the tomato sauce evenly over the top of one pizza, to within ½ inch (1 cm) from the edge. Top with a quarter of the mozzarella cheese. Arrange half the sun-dried tomatoes evenly over the cheese. Top with another quarter of the mozzarella. This thin cheese layer will prevent the sun-dried tomatoes from burning in the oven.
4. Top with half the shallots, half the roasted red peppers and 6 artichoke quarters.
5. Sprinkle the toppings with half the Parmesan cheese.
6. Repeat the steps with the second pizza using the remaining ingredients.
7. If using a pizza stone, load the pizzas onto the stone and bake in the preheated oven for 10 minutes. If not using a pizza stone, bake on the tray for 10 to 15 minutes or until the cheese is melted and the crust is golden brown.
8. Garnish with some torn basil leaves or finely chopped parsley. Cut into slices and serve.

CALIFORNIA SHRIMP PIZZA

One of the restaurants Larry cooked at before joining us was Calgary's then revolutionary, now legendary Fourth Street Rose, which took its inspiration from innovators like Wolfgang Puck and Alice Waters, who during the 1980s made California's Bay Area the centre of the culinary universe. After our first forno ovens arrived, Larry came up with this recipe, which makes it possible to put words like "complex," "light-tasting" and "pizza" in the same sentence.

1980s **1990s** 2000s 2010s

MAKES 2 PIZZAS

2 portions pizza dough (page 135)

Cornmeal (optional)

2 tbsp (30 mL) confit garlic oil (page 242)

1½ cups (375 mL) shredded mozzarella or Provolone cheese

¼ cup (60 mL) chopped sun-dried tomatoes, rehydrated if not oil-packed (see note)

½ cup (125 mL) crumbled feta

6 oz (170 g) raw shrimp (90 to 130 count), peeled and deveined

1 tsp (5 mL) vegetable oil

¼ cup (60 mL) pesto (page 242)

2 lemon wedges

1. Preheat the oven to 500°F (260°C). If you have a pizza stone, preheat on the rack in the middle position of the oven.
2. Stretch out the pizza dough to a 12-inch (30 cm) circle, trying to achieve an even thickness throughout. Place on a floured baking tray or use cornmeal if you have some on hand. Repeat with the second portion of dough.
3. Brush half the confit garlic oil evenly all over the top of one pizza, to within ½ inch (1 cm) from the edge. Top with a quarter of the mozzarella cheese. Arrange half the sun-dried tomatoes evenly over the cheese. Top with another quarter of the mozzarella and half the feta cheese. This thin cheese layer will prevent the sun-dried tomatoes from burning in the oven.
4. Drizzle the shrimp with the vegetable oil and mix to coat evenly. Arrange half the shrimp over the mozzarella and feta. Repeat all the steps with the second pizza using the remaining ingredients.
5. If using a pizza stone, load the pizzas onto the stone and bake in the preheated oven for 10 minutes. If not using a pizza stone, bake on the tray for 10 to 15 minutes or until the cheese is melted and the crust is golden brown.
6. Garnish with a generous drizzle of pesto and lemon wedges for serving. Cut into slices and serve.

There are two types of sun-dried tomatoes, oil-packed or regular dried. If you use regular (not oil-packed) sun-dried tomatoes, rehydrate them in warm water for 20 minutes before use. You can use larger shrimp for this pizza, but you will need to halve them lengthwise so that they cook evenly. Note the subbing of pesto for tomato sauce. Do make your own, especially in season (page 240), but if not, use a fresh, refrigerated version rather than from a jar.

CONFIT DUCK AND BLUE BRIE PIZZA

1980s 1990s **2000s** 2010s

MAKES 2 PIZZAS

2 tsp (10 mL) butter

1 cup (250 mL) finely sliced peeled and cored apples

2 portions pizza dough (page 135)

Cornmeal (optional)

2 tbsp (30 mL) olive oil

1½ cups (375 mL) shredded mozzarella

½ cup (125 mL) 1-inch (2.5 cm) chunks blue brie cheese (Cambozola)

½ cup (125 mL) shredded duck confit

2 tbsp (30 mL) candied pecans (page 89)

If pizza had been invented in France, would they have bothered with French fries? We can't say, but we do think that this Chef Michael Noble recipe is the pizza the French might have given us. Incidentally, duck confit is a treasure—a traditional method of preserving that easily beats freezing—but if you don't have a duck handy or aren't up to the hours of work involved, be assured that frozen confits can be found at gourmet-oriented shops, like Vancouver's Gourmet Warehouse, as they would be at any French supermarket.

1. Heat butter in a small skillet and allow to melt. Add the apple slices and sauté for 1 minute. Remove from heat and set aside.
2. Preheat the oven to 500°F (260°C). If you have a pizza stone, preheat on the rack in the middle position of the oven.
3. Stretch out the pizza dough to a 12-inch (30 cm) circle, trying to achieve an even thickness throughout. Place on a floured baking tray or use cornmeal if you have some on hand. Repeat with the second portion of dough.
4. Brush some olive oil evenly all over the top of one pizza dough, within ½ inch (1 cm) from the edge. Top with a half of the mozzarella cheese.
5. Arrange half the apples, half the blue brie and half the shredded duck confit over the mozzarella.
6. Repeat the steps with the second pizza using the remaining ingredients.
7. If using a pizza stone, load the pizzas onto the stone and bake in the preheated oven for 10 minutes. If not using a pizza stone, bake in the tray for 10 to 15 minutes or until the cheese is melted and the crust is golden brown.
8. Garnish the pizzas with the candied pecans. Cut into slices and serve.

A TODA MADRE PIZZA

1980s 1990s 2000s **2010s**

MAKES 2 PIZZAS

2 portions pizza dough (page 135)

Cornmeal (optional)

Refried beans (recipe follows)

Salsa (page 241)

1 cup (250 mL) shredded Jalapeño Jack and cheddar blend

Seasoned ground beef (recipe follows)

½ cup (125 mL) sour cream

1 cup (250 mL) shredded romaine lettuce

½ cup (125 mL) halved grape tomatoes

½ cup (125 mL) medium-diced avocado

¼ cup (60 mL) jalapeño or banana pepper rings (optional)

A toda madre is a Mexicanism meaning, basically, awesome! This pizza from Dawn Doucette (her very first recipe for us) is also a Mexicanism, a variation on the original southern Italian theme that would leave a Neapolitan perplexed. Still, on a continent gone mad for both pizza and Mexican, it surely represents the ultimate fusion food. And you know what? Fusion food sometimes does mean confusion food, but other times it's a *toda madre.*

1. Preheat the oven to 500°F (260°C). If you have a pizza stone, preheat on the rack in the middle position of the oven.
2. Stretch out the pizza dough to a 12-inch (30 cm) circle, trying to achieve an even thickness throughout. Place on a floured baking tray or use cornmeal if you have some on hand. Repeat with the second portion of dough.
3. Use the back of a spoon or an offset spatula to spread a generous layer of refried beans over the dough. Spread salsa over the refried beans, getting even coverage of both sauces right to ½ inch (1 cm) from the edge. Repeat with the second pizza.
4. Evenly distribute the cheese and ground beef between the two pizzas.
5. If using a pizza stone, load the pizzas onto the stone and bake in the preheated oven for 10 minutes. If not using a pizza stone, bake in the tray for 10 to 15 minutes or until the cheese is melted and the crust is golden brown.
6. Remove from the oven and top with sour cream, lettuce, tomatoes, avocados and jalapeños or banana peppers (if using).
7. Cut into slices and serve.

SEASONED GROUND BEEF

8 oz (225 g) ground beef

1 tsp (5 mL) fine salt

1 tsp (5 mL) ground black pepper

1. Heat a nonstick frying pan over medium heat. Add the ground beef and break it up into small chunks. Season with salt and pepper.
2. Cook until fully browned, stirring occasionally.
3. Drain meat thoroughly before using as pizza topping.

REFRIED BEANS

1 cup (250 mL) dried black or pinto beans

1 bay leaf

Salt to taste

1 tsp (5 mL) vegetable oil

½ cup (125 mL) diced white onions

2 tsp (10 mL) minced garlic

1 tsp (5 mL) ground cumin

1 tsp (5 mL) fine salt

½ tsp (2.5 mL) cayenne pepper

1 tbsp (15 mL) soy sauce

1 tbsp (15 mL) white vinegar

1 tbsp (15 mL) lime juice

2 tbsp (30 mL) finely chopped cilantro

1. In a large pot, cover the beans with cold water by at least 2 inches (5 cm). Add the bay leaf and bring to a boil over high heat.
2. Reduce heat to a simmer and cook until beans are very tender, about 1 to 2 hours. Replenish with water as necessary, maintaining at least 1 inch (2.5 cm) above the beans. Season with salt. Drain beans, reserving the cooking liquid. You should have about 2 cups (500 mL) of cooked beans. Discard the bay leaf.
3. Using the same pot, heat the vegetable oil until it ripples. Sauté the onions, garlic, cumin, salt and cayenne until the onions are soft and translucent.
4. Add the drained beans and ½ cup (125 mL) of bean cooking liquid. Using a potato masher, mash until half the beans are puréed.
5. Stir in the soy sauce, white vinegar and lime juice. Cook for 10 minutes, stirring often, until the mixture has reduced slightly. Remove from heat and fold in the cilantro.
6. Set aside to cool slightly before topping the pizza.

The refried beans in this recipe can be used as a
stuffing for burritos or soft tacos or even served with nachos!
They keep well for about a week in the refrigerator.

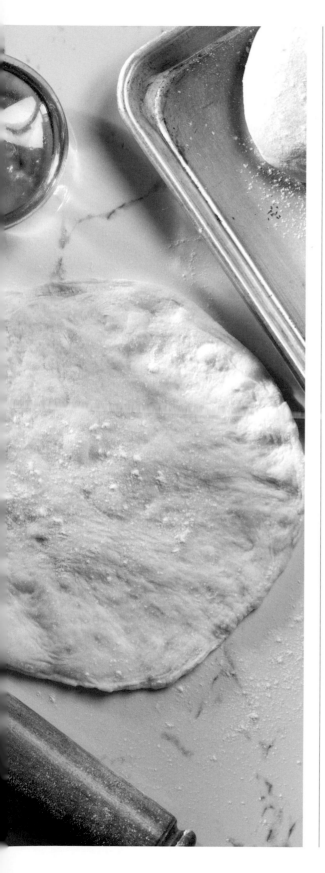

PIZZA DOUGH

The whole process in making this pizza dough takes forty-eight hours. The dough is allowed to rest in the refrigerator to develop gluten that is essential in creating a chewy yet crisp crust. The complex flavours that develop in this time are unattainable with a typical two-hour pizza dough method. Plan ahead and give it a try!

MAKES 6 DOUGH BALLS

2⅓ cups (560 mL) bread flour

1¼ cups (310 mL) cold water (60°F/15°C)

2 tsp (10 mL) sugar

1 tsp (5 mL) active dry yeast

1½ tbsp (22.5 mL) olive oil

1 tsp (5 mL) fine salt

1⅛ cups (280 mL) bread flour

1. Combine 2⅓ cups (560 mL) bread flour, water, sugar and yeast in the bowl of a stand mixer. Using the dough hook, mix on low speed until no traces of dry flour remain. Cover with a damp towel and allow to rest for 20 minutes. This step is called the autolysis and allows the flour cells to swell and develop strong gluten strands that result in a chewy and crisp crust.
2. Start the mixer on the lowest speed and add the olive oil and salt. Knead until fully incorporated.
3. Add the remaining 1⅛ cups (280 mL) flour, kneading on medium speed until no dry flour remains, approximately 5 minutes. The dough should look smooth and have formed into a ball.
4. Coat the surface of the dough with olive oil. Transfer to a greased, lidded container and refrigerate for 6 hours or overnight.
5. Punch down the cold dough and divide equally into 3 portions. Create a smooth surface by pulling all the sides of the dough to the bottom and pinching them together. Using a circular motion with the palm of your hand, gently roll the dough on a floured surface to create a ball shape.
6. Coat with a thin layer of flour, place on a parchment-lined baking tray and wrap with plastic wrap. Place in the refrigerator for a minimum of 6 hours or overnight.
7. Allow to come to room temperature before using, approximately 2 hours.

noodles and rice bowls

Tell us if this is a humblebrag, but we introduced an Asian noodle bowl before we had Asian noodles. In fact, Chuck came up with our first dish using the same fettuccine we used for our Alfredo. That wasn't quite the right thing to do and we knew it, so we recorded a radio spot beckoning people to "Bring your accordion and your chopsticks down to Earls."

Noodle pioneers that we were, we listened intently when George Piper started talking and just wouldn't stop about a dish he'd eaten in San Francisco's Chinatown at a place called Henry's Hunan Restaurant. He even brought back a cookbook and urged Chuck to make the dish, called kung pao. Always up to a challenge, Chuck did so, but no one really cared for it, not even George.

Fortunately, Chuck and George returned to San Francisco soon afterward on one of those inspiration trips they rewarded themselves with so regularly, and they stumbled, rather late at night, into Henry's. Even in their state, the two could tell that the cookbook had lied: the food in the restaurant was way spicier, more complex, more tightly knit and just plain better. Now acquainted with the true flavour profile, Chuck came back to Vancouver and knocked off our own version, which we called Hunan Kung Pao, and which started out slow but gradually grew into one of the bestselling items on our menu. Ironically, a few years later we switched up the dish to make it more authentically Hunanese, but guests complained, so the recipe you'll find here is Chuck's original.

There was one other thing about that dish, which is plenty spicy. We decided to give guests the option of ordering it as hot as they wanted, and someone came up with the idea of rating the options with from one to five peppers. As far as we know, that was the first time a restaurant had ever done that, though it certainly wasn't the last.

FETTUCCINE ALFREDO

This most fundamental of Roman dishes can be found in fifteenth-century cookbooks, but in Earls years it's even more ancient, dating all the way back to our first year. Our recent addition of a little cream cheese, on the advice of Robert Byford, at the time chef at West Vancouver's Beach House restaurant, sets it apart from most other versions, which rely on not much more than Parmesan and cream. When we introduced this it could be ordered as a main or as a side, with, say, a bacon cheddar burger. Calories? Never heard of 'em.

1980s 1990s 2000s 2010s

SERVES 4-6

1 lb (450 g) dried fettuccine, uncooked

2 cups (500 mL) heavy cream

4 oz (115 g) room-temperature cream cheese, cubed (half a package)

1 tsp (5 mL) fine salt

¼ tsp (1.25 mL) nutmeg

¼ tsp (1.25 mL) ground white pepper

1 lb (450 g) diced chicken breast or shelled prawns (optional)

½ cup (125 mL) finely grated Parmesan cheese

1 tbsp (30 mL) finely chopped parsley, for garnish (optional)

1. Cook the fettuccine according to package directions in salted water.
2. Meanwhile, heat 1 cup (250 mL) of the cream with the cream cheese in a saucepan over medium heat, whisking well until the cream cheese is completely melted and the sauce is smooth. Add the rest of the cream and seasonings, and cook, whisking well, until the sauce simmers. Remove from heat.
3. If adding protein (chicken or prawns) sauté until cooked through.
4. Drain the cooked fettuccine, but do not rinse. Add the pasta and optional cooked protein into the sauce and toss well to coat each noodle.
5. Divide into bowls and top with Parmesan cheese and cooked protein, if using. Garnish with chopped parsley.
6. Serve immediately.

Before you get started, make sure your cream cheese is at room temperature so that it melts evenly when cooked.

NASI GORENG

Chuck formulated this recipe using ingredients that were generally available at the time, so they should be universally available today. Later he spent time living and cooking in Indonesia, and although he says he would do this recipe differently now, he thinks it stands up nicely: the key to making it come alive lies not so much with what's in it but in how it's garnished, with the more fruits and vegetables the better. And now that he's the expert, maybe Chuck can tell us what the heck "nasi goreng" means. Well, he translates, "fried rice."

SERVES 4–6

2 tsp (10 mL) vegetable oil

1 lb (450 g) sliced chicken breast, sliced sirloin, shelled prawns or cubed firm tofu

1 cup (250 mL) ½-inch (1 cm) chopped celery

1 cup (250 mL) medium-diced red onion

1 cup (250 mL) medium-diced red pepper

Cooked rice (recipe follows)

Stir-fry sauce (recipe follows)

½ cup (125 mL) pineapple wedges

½ cup (125 mL) cored apple, 1/16-inch (2 mm) slices lengthwise

¼ cup (60 mL) currants

¼ cup (60 mL) coarsely chopped cilantro

¼ cup (60 mL) plain yogurt

1. Heat a nonstick skillet or wok over medium heat. Pour in vegetable oil and allow to heat until it ripples.
2. If adding protein (chicken, beef, prawns or tofu), sauté in the hot oil until almost cooked through.
3. Add celery, red onion and red pepper, cooking for 2 minutes until vegetables are slightly tender.
4. Toss in the rice and stir well, evenly distributing all ingredients.
5. Drizzle in the stir-fry sauce and continue tossing, coating each grain of rice with the sauce until the rice is thoroughly heated.
6. Divide into bowls.
7. Garnish each bowl evenly with pineapple, apple, currants and cilantro.
8. Dollop 1 tablespoon (15 mL) of yogurt over each bowl and serve immediately.

STIR-FRY SAUCE

¼ cup (60 mL) soy sauce

1 tbsp (15 mL) brown sugar

1 tbsp (15 mL) minced ginger

1 tbsp (15 mL) minced garlic

1 tbsp (15 mL) rice vinegar

2 tsp (10 mL) sesame oil

1. Mix all the ingredients together. Can be prepared and stored refrigerated up to 4 days ahead.

Prepare the rice a day before if time allows it. This will produce the best results when stir-frying the rice and allow the flavours to really develop overnight.

COOKED RICE

1½ cups (375 mL) shredded green cabbage (tightly packed)

¾ cup (180 mL) sushi rice or jasmine rice

¾ cup (180 mL) converted long-grain rice

⅓ cup (80 mL) mango chutney

1 tbsp (15 mL) sambal oelek (a chili and garlic paste found in the Asian food section of your grocery store)

1 tbsp (15 mL) curry powder

1 tsp (5 mL) salt

2 cups minus 1 tbsp (485 mL) water

Rice cooker method

1. Place all ingredients in a rice cooker insert with a minimum capacity of 6 cups (1.5 L).
2. Mix all the ingredients well so that all the sauces and spices are evenly distributed.
3. Cover the rice cooker and start the cook cycle. Once the cycle is finished, allow the rice to rest for 20 minutes to complete cooking. This allows the grains of rice to set properly and prevents gummy rice.
4. Remove the rice from the cooker and spread it onto a clean baking sheet. Allow to cool to room temperature before proceeding to the rest of the recipe. If preparing ahead, transfer to a sealed container and refrigerate overnight.

Saucepan method

1. Place all ingredients into a deep saucepan or Dutch oven with a tight-fitting lid. Mix all ingredients well and bring to a boil, stirring constantly to prevent it from sticking to the bottom.
2. Once the water has come to a full boil, lower to a simmer, stirring occasionally until three-quarters of the water is absorbed and steam holes begin to emerge in the surface of the rice, about 10 minutes.
3. Reduce the heat to the lowest setting and cover. Cook for a further 10 minutes, and then turn off the heat. Do not lift the lid! Allow the rice to rest for 20 minutes.
4. Spread the rice onto a clean baking sheet. Allow to cool to room temperature before proceeding to the rest of the recipe. If preparing ahead, transfer to a sealed container and refrigerate overnight.

HUNAN KUNG PAO WITH CHICKEN

This is the dish that Chuck borrowed from Henry's Hunan Kitchen and that many others have since borrowed from us. Recently, the test kitchen decided to give the recipe a hard look and switch it up if necessary, but the changes proved to be minuscule. It remains a quick meal that's easy to prepare yet massively addictive.

1980s **1990s** 2000s 2010s

SERVES 4–6

1½ lb (680 g) fresh steamed Chinese egg noodles

2 tbsp (30 mL) vegetable oil, divided

2 bird's-eye chilies (optional, or use more if desired)

8 oz (225 g) ½-inch (1 cm) diced chicken tenders or chicken breast

½ cup (125 mL) 1-inch (2.5 cm) diced red onion

½ cup (125 mL) 1-inch (2.5 cm) diced red pepper

½ cup (125 mL) ⅛-inch (3 mm) diagonally cut carrot

½ cup (125 mL) ¼-inch (½ cm) diagonally cut celery

2 cups (500 mL) 1-inch (2.5 cm) chopped yu choy

Hunan sauce (recipe follows)

¼ cup (60 mL) roasted peanuts

1. Bring a pot of salted water to a full boil. Blanch the noodles for 2 minutes, stirring well to loosen up the clumps of noodles.
2. Drain the noodles immediately and flush them with cold water to stop cooking. Allow to drain and cool completely. Coat lightly with 1 tablespoon (15 mL) of vegetable oil to prevent sticking.
3. Heat the remaining tablespoon (15 mL) of vegetable oil in a wok or nonstick skillet over high heat until it ripples.
4. Add the desired amount of chilies to the oil and cook until blistered. Toss in the chicken and allow to sear on one side, separating each piece to ensure that the chicken cooks evenly, approximately 2 minutes. Flip each piece of chicken to sear the second side.
5. Add the onion, pepper, carrots and celery, cooking for 2 minutes until the vegetables are blistered and begin to soften.
6. Toss in the yu choy and continue cooking until it turns bright green from the heat, approximately 1 minute.
7. Add the Hunan sauce and bring to a simmer.
8. Push the chicken and vegetables to one side of the pan. Add the noodles to the empty side.
9. Toss very well to coat each ingredient with sauce. The sauce will thicken slightly as the chicken and vegetables cook thoroughly. Check to see if the largest piece of chicken is cooked. The vegetables should be tender but not limp.
10. Divide into bowls and garnish each bowl evenly with roasted peanuts.

HUNAN SAUCE

½ cup (125 mL) soy sauce

½ cup (125 mL) chicken stock

2 tbsp (30 mL) brown sugar

2 tbsp (30 mL) minced ginger

2 tbsp (30 mL) minced garlic

2 tbsp (30 mL) rice vinegar

1 tbsp (15 mL) sesame oil

1 tbsp (15 mL) cornstarch

1. Mix all ingredients together. Can be prepared ahead and stored refrigerated up to 4 days. Stir well before use.

THAI GREEN CURRY WITH CHICKEN

1980s **1990s** 2000s 2010s

SERVES 4–6

2 14 fl oz cans (400 mL each) coconut milk, divided

⅓ cup (80 mL) Thai green curry paste

2 lime leaves

¼ cup (60 mL) Thai basil leaves and stems

¼ cup (60 mL) cilantro leaves and stems

2 tbsp (30 mL) brown sugar

1½ tbsp (22.5 mL) fish sauce

1 tbsp (15 mL) lime juice

1½ lb (680 g) boneless skinless chicken breasts

2 tbsp (30 mL) vegetable oil

1½ cups (375 mL) diagonally sliced zucchini

½ tsp (2.5 mL) fine salt

½ tsp (2.5 mL) ground black pepper

¼ cup (60 mL) medium-diced pineapple

¼ cup (60 mL) shelled pistachios, roughly chopped

Cilantro sprigs (optional)

Thai cooking is complex, and there's no shame in cutting out several steps from this recipe through the use of a prepared curry paste, as we've done here. Still, says Karen Lyons, she had no trouble finding all the ingredients in Vancouver's Chinatown—and it was almost twenty years ago that the pastry cook turned development chef worked with us. On our summer menus, this dish was often served with coconut rice and a grilled peach, which both complements the flavours and brings the dish on home to the region.

1. Combine 1 cup (250 mL) of coconut milk, green curry paste, lime leaves, Thai basil leaves and cilantro in a large saucepan over medium heat. Bring to a simmer and cook for 10 minutes, uncovered. The sauce will reduce slightly.

2. Add the remaining coconut milk and the brown sugar. Bring to a gentle simmer and cook for 15 minutes, uncovered. Again, the sauce will reduce slightly.

3. Add the fish sauce and lime juice. Remove from the heat and strain out the leaves and stems with a coarse sieve. Keep warm while preparing the chicken, or if made ahead, the curry can be stored refrigerated in an airtight container for up to 5 days.

4. Cut the chicken breasts into 1½-inch (4 cm) dice.

5. Heat the vegetable oil in a nonstick skillet over medium heat.

6. Sauté the chicken until it is golden brown on all sides and the largest pieces are 90 percent cooked through, approximately 4 to 5 minutes.

7. Add the zucchini slices and continue cooking until the zucchini is tender, but not wilted.

8. Season evenly with the salt and pepper, and then add the Thai green curry sauce.

9. Simmer for 3 minutes until the sauce is fully heated. Serve over steamed jasmine rice and garnish with pineapple, chopped pistachios and cilantro sprigs.

You can substitute prawns, fish or even pork for the chicken.
Proper reduction is the key to developing the rich, complex flavours of this sauce.

GRILLATO BASIL FETTUCCINE

During the 1990s, when we called on him to work on a pasta for us, Julio Gonzalez Perini ran his own restaurant, a charming and ambitious little Italian spot called Villa del Lupo. Twenty years later, after many travels, he's back in the same spot but with a more casual and contemporary restaurant called Lupo. While Julio's restaurant may have changed, the pasta he gave us hasn't needed to. For a dish that takes a half-hour to prepare using ingredients available in any supermarket (well, maybe not the brandy), it punches plenty hard.

1980s **1990s** 2000s 2010s

SERVES 4–6

1 lb (450 g) dried fettuccine, uncooked

¼ cup (60 mL) olive oil

2 cups (500 mL) thinly sliced tomatoes

1 cup (250 mL) thinly sliced red onion

¼ cup (60 mL) rehydrated sun-dried tomatoes, cut into strips

¼ cup (60 mL) canned diced green chilies

2 tbsp (30 mL) drained green peppercorns

2 tbsp (30 mL) minced garlic

1 tbsp (15 mL) lemon juice

¼ cup (60 mL) brandy

2 cups (500 mL) heavy cream

2 tsp (10 mL) fine salt

2 tsp (10 mL) black pepper

½ cup (125 mL) finely chopped basil (chiffonade)

1 tbsp (15 mL) finely chopped parsley

1. Cook the fettuccine according to package directions in salted water.
2. Heat the olive oil in a skillet until shimmering.
3. Add the tomatoes, onion, sun-dried tomatoes, green chilies, green peppercorns, garlic and lemon juice. Sizzle for 3 minutes.
4. Add the brandy and allow to flambé by tipping the pan over the flame. Be careful to keep your distance, as the flames can burn quite high. If using an electric or induction burner, you can use a lighter or matches to carefully flambé the brandy.
5. Once the flames have died down, add the cream, salt and black pepper.
6. Toss in the drained fettuccine and incorporate into the sauce. Allow the pasta to return to a simmer, and then remove from heat.
7. Stir the basil in well, ensuring even distribution of all the ingredients. The sauce should be creamy and coat each noodle lightly.
8. Divide into bowls and garnish with chopped parsley. Serve immediately.

Basil is the key element of this dish—add it at the last minute so as not to cook out its bright flavour. Make sure to evenly distribute it so there's a bit of basil in each bite. You can find canned brined green peppercorns in the spice aisle of your local market.

MEDITERRANEAN LINGUINE

Michael Noble joined us in 2005 after two decades as chef at some of the finest spots in Vancouver and Calgary and an appearance on the original Japanese *Iron Chef*. During his two years with us, he refined a lot of recipes and developed several others, always with an eye for nuance and concentration—both of which shine through here. Only later did we discover that he maintained a tasting panel of his own, a group he called the "tasty ladies." This bright, sparkly and easy-to-prepare pasta lit them up, as it proved to do with our guests.

1980s 1990s **2000s** 2010s

SERVES 4–6

1 lb (450 g) dried linguine, uncooked

1 tbsp (15 mL) olive oil

1 lb (450 g) diced chicken breast or shelled prawns (optional)

1 dry pint (1½ cups/375 mL) grape tomatoes

¼ cup (60 mL) roughly chopped kalamata olives

¼ cup (60 mL) thinly sliced roasted red peppers (page 243)

1 tbsp (15 mL) minced garlic

1 cup (250 mL) vegetable stock

1 tbsp (15 mL) cornstarch

2 cups (500 mL) Mediterranean tomato sauce (recipe follows)

¼ cup (60 mL) thinly chopped basil (chiffonade)

⅓ cup (80 mL) finely grated Parmesan cheese

½ cup (125 mL) crumbled feta cheese

2 tbsp (30 mL) finely chopped parsley

1. Cook linguine according to package directions in salted water. Drain, but do not rinse.
2. Heat olive oil in a skillet until shimmering.
3. If adding protein (chicken or prawns), sauté in the hot oil until almost cooked through.
4. Toss the grape tomatoes, kalamata olives, roasted red peppers and minced garlic into the skillet and cook until tomatoes have blistered slightly.
5. Stir together the vegetable stock and cornstarch to form a slurry and then add to the skillet. Immediately add the Mediterranean tomato sauce and allow it to come to a simmer, approximately 5 minutes. The sauce will thicken slightly.
6. Add the pasta to the sauce and toss well to coat each noodle.
7. Remove from the heat and add the basil and Parmesan to the noodles, twisting with a pair of tongs until well incorporated into the pasta.
8. Divide equally into bowls. Top with the feta and parsley. Serve immediately.

MEDITERRANEAN TOMATO SAUCE

1 cup (250 mL) San Marzano tomato sauce (page 241)

½ cup (125 mL) olive oil

⅓ cup (80 mL) sherry vinegar

1 tbsp (15 mL) lemon zest

2 tsp (10 mL) red pepper flakes

½ tsp (2.5 mL) fine salt

½ tsp (2.5 mL) ground black pepper

1. Place all the ingredients in a mixing bowl and whisk until all ingredients are combined.
2. Transfer to an airtight container and refrigerate. The sauce can be stored refrigerated for 5 days.

VINDALOO CURRY

For many years, George Piper and Bus lunched at a tiny restaurant called Flavours of India, where they got to know the chef/proprietor, Manjeet, and fell in love with her chicken curry. They offered her more and more money to come in and give us the recipe, but she steadfastly refused until the day she was about to close up shop. That dish, called Jeera Chicken Curry, still shows up on our menus, as does this one, from another chef/proprietor, Krishna Jamal, who operated the landmark Rubina Tandoori. Mo Jessa, who knows his curries, was her courter, but like Manjeet, she refused to divulge her recipe, eventually allowing only that she and her son would supply a paste for us to use, a deal that we were happy to make. For you we've subbed in a paste from Patak's, which is also very good.

1. Preheat a deep fryer or a large Dutch oven half full of vegetable oil to 375°F (190°C).
2. Fry the potatoes for 4 minutes, stirring well to avoid sticking. Set aside.
3. Drizzle a tablespoon of vegetable oil in a hot work and heat until the oil begins to ripple.
4. Sear the beef, ginger, garlic, salt and pepper until the beef is golden brown on the outside and around 90 percent cooked through.
5. Add the potatoes and the vindaloo sauce to the beef and bring to a simmer.
6. Cook for 2 minutes or until the beef is cooked to your desired doneness. Remove from heat and add the chopped cilantro. Toss well.
7. Divide into portions and ladle over rice. Dollop 1 tablespoon (15 mL) of yogurt over each vindaloo. Serve immediately.

SERVES 4–6

Vegetable oil for deep-frying

1 lb (450 g) halved mini gold or red potatoes

1 tbsp (15 mL) vegetable oil

1½ lb (680 g) cubed beef sirloin

2 tsp (10 mL) minced ginger

2 tsp (10 mL) minced garlic

1 tsp (5 mL) fine salt

1 tsp (5 mL) ground black pepper

Vindaloo sauce (recipe follows)

¼ cup (60 mL) finely chopped cilantro

¼ cup (60 mL) plain yogurt

VINDALOO SAUCE

¼ cup plus 1 tsp (65 mL) vegetable oil, divided

3 cloves

2 black cardamom pods

1 cinnamon stick

1 cup (250 mL) thinly sliced onions

1 tsp (5 mL) minced ginger

1 tsp (5 mL) minced garlic

2 serrano peppers, seeded and finely minced

2 tbsp (30 mL) tomato paste

⅓ cup (80 mL) Patak's hot vindaloo paste

¼ cup (60 mL) crispy fried onions, which you can find in the ethnic aisle of your grocery store

2¾ cups (660 mL) water

1 cup (250 mL) diced tomatoes with juice

1 tsp (5 mL) fine salt

2 tsp (10 mL) lemon juice

2 tbsp (30 mL) garam masala, divided

1 tbsp (15 mL) brown sugar

½ tsp (2.5 mL) ground turmeric

1. Heat 1 teaspoon (5 mL) of vegetable oil in a heavy-bottomed pot or Dutch oven over medium heat until rippling. Add the cloves and cardamom pods and cook until the spices crackle and become fragrant, approximately 30 seconds. Remove from heat and crush in a mortar or grind in a spice grinder. Set aside.

2. Heat the remaining ¼ cup (60 mL) of vegetable oil in the same pot until the oil ripples. Add the cinnamon stick and cook until it begins to crackle and release fragrance, approximately 30 seconds. Add the onions and cook for 5 to 6 minutes, stirring occasionally, until the onions are soft and golden brown.

3. Add the ginger, garlic, peppers and tomato paste. Cook until the peppers are softened and the tomato paste is a deep dark brown.

4. Stir the vindaloo paste and fried onions, incorporating into the other aromatics. Cook for 2 to 3 minutes or until the fried onions are softened.

5. Add the water, diced tomatoes, salt, lemon juice, 1 tablespoon (15 mL) of garam masala, brown sugar, turmeric and reserved cloves and cardamom to the pot and bring to a simmer. Mix well and simmer, covered, for 10 minutes.

6. Remove from heat and add the remaining 1 tablespoon (15 mL) of garam masala.

7. Retrieve the cinnamon stick and discard. Allow the sauce to cool to room temperature and transfer to a lidded container. Refrigerate overnight to allow the flavours to marry. If made ahead, store for at most 5 days.

Originating in the Portuguese-influenced state of Goa, vindaloo is one of the spicier curries, with predominant flavour components of vinegar, ginger, spices and chilies.

PRAWN SCALLOP LINGUINE

On our menu we had a dish called, unimaginatively enough, seafood penne. With its rosé sauce, the dish was rich and tasty, but Chef Reuben Major thought it could be transformed into something lighter and brighter, which led to all the greens, tomatoes and pine nuts seen here. At the same time, he wanted to ensure that the prawns and scallops remained the stars of the show, which explains the yummy but not overbearing lemon cream sauce.

1980s 1990s **2000s** 2010s

SERVES 4–6

1 lb (450 g) dried linguine noodles

1 tbsp (15 mL) vegetable oil

1 cup (250 mL) grape tomatoes

Shallot garlic paste (recipe follows)

10 oz (285 g) 26 to 30 count prawns, peeled, deveined and butterflied

6 oz (170 g) scallops, tendons removed

Lemon cream sauce (recipe follows)

½ cup (125 mL) arugula

¼ cup (60 mL) roughly chopped basil leaves

½ cup (125 mL) finely grated Parmesan cheese

¼ cup (60 mL) toasted pine nuts

1. Cook the linguine according to package directions in salted water.
2. In a large nonstick skillet, heat the vegetable oil over medium heat until it ripples.
3. Add the grape tomatoes and cook until beginning to blister, approximately 30 seconds to 1 minute.
4. Add the shallot garlic paste and cook until fragrant, approximately 30 seconds.
5. Add the prawns and scallops to the pan, searing on all sides until prawns turn pink and are 90 percent cooked through, 1 to 2 minutes.
6. Drain the cooked linguine, but do not rinse. Add the linguine and the lemon cream sauce to the pan and bring to a simmer. Toss well to incorporate each ingredient.
7. Remove from heat and combine with the arugula and basil, twisting into the noodles until slightly wilted from the residual heat.
8. Divide into portions and garnish evenly with Parmesan cheese and pine nuts.
9. Serve immediately.

SHALLOT GARLIC PASTE

¼ cup (60 mL) minced shallots

2 tbsp (30 mL) minced garlic

1 tsp (5 mL) fine salt

½ tsp (2.5 mL) ground black pepper

¼ tsp (1.25 mL) red chili flakes

⅓ cup (80 mL) olive oil

1. Combine all ingredients in a food processor and blend into a paste.
2. If made ahead, transfer to an airtight container and refrigerate. The sauce can be stored refrigerated for 7 days maximum.

LEMON CREAM SAUCE

1¼ cups (310 mL) heavy cream

¾ cup (180 mL) white wine

¾ cup (180 mL) chicken stock

2 tsp (10 mL) lemon zest

1. Combine all ingredients well using a whisk.
2. If made ahead, transfer to an airtight container and refrigerate. The sauce can be stored refrigerated for 5 days maximum.

The shallot garlic paste is a great condiment to have in your refrigerator, as it can be used as the aromatic base to many pasta, sauté or stir-fry dishes. Try it and see if you agree!

CHICKEN PANCETTA TAGLIATELLE

David Wong is a master of the one-dish meal, which is great for us, even if it isn't really part of the cultural tradition in Italy, where multiple courses are the norm. Still, there's nothing inherent in Italian cooking that would prevent the blending of food groups, as is on display here. Rather, the test is always, is the dish delicious? And yes, the dish is delicious.

1980s 1990s 2000s **2010s**

SERVES 4–6

1 lb (450 g) dried tagliatelle

2 tbsp (30 mL) olive oil

½ cup (125 mL) finely diced pancetta

8 oz (225 g) brined chicken breast (page 239)

1 cup (250 mL) 1½-inch (4 cm) asparagus pieces

¾ cup (180 mL) marinated artichokes, quartered

Parmesan cream sauce (recipe follows)

½ cup (125 mL) finely grated Parmesan cheese, divided

2 tbsp (30 mL) parsley leaves

¼ cup (60 mL) oven-dried grape tomatoes (page 48)

1 tbsp (15 mL) toasted pine nuts

¼ cup (60 mL) roughly chopped basil leaves

¼ cup (60 mL) arugula

Freshly ground black pepper

1. Cook the tagliatelle according to package directions in salted water.
2. In a large nonstick skillet, cook the olive oil and pancetta over medium heat without shaking the pan, approximately 1 minute or until golden brown on the bottom.
3. Cut the chicken into 1-inch (2.5 cm) dice and add to the pan, searing on all sides until golden and 90 percent cooked through, 4 to 5 minutes.
4. Add the asparagus and cook for 30 seconds. Toss in the marinated artichokes and cook for another 30 seconds.
5. Drain the cooked tagliatelle, but do not rinse. Add the pasta and the Parmesan cream sauce to the pan and bring to a simmer. Toss well to incorporate each ingredient.
6. Remove from heat and add half the Parmesan cheese together with the parsley and dried tomatoes. Toss thoroughly again to warm the tomatoes.
7. Divide into portions and garnish evenly with Parmesan cheese, pine nuts, basil leaves, arugula and pepper.
8. Serve immediately.

PARMESAN CREAM SAUCE

2¾ cups (660 mL) heavy cream

1¼ cups (310 mL) vegetable or chicken stock

2 tsp (10 mL) minced garlic

1 tsp (5 mL) fine salt

¼ cup (60 mL) finely grated Parmesan cheese

1. Bring the cream, vegetable stock, garlic and salt to a simmer in a medium-sized pot.
2. Using a hand-held blender, incorporate the Parmesan cheese into the simmering liquid until fully melted.
3. Remove from heat.
4. If made ahead, allow to cool to room temperature, then transfer to an airtight container and refrigerate. The sauce can be stored refrigerated for 5 days maximum.

Serve this pasta on its own or add a green salad or some green beans.

BEEF BIBIMBAP

At a Korean restaurant, this dish arrives at the table with a raw egg on top. First timers sometimes panic—until their server stirs the egg into the rice, and the hot stone bowl, called a *dolsot*, fries the mixture, creating a wonderful crispiness in the process. Our adaptation delivers all of the flavour and most of the crispiness with none of the panic. And local restaurant critics seem to agree it's one of the best in a town with lots of Korean options.

1980s 1990s 2000s **2010s**

SERVES 4

¼ cup (60 mL) sesame oil

3 cups (750 mL) steamed jasmine rice

¼ cup (60 mL) vegetable oil

12 oz (350 g) thinly sliced striploin

1 cup (250 mL) thinly sliced zucchini half moons

1 cup (250 mL) oyster mushrooms, torn into 1 inch (2.5 cm) pieces

1 cup (250 mL) thinly sliced carrot half moons

1 cup (250 mL) thinly sliced white onion, sliced lengthwise

1½ tsp (7.5 mL) minced garlic

2 tsp (10 mL) fine salt

Soy ginger vinaigrette (recipe follows)

4 poached eggs

1 tbsp (15 mL) salted cucumber (page 48)

1 tbsp (15 mL) pickled red pearl onions (recipe follows)

1 tbsp (15 mL) pickled red Fresno chilies (recipe follows)

2 tbsp (30 mL) thinly diagonally sliced green onions

4 tsp (20 mL) sesame seeds

Gochujang sauce (page 37)

1. If using dolsot (stone bowls), place each bowl over medium-high heat until piping hot, approximately 1 minute. Heat 1 tablespoon (15 mL) sesame oil per bowl and add ¾ cup (180 mL) steamed jasmine rice. Gently spread the rice over the entire surface of the bowl to maximize crisping the rice, approximately 4 minutes. Repeat with the remaining dolsot. Proceed to step 3. If you are using regular bowls, skip this step and proceed with step 2.

2. If you are using regular bowls for this dish, place a wok over medium-high heat and heat 1 tablespoon (15 mL) of the sesame oil until it ripples. Add ¾ cup (180 mL) steamed jasmine rice and spread out over the surface of the wok. Do not stir for at least 3 minutes. Cook until the rice crisps up and turns a golden brown on the bottom. Transfer to a bowl and repeat with the remaining portions. Wipe down the wok and proceed to step 3.

3. Heat a wok over medium-high heat until very hot, approximately 1 minute.

4. Add the vegetable oil and the striploin, immediately spreading out the beef in a single layer to promote searing. Do not flip or stir the beef for 1 to 2 minutes or until the beef is deep brown.

5. Flip the beef and return to a single layer to cook through.

6. Add the zucchini, mushrooms, carrots, white onion, garlic and salt. Toss well and cook until vegetables are tender, but still firm, approximately 2 minutes.

7. Add the soy ginger vinaigrette and bring to a simmer. Reduce the liquid slightly until it is thick enough to coat the vegetables.

8. Divide the beef and vegetables equally among the 4 rice bowls, leaving a divot in the centre of each portion for the poached egg.

9. Gently nestle the egg in the divot and arrange the garnishes around the egg. The salted cucumber, pearl onions, Fresno chilies and green onions should be arranged in separate piles over the rice. Repeat for all bowls.

10. Sprinkle each bowl with 1 teaspoon (5 mL) sesame seeds and serve with gochujang sauce on the side.

Bibimbap literally means "mixed rice" and is a very healthy and gluten-free meal. If you have the traditional stone *dolsot* pots, then the crispy layer of rice on the bottom is the best part. Otherwise, use regular bowls to build the individual portions, but keep in mind that the textural component of the crispy rice will be missing in the final dish.

P-48
P-37

SOY GINGER VINAIGRETTE

¼ cup (60 mL) vegetable oil

1½ tbsp (22.5 mL) soy sauce

2 tsp (10 mL) rice vinegar

2 tsp (10 mL) minced shallots

1 tsp (5 mL) minced ginger

1 tsp (5 mL) minced garlic

1. Using a food processor or hand-held blender, purée all ingredients until emulsified.
2. Transfer to an airtight container and refrigerate. The vinaigrette can be stored refrigerated for 5 days. Mix well before use.

PICKLED RED PEARL ONIONS AND PICKLED RED FRESNO CHILIES

1¼ cups (310 mL) water

⅔ cup (160 mL) white wine vinegar

½ cup (125 mL) peeled and trimmed red pearl onions

½ cup (125 mL) ⅛-inch (3 mm) sliced Fresno chilies, seeded

1. Bring the water and vinegar to a boil.
2. Place the pearl onions in an appropriately sized container. Place the chilies in a separate container.
3. Pour half the pickling liquid into the onion container and the remaining half into the chili container. Push the vegetables into the liquid if necessary to make sure they are fully submerged.
4. Allow to cool to room temperature before lidding and transferring to the refrigerator. Allow to pickle for 24 hours before using.

main plates

What age of vegetables are best in the recipes you'll find in this section? An odd question, but let us explain: baby vegetables are tender and sweet but don't store well, so they're best used within hours or at most days of leaving the field, which isn't always possible. Mature ones carry more intense flavours (for better or worse) and store better, but their tougher texture is more complicated to work with and may not be as pleasing. So there are advantages and disadvantages to each, which brings us to a third type: "teen" vegetables.

Fifteen years ago one of our primary vegetable suppliers, Roots Organic in Surrey, British Columbia, found that they had to throw a lot of their vegetables away about the day they turned (in human equivalents) thirteen. In the boutique restaurant trade they catered to, there was just no market for even slightly mature zucchini, carrots or several other types of vegetables. When we learned about this, our purchasing department got very interested very quickly, since it reduced the cost of organic produce to that of non-organic. But would our chefs play along? Why, yes, they would. In some cases recipes and cooking times had to be adjusted slightly, but the flavours were, if anything, more intense, which definitely works for us—plus, who wants to stand in the way of saving money while preventing waste?

That was the beginning of a program that has now spread chain-wide. To make sure the teen vegetables they supply to us are as cuddly and tousle-haired (we're speaking metaphorically here) as baby vegetables would be, Roots Organic hand-picks, hand-washes and hand-packs ours. They are the spoiled brats of the vegetable world, in other words—and despite that, we recommend them highly.

TERIYAKI-GLAZED CHICKEN

Restaurants like Earls (not that there were any restaurants like Earls back then) simply didn't offer Japanese dishes in the 1980s, and Chuck remembers that not many Earls guests were looking for them either, at least at first. That changed quickly, and nowadays, an old-school dish like this qualifies as comfort food and goes over especially well with children.

1980s 1990s 2000s 2010s

SERVES 4

1 whole chicken (3 lb/1.5 kg), cut into 6 pieces, or 6 bone-in breasts or thighs

3 cups (750 mL) teriyaki marinade, divided (recipe follows)

1½ tbsp (22.5 mL) cornstarch

1 tsp (5 mL) butter

4 pineapple wedges

TERIYAKI MARINADE

1 cup (250 mL) hot water

1 cup (250 mL) soy sauce

½ cup (125 mL) pineapple juice

½ cup (125 mL) brown sugar

1 tsp (5 mL) minced garlic

1 tsp (5 mL) minced ginger

1. Mix all ingredients together. Can be prepared and stored refrigerated up to 4 days ahead.

1. Marinate chicken pieces in 1½ cups (375 mL) of teriyaki marinade. Cover and refrigerate for at least 6 hours and up to 8 hours, rotating the chicken halfway through to ensure even marinating.
2. While chicken is marinating, make the teriyaki glaze using the reserved 1½ cups (375 mL) of teriyaki marinade.
3. Bring 1 cup (250 mL) of the reserved teriyaki marinade to a boil.
4. Whisk the cornstarch into the remaining ½ cup (125 mL) of marinade. Slowly pour into the boiling teriyaki marinade, whisking constantly to avoid lumps, until the marinade has thickened to a glaze consistency.
5. Pour through a strainer. Set aside to cool thoroughly.
6. Preheat the oven to 350°F (180°C). Arrange the marinated chicken on a foil-lined tray, leaving ample space between each piece. This will encourage even cooking and caramelization.
7. Bake for 30 minutes. Remove from the oven and baste all surfaces with the teriyaki glaze. Return to the oven and broil at 450°F (230°C) for an additional 4 to 5 minutes, watching carefully to avoid burning the skin of the chicken.
8. Check the internal temperature of the chicken for doneness. Chicken breast pieces must be cooked to 160°F (71°C), while the thickest part of the thighs must be cooked to 170°F (77°C). Return the chicken to the 350°F (180°C) oven if necessary.
9. Once chicken is cooked, let it rest for 10 minutes to allow juices to settle back into the meat.
10. While the chicken is resting, heat the butter in a nonstick pan or grill over medium heat. Sauté or grill the pineapple wedges until golden brown on each side, approximately 3 minutes. Remove from heat.
11. Brush the remaining teriyaki glaze on the chicken right before serving.
12. Garnish each dish with a warm pineapple wedge.

The simplicity and versatility of this marinade make it an easy weeknight meal. Make a double batch of the teriyaki glaze and use it as a stir-fry sauce or even as a dip for steamed veggies. Chuck says he'd consider switching things up from the original recipe shown here by subbing mirin for half the pineapple juice, and notes that pineapple juice is way better when it's not from concentrate.

TANDOORI CHICKEN

When we first rolled out our forno ovens, they were a smash hit with guests, but not so much with Chuck, who noticed that the designated pizza cook wasn't busy enough. Thinking quickly, he came up with a few more recipes that could use a 600°F (315°C) oven, including this Indian classic. Yes, it uses a commercially prepared tandoori paste (he still swears by Patak's), which was unusual for us, but utterly sensible for the home cook. And the dish works just as well at a conventional oven temperature too.

1980s **1990s** 2000s 2010s

SERVES 4–6

1 whole chicken (3 lb/1.5 kg), cut into 6 pieces, or 6 bone-in breasts or thighs

2 cups (500 mL) tandoori marinade (recipe follows)

1 cup (250 mL) mango chutney (found in the Asian food section of your grocery store)

1. Marinate the chicken in the tandoori marinade, making sure each piece is evenly coated with sauce. Refrigerate overnight or 8 hours minimum.
2. Preheat the oven to 350°F (180°C). Arrange the marinated chicken on a foil-lined tray, leaving ample space between each piece. This will encourage even cooking and caramelization.
3. Bake for 30 minutes. Set the oven to broil at 450°F (230°C).
4. Broil for an additional 4 to 5 minutes, watching carefully to avoid burning the chicken.
5. Check the internal temperature of the chicken for doneness. Chicken breast pieces must be cooked to 160°F (71°C), while the thickest part of the thighs must be cooked to 170°F (77°C). Return the chicken to the 350°F (180°C) oven if necessary.
6. Once the chicken is cooked, let it rest for 10 minutes to allow juices to settle back into the meat.
7. Serve with the mango chutney.

TANDOORI MARINADE

1 cup (250 mL) yogurt

¾ cup (180 mL) tandoori paste

2 tbsp (30 mL) vegetable oil

1½ tbsp (22.5 mL) minced ginger

1½ tbsp (22.5 mL) lemon juice

2 tsp (10 mL) minced garlic

½ tsp (2.5 mL) fine salt

1. Combine all ingredients until fully incorporated.
2. Can be stored refrigerated for up to 5 days.

For best results, the chicken should marinate overnight.
The yogurt and ginger permeate the meat and make for
very tender and juicy chicken.

ROASTED HUNTER CHICKEN

Way back when, Larry introduced this hunter sauce to luxurious effect with our forno-roasted chicken. Mention it in passing that your *sauce chasseur* was invented by the same guy who came up with Mornay, lyonnaise, and béchamel, and you'll be golden.

1980s **1990s** 2000s 2010s

SERVES 4–6

1 whole chicken (3lb/1.5kg) cut into 6 pieces, or 6 boneless chicken breasts, brined (page 239)

Hunter sauce

1. Preheat the oven to 350°F (180°C). Thoroughly pat dry the brined chicken to encourage crisp skin.
2. Arrange the chicken on a foil-lined tray, leaving ample space between each piece to help caramelization and even cooking.
3. Bake for 30 minutes for bone-in chicken, or 10 minutes for boneless breasts. The internal temperature of the cooked chicken should register 160°F (71°C).
4. Broil for 4 to 5 minutes, watching carefully to avoid burning the skin. Allow a rest for 1 minute before plating with desired sides.
5. Pour ¼ cup (160mL) of hunter sauce over the chicken breasts. Serve immediately with additional sauce on the side.

Serve this dish with mashed potatoes, roasted potatoes, seasonal vegetables or salad.

HUNTER SAUCE

1 tsp (5 mL) vegetable oil

2 cups (500 mL) quartered mushrooms

1½ tsp (7.5 mL) green peppercorns

1½ tbsp (22.5 mL) brandy

¾ cup (180 mL) demi-glace (page 245)

3 tbsp (45 mL) white wine

2 tbsp (30 mL) sun-dried tomatoes, rehydrated if not oil-packed

1 tbsp (15 mL) finely chopped parsley

1 tsp (5 mL) Dijon mustard

1. Heat the oil in a heavy-bottomed pot until it ripples. Sauté mushrooms until golden brown and fragrant, approximately 5 minutes. Add the peppercorns and continue to sauté for another 2 minutes.
2. Add the brandy and allow to flambé by tipping the pan over the flame. Be careful to keep your distance, as the flames can burn quite high. If using an electric or induction burner, you can use a lighter or matches to carefully flambé the brandy. Allow brandy to evaporate.
3. Add the demi-glace, white wine, sun-dried tomatoes, parsley and mustard. Reduce heat to low and simmer gently until the sun-dried tomatoes are softened, approximately 3 minutes. Do not reduce!
4. Remove from heat. Serve immediately or allow to come to room temperature.
5. The sauce can be stored refrigerated for up to 5 days.

HALIBUT WITH TOMATO OLIVE BALSAMIC STEW

1980s 1990s **2000s** 2010s

SERVES 4–6

1½ lb (680 g) fresh halibut fillets (4 to 6 pieces)

1 tsp (5 mL) fine salt

1 tsp (5 mL) ground black pepper

1 tbsp (15 mL) olive oil

Tomato olive balsamic stew (recipe follows)

2 tbsp (30 mL) balsamic glaze, which you can find in the vinegar section of most gourmet stores

With his Pear Tree restaurant, Bocuse d'Or veteran Scott Jaeger became one of the leading lights of a generation of young chefs who transformed Vancouver's restaurant scene by adapting their classical training to the local larder and more casual dining culture. All of which made perfect sense to us, so we were thrilled when Scott came into the test kitchen and left us with this zippy dish, which he created originally for the Bocuse d'Or, a fresh take on one of our favourite North Pacific fish.

1. Pat the halibut fillets dry with a paper towel. Season evenly with salt and pepper.
2. In a large nonstick skillet, heat the olive oil over medium-high heat until it ripples. Sear the halibut, presentation side down, for 5 minutes. Do not touch the fish at this point as you are trying to develop a nice sear. The halibut will release from the pan once a crust has developed.
3. Flip the halibut and continue cooking on the other side for an additional 5 to 6 minutes, depending on the thickness of the halibut fillets.
4. Remove from heat as soon as the internal temperature of the fish reaches 135°F (57°C). Allow to rest for 5 minutes before topping with ¼ cup (60 mL) of tomato olive balsamic stew over each fillet.
5. Drizzle each piece of halibut with balsamic glaze.

Halibut overcooks very easily, so keep an eye on the temperature and remove it from the heat immediately when it reaches an internal temperature of 135°F (57°C). This fish goes from moist and succulent to tough and dry in minutes!

TOMATO OLIVE BALSAMIC STEW

3 tbsp (45 mL) olive oil, divided

¼ cup (60 mL) medium-diced onions

2 tsp (10 mL) minced garlic

2½ cups (600 mL) canned San Marzano tomatoes

2 tbsp (30 mL) balsamic vinegar

½ tsp (2.5 mL) fine salt

¼ tsp (1.25 mL) ground black pepper

¼ cup (60 mL) roughly chopped kalamata olives

2 tbsp (30 mL) coarsely chopped basil leaves

1. Heat 1 tablespoon (15 mL) of the olive oil in a heavy-bottomed saucepan until it ripples.
2. Sauté the onions until translucent, approximately 5 minutes, then add the garlic and continue cooking until fragrant.
3. Drain the San Marzano tomatoes well and add to the pan along with the balsamic vinegar, salt and pepper.
4. Bring the mixture to a simmer, lower the heat and cook for 10 minutes.
5. Add the olives and remaining 2 tablespoons (30 mL) of olive oil, stirring well to incorporate all the ingredients.
6. Continue to simmer the sauce until it reduces to 2 cups (500 mL). The sauce should take on a deep-red colour and have a thick consistency.
7. Remove from the heat and allow to cool completely. Once cooled, add the basil and stir well.
8. Use immediately or transfer to an airtight container. Can be stored refrigerated for 3 days.

BRAISED BEEF SHORT RIBS

Looking to impress people without going to ridiculous lengths? An elaborate salad like our Jerusalem Salad with Moroccan Spiced Chicken (page 91) would be a nice summer option. The wintertime alternative might be a slow braise, like this one from Michael Noble. Prepare it the day before so that the flavours knit and you can easily remove the layer of fat that rises, while simultaneously providing the illusion that you somehow whipped it up in the minutes before your guests' arrival. Ta-da!

SERVES 4–6

4 lb (1.8 kg) 3-inch (8 cm) thick-cut bone-in beef short ribs or 2½ lb (1.15 kg) 3-inch (8 cm) cut boneless short ribs

1 tbsp (15 mL) coarse salt

1 tbsp (15 mL) ground black pepper

2 tbsp (30 mL) vegetable oil

1 cup (250 mL) medium-diced onion

¼ cup (60 mL) whole peeled garlic cloves

¼ cup (60 mL) tomato paste

2 cups (500 mL) red wine

4 sprigs rosemary

4 sprigs thyme

1 bay leaf

4 cups (1 L) beef stock

1 15 oz can (approximately 1¾ cups/ 435 mL) crushed tomatoes

1½ cups (375 mL) demi-glace (page 245)

Horseradish cream (recipe follows)

Ask your butcher to give you the meatier pieces for the short ribs. The bones will most likely fall out after cooking, so don't worry too much about portioning until after the meat is fully cooked. Serve with mashed potatoes and roasted vegetables if desired.

1. Preheat the oven to 350°F (180°C).
2. Season the short ribs generously with coarse salt and pepper.
3. Heat oil in a large, heavy-bottomed ovenproof pot over high heat. Add the seasoned short ribs and brown on all sides. Work in batches if you need to so that the short ribs don't get overcrowded, which makes it difficult to get a proper sear. Sear the short ribs without moving them for several minutes on each side, letting them brown deeply. Use tongs to turn and sear all sides. This will take about 15 minutes total. Once seared, transfer to a baking tray.
4. Remove the excess fat from the pot, retaining approximately 2 tablespoons (30 mL) to cook the onions.
5. Turn the heat down to medium and add the onion and garlic, cooking until the onions are translucent, approximately 5 minutes.
6. Add the tomato paste and cook until the paste turns a brownish red, stirring frequently to avoid burning.
7. Deglaze the pot with the red wine, scraping the bottom and edges of the pot. Bring to a simmer.
8. Add the rosemary, thyme, bay leaf and the short ribs. Bring to a simmer.
9. Add the beef stock, crushed tomatoes and demi-glace. Return to a simmer.
10. Cover the pot tightly and place in the oven. Cook for 3¼ hours or until the ribs are extremely tender.
11. Remove the short ribs from the roasting liquid carefully so that the pieces do not break apart. Strain the solids from the liquid and skim the fat. Discard the strained onions and herbs.
12. Continue to simmer the liquid over medium heat until it is reduced by half and has thickened nicely.
13. Serve each portion of short rib with the reduced jus and some horseradish cream. Mashed potatoes and roasted vegetables make an excellent accompaniment.

HORSERADISH CREAM

¾ cup (180 mL) sour cream

¼ cup (60 mL) mayonnaise

¼ cup (60 mL) prepared horseradish

2 tsp (10 mL) lemon juice

½ tsp (5 mL) fine salt

1. Combine the ingredients and mix well. Use immediately, as the horseradish loses its potency over time.

PORK CHOPS WITH BURNT ORANGE SAUCE

1980s 1990s **2000s** 2010s

SERVES 4–6

4 to 6 pork chops, 1½ to 2 inches thick (4 to 5 cm)

Chicken brine (page 239)

Vegetable oil, for coating chops

1 tsp (5 mL) coarse salt

1½ tsp (7.5 mL) coarse black pepper

1¼ cups (310 mL) orange juice

½ cup (125 mL) white wine vinegar

¼ cup (60 mL) honey

¼ cup (60 mL) thinly sliced shallot (about 1 small shallot)

2 tsp (10 mL) fresh thyme leaves, divided

1¼ cups (310 mL) demi-glace (page 245)

⅓ cup (80 mL) heavy cream

2 tbsp (30 mL) sherry wine

Here's another example of the way that the classical French techniques mastered by so many of our chefs, in this case Michael Noble, have helped elevate some of our dishes. Beyond the rich sauce, the key here is to brine the chops a day ahead, which keeps them moist, flavourful and so different from a quick-fry chop pulled out of a shopping bag. As the French say, *vive la différence!*

1. Submerge the pork chops in enough chicken brine to cover. Allow to brine overnight or at least 5-6 hours.
2. Preheat the oven to 400°F (200°C). Preheat a skillet or grill pan over medium-high heat.
3. Pat the pork chops dry with paper towels. Rub each pork chop with a light coating of vegetable oil. Season with coarse salt and black pepper.
4. Sear each pork chop for 5 minutes, then flip and continue searing for 4 minutes.
5. Transfer to the oven and cook for 10 minutes. The internal temperature of the pork should register 145°F to 160°F (63°C to 71°C) for medium-rare to medium respectively.
6. Set aside to rest on a platter. Cover with foil to keep warm.
7. Combine the orange juice, vinegar, honey, shallot and half the thyme in a saucepan and bring to a boil. Lower heat to medium and reduce until the sauce has a syrupy consistency.
8. In a separate bowl, mix together the demi-glace and heavy cream. Add it to the orange syrup and stir constantly with a whisk until the sauce thickens enough to coat the back of a spoon.
9. Add the sherry and the rest of the thyme. Remove from heat and set aside.
10. If made ahead, transfer the sauce to an airtight container. Can be stored refrigerated for up to 5 days.
11. Serve the pork chop with desired sides and the burnt orange sauce.

MOROCCAN SALMON WITH PERSIAN CAULIFLOWER

1980s 1990s 2000s **2010s**

SERVES 4–6

1½ lb (680 g) salmon fillet

2 tsp (10 mL) melted salted butter

1 tsp (5 mL) coarse salt

1 tsp (5 mL) ground black pepper

1 cup (250 mL) peas, thawed if frozen

½ cup (125 mL) pearl onions, thawed if frozen

¼ cup (60 mL) vegetable stock

2 oz (57 g or ¼ cup/60 mL) butter

1 tsp (5 mL) lemon juice

½ cup (125 mL) basil leaves, torn in half crosswise if longer than 2 inches (5 cm)

½ tsp (2.5 mL) salt

Charmoula (recipe follows)

Persian cauliflower (recipe follows)

1 tbsp + 1 tsp (20 mL) smoked paprika oil (recipe follows)

2 tsp (10 mL) lemon juice

1 bunch watercress, cleaned and dried

A native of Iran, Hamid Salimian knows northern Africa and the Middle East, and as a part-captain of Canada's team at the 2016 Culinary Olympics, he certainly knows his way around a kitchen, especially a Persian kitchen. Because of that, he'll find the preparation of this dish, ideal for late summer, a little simpler than most other people, but if the *charmoula* is prepped in advance, it's not so complicated. And oh my, the result!

1. Preheat the oven to 450°F (230°C).
2. Cut the salmon fillet into the desired number of servings (4 to 6 portions). Arrange on a parchment-lined rimmed baking tray. Brush a thin film of melted butter over each portion and season with coarse salt and pepper.
3. Place in the preheated oven and cook for 8 to 10 minutes or until the salmon is firm to the touch when pressed in the thickest part and registers an internal temperature of 130°F (54°C).
4. Combine the peas, pearl onions, vegetable stock, butter and lemon juice in a small pot and heat until just beginning to simmer. Add the basil leaves and salt.
5. Brush 1 tablespoon (15 mL) of charmoula on each plate in the shape of an arch off the centre of the plate.
6. Plate the peas and onion mixture in the centre of the arch. Arrange the cauliflower over the charmoula.
7. Plate the salmon over the peas and pearl onions and drizzle with 1 teaspoon (5 mL) of smoked paprika oil and ½ teaspoon (2.5 mL) of lemon juice. Garnish with watercress leaves. Serve immediately.

CHARMOULA

¼ cup + 2 tbsp (90 mL) olive oil, divided

2 tsp (10 mL) minced ginger

2 tsp (10 mL) minced garlic

2 tsp (10 mL) smoked paprika

1 tsp (5 mL) ground cumin

1 tsp (5 mL) ground coriander

1 tsp (5 mL) fine salt

¼ tsp (1.25 mL) cayenne

⅓ cup (80 mL) tomato paste

2 tbsp (30 mL) lemon juice

1 tbsp (15 mL) lime juice

2 tbsp (30 mL) cilantro leaves

2 tbsp (30 mL) parsley leaves

4 lime leaves (common in the Asian freezer section of your grocery store)

2 tsp (10 mL) lemon zest

Small pinch saffron powder or threads

1. In a small saucepan, heat 2 tablespoons (30 mL) of the olive oil over medium heat until it ripples. Add the ginger and garlic and sauté until fragrant and beginning to soften, approximately 2 minutes.
2. Stir in the smoked paprika, cumin, coriander, salt and cayenne. Sauté until fragrant, approximately 30 seconds.
3. Stir in the tomato paste, lemon and lime juice, cilantro, parsley, lime leaves, lemon zest and saffron. Simmer for 2 minutes to allow the flavours to combine. Do not reduce. Discard the lime leaves after simmering.
4. Transfer all the ingredients, including the remaining olive oil, into a food processor. Blend well. The ingredients must be finely puréed and the sauce should be smooth.
5. Pass through a sieve. Keep warm.
6. If made ahead, transfer to an airtight container and refrigerate. The sauce can be stored refrigerated for 5 days.

PERSIAN CAULIFLOWER

¼ cup (60 mL) vegetable oil

½ tsp (2.5 mL) garam masala

¼ tsp (1.25 mL) turmeric

1 lb (450 g) cauliflower, cut into florets approximately 1 to 2 inches (2.5 to 5 cm)

1. Preheat the oven to 450°F (230°C).
2. Combine the vegetable oil, garam masala, and turmeric in a small pot. Heat oil until it reaches 320°F (160°C).
3. Remove from heat and let cool to room temperature.
4. Toss with the cauliflower florets until well coated and transfer to a parchment-lined rimmed baking tray.
5. Bake for 20 to 25 minutes or until the cauliflower is dark golden brown. Stir occasionally to encourage even cooking.
6. Remove from the oven and serve immediately.

SMOKED PAPRIKA OIL

1 cup minus 2 tbsp (220 mL) vegetable oil, divided

1 tbsp (15 mL) thinly sliced shallots

1 tsp (5 mL) cumin seeds

½ tsp (2.5 mL) fennel seeds

½ tsp (2.5 mL) coriander seeds

½ tsp (2.5 mL) red chili flakes

2 tsp (10 mL) smoked paprika

1. In a small saucepan, heat 3 tablespoons (45 mL) of the vegetable oil over medium heat until it ripples. Add the shallots and cook until they are a golden brown.
2. Add the cumin, fennel, coriander and chili flakes and cook until fragrant, approximately 30 seconds.
3. Add the remaining vegetable oil and the smoked paprika with the sautéed shallot and spice mixture.
4. Place on the lowest heat setting and allow the flavours to steep for at least 1 hour. Remove from heat and allow to rest overnight.
5. Strain through a cheesecloth and discard solids.
6. If made ahead, transfer to an airtight container and refrigerate. The oil can be stored refrigerated for 5 days.

QUINOA CRUSTED SALMON

Here's a meal that's had the starch taken out of it. That was Dawn Doucette's goal, in fact, and the captivating thing about it is her use of quinoa, which is always nutritious and often tasty, but less often interesting. Here, though, it's used in an unfamiliar role to crust the salmon, and also served on the side but in living colour. Try it and you'll understand why so many people are keen on the South American staple.

1980s 1990s 2000s **2010s**

SERVES 4-6

2 lb (1 kg) salmon fillet

2 tbsp (30 mL) melted salted butter

1 tsp (5 mL) coarse salt

1 tsp (5 mL) ground black pepper

Red and white quinoa (recipe follows)

Carrot purée (recipe follows)

Herb and ginger vinaigrette (recipe follows)

1. Preheat the oven to 450°F (230°C).
2. Cut the salmon fillet into the desired number of servings (4 to 6 portions). Arrange on a parchment-lined rimmed baking tray. Brush a thin film of butter over each portion and season with coarse salt and pepper.
3. Press 2 tablespoons (30 mL) of quinoa onto the presentation side of each salmon portion. Use your fingers to gently spread the quinoa out evenly over the entire surface so that each bite of salmon will have some quinoa. Repeat with the remaining salmon portions.
4. Place in the preheated oven and cook for 8 to 10 minutes or until the salmon is firm to the touch when pressed in the thickest part and registers an internal temperature of 130°F (54°C).
5. Serve with the carrot purée and a drizzle of the herb and ginger vinaigrette.

RED AND WHITE QUINOA

½ cup (125 mL) white (regular) quinoa

½ cup (125 mL) red quinoa

2 cups (500 mL) water

½ tsp (2.5 mL) fine salt

1. Rinse both kinds of quinoa under running water. Drain well.
2. Bring the water and salt to a boil and immediately add the drained quinoa.
3. Lower the heat to medium and stir occasionally to prevent sticking.
4. Simmer until all the water has been absorbed and quinoa has doubled in size, approximately 15 to 20 minutes.
5. Test for doneness: the quinoa should retain a slight chew. If the quinoa is undercooked, cover with a lid and allow the residual steam to continue cooking the quinoa.
6. Spread out the cooked quinoa onto a parchment-lined baking tray and allow to cool completely.
7. Use in the salmon recipe or transfer to an airtight container and refrigerate. The quinoa can be stored refrigerated for 5 days.

Quinoa Crusted Salmon

CARROT PURÉE

2 lb (1 kg) peeled carrots

1 small handful cilantro, whole sprigs

¾ cup (180 mL) olive oil, divided

1 cup (250 mL) medium-diced white onion

1 tsp (5 mL) fine salt

¼ tsp (1.25 mL) ground black pepper

1. Chop the carrots in half lengthwise, then in half again crosswise. Place in a steamer basket along with the cilantro sprigs and steam for approximately 20 to 25 minutes or until the carrots are completely soft.
2. Remove the cilantro and discard.
3. In a large heavy-bottomed pot or Dutch oven, heat ½ cup (125 mL) of olive oil until it ripples. Sauté the onions until translucent and softened, approximately 5 minutes.
4. Add the carrots and continue sautéeing until the carrots begin to stick to the bottom of the pot, approximately 8 minutes.
5. Remove from heat and add the remaining ¼ cup (60 mL) of olive oil. Season with salt and pepper.
6. Using a hand-held blender, purée until all ingredients are emulsified and smooth. Scrape down the sides of the pot to make sure no chunks of carrot remain. The purée should be velvety smooth.
7. Keep warm while preparing the salmon.

HERB AND GINGER VINAIGRETTE

1 tbsp (15 mL) roughly chopped mint leaves

1 tbsp (15 mL) roughly chopped cilantro

1 tbsp (15 mL) minced shallots

2 tsp (10 mL) minced ginger

1 tsp (5 mL) minced seeded serrano pepper

1 tsp (5 mL) minced garlic

⅓ cup (80 mL) olive oil

⅓ cup (80 mL) vegetable oil

1 tbsp (15 mL) lime juice

½ tsp (2.5 mL) fine salt

¼ tsp (1.25 mL) ground black pepper

1. Using a food processor or hand-held blender, purée all ingredients until emulsified and the herbs, shallots, ginger, serrano peppers and garlic are finely chopped.
2. Transfer to an airtight container and refrigerate. The vinaigrette can be stored refrigerated for 5 days. Mix well before use.

SALMON WITH GRILLED CORN AND CILANTRO PURÉE

1980s 1990s 2000s **2010s**

SERVES 4–6

1½ lb (680 g) mini new potatoes

2 tbsp (30 mL) olive oil, divided

1½ lb (680 g) salmon fillet

¾ tsp (3.75 mL) fine salt, divided

½ tsp (2.5 mL) ground black pepper

1 cup (250 mL) corn kernels

1 cup (250 mL) oven-dried grape tomatoes (page 48)

½ cup (125 mL) thinly shaved fennel

½ cup (125 mL) marinated artichokes

¼ cup (60 mL) melted salted butter

1 tbsp (15 mL) lemon juice

¼ cup (60 mL) 1-inch (2.5 cm) torn basil leaves

½ cup (125 mL) jalapeño cilantro purée (recipe follows)

¼ cup (60 mL) chimichurri sauce (page 185)

1½ tbsp (22.5 mL) lemon coriander gastrique (recipe follows)

1 tbsp (15 mL) lemon juice

1 cup (250 mL) watercress leaves

This is another showstopper from Hamid Salimian that we serve every day, but we are pretty sure, given its complication, that you won't. That said, for a dinner party where meat can't be on the menu, it's the kind of knock-out dish that can turn cavemen into pescatarians. Most of the prep work goes into the chimichurri and the jalapeño cilantro purée, so make lots and refrigerate them to use with something that you do serve yourself every day.

1. Blanch the mini new potatoes in salted water until a knife slides easily through the largest piece. Drain and toss with 1 tablespoon (15 mL) of the olive oil.
2. Preheat the oven to 450°F (230°C). Place the mini potatoes on the lowest rack.
3. Cut the salmon fillet into 4 to 6 even pieces. Place the salmon on a foil-lined rimmed baking tray. Drizzle with 2 teaspoons (10 mL) of the olive oil. Season lightly with ½ teaspoon (2.5 mL) each salt and pepper. Roast in the oven for 6 to 8 minutes or until the salmon registers an internal temperature of 130°F (54°C) on an instant-read thermometer. Immediately remove from the oven.
4. Remove the potatoes from the oven and keep warm. Switch the oven to broil.
5. Spread the corn out on a foil-lined baking tray, drizzle with the remaining 1 teaspoon (5 mL) of olive oil and broil for 3 to 5 minutes or until slightly browned. Stir well to ensure even browning and allow to brown for a further 2 to 3 minutes.
6. To the same tray, add the oven-dried grape tomatoes, fennel, artichokes, butter and lemon juice. Return to the oven and cook for 3 minutes or until all ingredients are warmed through.
7. Transfer all the ingredients to a mixing bowl and add the basil leaves. Season with the remaining ¼ teaspoon (1.25 mL) salt. Toss all ingredients to combine.
8. Using a spoon, smear 2 tablespoons (30 mL) of jalapeño cilantro purée on each plate in a neat line. Arrange a portion of the roasted corn salad over one side of the jalapeño cilantro purée, then plate the mini potatoes around the roasted corn salad.
9. Place the salmon over the other side of the jalapeño cilantro purée and drizzle with 2 tablespoons (30 mL) of chimichurri, 1 teaspoon (5 mL) of lemon coriander gastrique and a drizzle of lemon juice.
10. Garnish with some watercress leaves. Repeat with the remaining plates.

JALAPEÑO CILANTRO PURÉE

⅓ cup (80 mL) garlic cloves

1 poblano pepper, halved and seeded

1 jalapeño pepper, halved and seeded

¼ cup (60 mL) finely chopped cilantro

½ tsp (2.5 mL) fine salt

2 tbsp (30 mL) olive oil

1. In a medium-sized pot of boiling salted water, blanch the garlic for 15 minutes until soft throughout. Immediately shock in an ice bath until completely cool, and then drain well.
2. Place the poblano and jalapeño peppers on a rimmed baking tray, cut side down, pressing firmly to flatten the peppers. Broil under medium-high heat until all the skin is fully charred and the peppers are soft, approximately 10 minutes. Cool to room temperature.
3. Combine the peppers, blanched garlic, cilantro, salt and olive oil in a food processor and purée until very smooth.
4. Pass through a sieve, discarding any solids or bits of skin.
5. If made ahead, transfer to an airtight container and refrigerate. The purée can be stored refrigerated for 5 days maximum.

LEMON CORIANDER GASTRIQUE

½ cup (125 mL) apple cider vinegar

¼ cup (60 mL) sugar

1 tsp (5 mL) coriander seed

1 tsp (5 mL) lemon zest

1. Bring all the ingredients to a boil in a small pot. Reduce to a simmer and allow to cook uncovered until the liquid is reduced to ¼ cup (60 mL) after straining.
2. Remove from heat and strain the gastrique through a fine sieve.
3. If made ahead, transfer to an airtight container and refrigerate. The gastrique can be stored refrigerated for 9 days maximum.

ROASTED ROMESCO CHICKEN

In Spain, romesco sauce is traditionally served with fish, but in recent years it's come to the attention of a lot of chefs as being rich, smooth and delicious yet also magically healthy and even nutritious. And of course, we have those forno ovens crying out for things to be roasted in them—things like, for example, chicken.

1980s 1990s 2000s **2010s**

SERVES 4–6

4 to 6 brined full chicken breasts, boneless (page 239)

Romesco sauce (recipe follows)

1. Preheat the oven to 500°F (260°C). Thoroughly pat dry the brined chicken breasts to encourage crisp skin.
2. Arrange the chicken skin side down on an oiled rimmed baking tray.
3. Bake in the oven for approximately 4 minutes then flip and continue cooking for 4 minutes. The internal temperature of the cooked chicken should register 160°F (71°C).
4. Allow to rest for 1 minute before cutting each full breast in half and plating with desired sides.
5. Pour ¼ cup (60 mL) of romesco sauce over the chicken breasts. Serve immediately with additional sauce on the side.

ROMESCO SAUCE

1 28 oz can (approximately 3½ cups/ 800 mL) San Marzano tomatoes

1 tbsp (15 mL) chipotle peppers in adobo, puréed

1 tbsp (15 mL) confit garlic (page 242)

2 slices bread, crusts removed

½ cup + 1 tbsp (140 mL) olive oil, divided

2 tbsp (30 mL) slivered almonds, toasted

1 tbsp (15 mL) red wine vinegar

2 tsp (10 mL) finely chopped parsley

½ tsp (5 mL) fine salt

1. Use your hands to crush the tomatoes in half, being careful not to lose any of the juices that might spill out of the tomatoes.
2. Transfer the tomatoes, puréed chipotle peppers and the confit garlic to a 9- × 13-inch (23 × 33 cm) pan.
3. Broil over medium heat until the tomatoes are slightly charred and the liquid has reduced by a quarter. The sauce should have a thick consistency.
4. Brush the two slices of bread on all sides with 1 tablespoon (15 mL) of the olive oil. Broil the two slices of toast until light brown. The darker the toast, the more flavour it will give to the sauce (but do not burn!). Tear into 1-inch (2.5 cm) chunks.
5. Place the almonds in a food processor and pulse until the almonds are the size of coarse bread crumbs or panko crumbs, approximately ⅛ inch (3 mm).
6. Add the charred tomato mixture and toast to the almonds and pulse until the pieces of bread are maximum ¼ inch (½ cm). Do not overmix; the texture should stay coarse.
7. Add the remaining olive oil, red wine vinegar, parsley and salt. Pulse until well combined.
8. Place in an airtight container and store refrigerated overnight to let the flavours develop. Store a maximum of 4 days refrigerated.

CHIMICHURRI SKIRT STEAK

We served this dish from Chef Hamid Salimian at the Chicago Gourmet Food Festival to great acclaim. Is your mouth watering? We thought so.

1980s 1990s 2000s **2010s**

SERVES 4–6

1½ lb (680 g) skirt steak

Skirt steak marinade (recipe follows)

1 lb (450 g) baby potatoes

1 tsp (5 mL) coarse salt

1 lb (450 g) strawberry tomatoes or grape tomatoes

½ tsp (2.5 mL) fine salt

½ lb (225 g) bunch of green onions whole

Chimichurri sauce (recipe follows)

Poblano purée (recipe follows)

1 bunch watercress, washed and dried

1. Cut the skirt steak into 6 oz (170 g) portions. Trim away any excess fat or sinew until you have 4 clean portions of steak.
2. Coat each portion of steak with 2 tablespoons (30 mL) skirt steak marinade. Ensure all surfaces are exposed to the marinade. Transfer to a sealed container or ziplock bag and allow to marinate for 24 to 48 hours before use.
3. Boil the baby potatoes in well-salted water until a knife poked through the centre of the largest potato meets no resistance. Allow to cool completely before slicing in half.
4. Remove the steak from the refrigerator 1 hour before grilling. This will allow the beef to cook evenly. Preheat the grill or if using a grill pan, preheat until smoking hot.
5. Season the skirt steak well with coarse salt and cook for approximately 2 minutes on the first side. Flip and continue cooking for another 2 minutes for medium-rare. Cook 1 minute longer for medium. Allow to rest for 3 minutes before slicing.
6. Preheat a nonstick skillet over medium heat and place the potatoes cut side down, cooking until the cut side is golden brown, approximately 2 minutes. Remove potatoes and set aside.
7. Using the same pan, blister the tomatoes over medium-high heat and season with some fine salt. Transfer to a plate, keeping warm while all the other components are being prepared.
8. Trim the root end of the green onions and sauté on all sides on the grill or using a grill pan.
9. Chop the green onions into ½-inch (1 cm) pieces and coat lightly with some chimichurri sauce.
10. Slice the skirt steak portions on a 45-degree angle, across the grain, into 1½-inch (4 cm) strips. Serve with some baby potatoes, poblano purée, blistered tomatoes and grilled onions. Drizzle chimichurri sauce over the steak and garnish with some watercress leaves.

SKIRT STEAK MARINADE

½ cup (125 mL) dark tamarind paste (common in the Asian food section of your grocery store)

½ cup (125 mL) finely chopped green onion

½ cup (125 mL) finely chopped cilantro

¼ cup (60 mL) brown sugar

2 tbsp (30 mL) minced shallots

1 tbsp (15 mL) minced serrano peppers

2 tsp (10 mL) minced garlic

2 tsp (10 mL) fine salt

1 tsp (5 mL) ground cumin

1 tsp (5 mL) ground coriander

1. Combine all the ingredients in the bowl of a food processor. If using a hand-held blender, use a deep container to finely mince all the ingredients effectively.
2. Pulse all the ingredients until you have ⅛-inch (3 mm) pieces.
3. Transfer to an airtight container and refrigerate. The marinade can be stored refrigerated for 2 days.

Tamarind paste comes in seeded and seedless varieties. This recipe calls for the seedless type. If you can find only seeded blocks of tamarind, soak it first in a little hot water to soften the seeds and create a paste. Then strain the seeds out by pushing the pulp through a coarse sieve. Use as directed in the recipe.

POBLANO PURÉE

10 oz (285 g) poblano peppers, whole

1 oz (30 g) jalapeño peppers, whole

2 tbsp (30 mL) olive oil

¼ cup (60 mL) thinly sliced shallots

½ cup (125 mL) roughly chopped cilantro

1 tbsp (15 mL) confit garlic

½ tsp (2.5 mL) fine salt

½ tsp (2.5 mL) ground coriander

½ tsp (2.5 mL) ground cumin

1. Place the poblano and jalapeño peppers on a rimmed baking tray and broil under medium-high heat, turning peppers as necessary, until all the sides are fully charred.
2. Remove from heat and preheat the oven to 400°F (200°C).
3. Bake the peppers for approximately 30 minutes or until soft. Allow to cool to room temperature before proceeding with the rest of the recipe.
4. In a medium-sized pot, heat the olive oil over medium heat until it ripples. Sauté the shallots until soft, approximately 10 minutes.
5. Remove the stems and seeds from the charred peppers, but leave the charred skins intact.
6. Combine the peppers, sautéed shallots, cilantro, confit garlic, salt, coriander and cumin in a food processor and purée until very smooth.
7. Pass through a sieve, discarding any solids or bits of skin.
8. Keep warm, or if made ahead, transfer to an airtight container and refrigerate. The purée can be stored refrigerated for 5 days maximum.

CHIMICHURRI SAUCE

½ cup (125 mL) olive oil

2 tsp (10 mL) minced garlic cloves

3 tbsp (45 mL) lime juice

3 tbsp (45 mL) minced shallots

1 tbsp (15 mL) minced jalapeños, seeded

3 tbsp (45 mL) finely chopped cilantro

3 tbsp (45 mL) finely chopped parsley

1 tbsp (15 mL) finely chopped oregano leaves

1 tsp (5 mL) thyme leaves

½ tsp (2.5 mL) fine salt

1. Combine all the ingredients into the bowl of a food processor. If using a hand-held blender, use a deep container to finely mince all the ingredients effectively.
2. Pulse all the ingredients until you have ⅛-inch (3 mm) pieces.
3. Transfer to an airtight container and refrigerate. The sauce can be stored refrigerated for 2 days.

BEEF CHILI

So if Ryan Stone represented Canada at the Bocuse D'Or, the culinary equivalent of the Olympics, does that make his chili haute cuisine? Nope, but we're betting that you will find it just a touch more interesting than the last chili you ate or made, due to chefly touches such as charring the kidney beans, corn and green onions before combining them with the meat and spice mixture. We serve this on our game nights, the two or three nights a week when local heroes are on the tube.

1980s 1990s 2000s **2010s**

SERVES 4–6

¼ cup (60 mL) vegetable oil

1½ cups (375 mL) finely diced onion

2 cups (500 mL) canned crushed tomatoes

2 cups (500 mL) diced tomatoes

2 tbsp (30 mL) yellow mustard

1¼ cups (310 mL) beef or chicken stock

⅓ cup + 1 tbsp (95 mL) chili spice blend (recipe follows)

¾ cup (180 mL) pale ale

1 lb (450 g) ground beef, divided

10 oz (285 g) rinsed and drained canned kidney beans

1 cup (250 mL) corn kernels (thawed if frozen)

½ cup (125 mL) ½-inch (1 cm) chopped green onions

Sour cream

Jalapeño rings

Cheddar crackers (recipe follows)

1. Preheat the oven to 450°F (230°C).
2. In a large Dutch oven or heavy-bottomed pot, heat the vegetable oil until ripping. Add the onions and sweat until translucent. Turn off the heat.
3. Add the crushed tomatoes, diced tomatoes, mustard, stock, ⅓ cup (80 mL) of the chili spice blend and beer to the pot. Stir well until everything is well mixed.
4. Add ¾ of the ground beef to the liquid and mix well with a whisk until the beef is broken down to pieces no larger than ½ inch (1 cm).
5. Turn the heat back on and simmer, stirring occasionally, for 40 minutes.
6. Spread out the beans, corn and half the green onions in a single layer on a parchment-lined rimmed baking tray.
7. Roast for 10 to 12 minutes or until the edges of the corn and green onions begin to char.
8. Mix together the remaining ground beef and 1 tablespoon (15 mL) chili spice blend.
9. Heat a large skillet over medium-high heat and brown the reserved chili spiced beef. Break into ½-inch (1 cm) pieces, until well browned and fully cooked.
10. Once the chili has finished simmering for 40 minutes, add the roasted corn mixture and the browned spiced beef. Simmer for a further 10 minutes.
11. Remove from heat. Garnish each serving with sour cream, the remaining green onions and jalapeño rings. Serve with cheddar crackers or other side dishes.

CHILI SPICE BLEND

¼ cup (60 mL) brown sugar

3¼ tbsp (50 mL) cornstarch

2 tbsp (30 mL) ground cumin

1¾ tbsp (26 mL) ancho chili powder

1¾ tbsp (26 mL) chili powder

1 tbsp + 1 tsp (20 mL) sugar

¾ tbsp (12 mL) smoked paprika

¾ tbsp (12 mL) dried thyme

1 tsp (5 mL) cinnamon

1. Combine all ingredients well with a whisk. Store in an airtight container at room temperature for 3 months.

CHEDDAR CRACKERS

2 cups (500 mL) shredded white cheddar

3 tbsp (45 mL) all-purpose flour

¾ tsp (3.75 mL) sugar

¼ tsp (1.25 mL) fine salt

½ cup (125 mL) panko bread crumbs

1. Preheat the oven to 325°F (165°C).
2. Toss the white cheddar, flour, sugar, salt and bread crumbs together in a mixing bowl until the cheese is fully coated.
3. Spread out in an even layer on a parchment-lined rimmed 13- × 18-inch (33 × 45 cm) baking tray.
4. Bake for 20 to 25 minutes, rotating the tray after 10 minutes. The crackers should be golden brown.
5. Remove from the oven and allow to cool completely.
6. Once cooled, break into large pieces. Store in an airtight container at room temperature.

Left to right: Ryan Stone, Fay Duong, Bowen Lansdell, Dave Wong and Brian Skinner

CHEF COLLECTIVE

It's pretty much a given that at one time or another someone has cussed at someone else in one of our kitchens. Gosh knows we've all read the books and seen the TV shows about what's supposed to go on back there. But to understand what our kitchens are truly like, the thing to understand is that our head development chef, the person who in theory should be the most tyrannical and ego-driven—well, that isn't a single person at all, but a *collective*.

Yes, for the past several years our Vancouver test kitchen has been populated by a multiplicity of chefs. Typically for us, this situation came about pretty much on its own without anyone really deciding that it should. We had the institutional memory of Chuck Currie and Larry Stewart splitting duties during our first decade, of course, and then for years we made a habit of bringing in whoever we thought could help us push a particular dish or type of menu item over the top. Michael Noble ran culinary development for a while, and as you will see

from the recipes, some pretty interesting chefs contributed dishes. By 2013, most of the test kitchen duties were being shared by Reuben Major, Alym Hirji, Fay Duong, Andrew Hounslow, Bowen Lansdell and Dawn Doucette. But then Reuben left, Fay went on maternity leave and Dawn cut back her hours to take on other culinary projects. Mo Jessa, who'd just become our president, responded by blending in Hamid Salimian, a big-deal, gold medal-winning Culinary Olympics guy who turned out to be the least frightening person you can imagine, and David Wong, who got his start as a teenager in one of our kitchens and went on to run award-winning fine dining kitchens, as well as competing in the prestigious culinary competition Bocuse d'Or.

Too many cooks? Mo didn't think so. Next was the brilliant young chef Ryan Stone, whose résumé included yet more Culinary Olympics and Bocuse d'Or escapades, as well as time spent with France's Alain Ducasse and the San Francisco 49ers. Meanwhile, steeped in the

Earls tradition of eating anywhere and everywhere, Mo had become a fan of the vegetarian restaurant the Acorn, and wouldn't you know that the founding chef there, Brian Skinner, got his start at Earls before spending years cooking in London, as well as at Copenhagen's Noma. Into the test kitchen he came too, along with the late Tina Fineza, a prominent consulting chef with an amazing palate for Latin and Mexican flavours, who'd gotten a half-dozen Vancouver landmarks off the ground. Then, while in Miami opening our new place there, we discovered that city's Yardbird restaurant. As it happened, their chef, Jeff McInnis, was just leaving, and Mo took the opportunity to invite him up to Vancouver too. Jeff has since opened New York City's Root & Bone and a couple of restaurants back in Miami with his partner, Janine Booth, but he still drops by our kitchen when he can. And most recently we finally managed to get Colin Bedford, a Relais & Châteaux Grand Chef from North Carolina, to spend some time in our test kitchen.

So that's our Chef Collective, which at any given hour of any given week can add up to a half dozen people or, just as easily, one or two. All in all, it's definitely lucky that we also have a few people who keep more regular hours, led by our executive chef, Phil Gallagher.

Incidentally, our test kitchen isn't some satellite operation located in a strip mall somewhere in the burbs. Nope, it's right upstairs from our downtown Vancouver Hornby Street location, and guests who've booked into the seating there can watch the action and perhaps sample some of the goods. And every Friday the chefs present an assortment of dishes to our tasting panel, which often includes people like Mo, or Stan and Stew Fuller.

Feel the energy! Imagine the drama! Or more likely, sit back and watch as some very serious-minded but exceptionally pleasant people explain what they've come up with while eliciting feedback from a second group of serious-minded but pleasant people. That scandalous, behind-the-scenes TV series of ours is just going to have to wait.

The Chef Collective, circa 2014 (L to R): Dawn Doucette, Andrew Hounslow, the late Tina Fineza, Jeff McInnes, Hamid Salimian, David Wong

desserts

When the first Earls opened in 1982, the only dessert we offered was a cake, which—confession time—we picked up from a bakery. But before the year was out, we expanded the dessert list to three items, including Mocha Kahlua Ice Cream Pie, which proved to be an instant hit, for more reasons than meet the eye. Chuck remembers that the dish was Stan Fuller's idea, based on something he'd eaten during his European travels, but that the chef had to spend days in the kitchen trying to make it work.

The original idea was that both the ice cream and the sauce had to be laced with Kahlua because, after all, it was the 1980s. Chuck's problem was that ice cream needs to be served at a temperature much warmer than that of a typical deep freeze or else it's too hard—but Kahlua, with an alcohol content of 20 percent, won't freeze until it's fairly cold. The solution involved finding ice cream with very high butterfat content, then slowly paddling the slightly warmed ice cream together with the Kahlua, and finally blending at a higher speed to mix in some air. Between the ice cream and the sauce, there was about an ounce of Kahlua in each serving of that original dish.

Chuck added a jolt of chilled espresso to the Kahlua sauce to cut the sweetness a little, then put a base of crushed Oreos underneath to promote tooth decay all over again. By popular demand, the very retro dessert can still be found in some of our restaurants, although it now arrives with Kahlua-free ice cream. Sporting big hair and turning "My Sharona" up to 9 on the ghetto blaster are at the guest's discretion.

MOCHA KAHLUA PIE

This update of Chuck's recipe for our longest-serving dessert is now child-safe, with a fraction of the original's alcohol content.

1980s 1990s 2000s 2010s

MAKES ONE 9-INCH (23 CM) CAKE

1½ cups (375 mL) Oreo crumbs

2.67 oz (75 g or ⅓ cup/80 mL) salted butter

12 cups (3 L) vanilla ice cream

¼ cup (60 mL) cold espresso

Mocha Kahlua sauce (recipe follows)

1. Combine the Oreo crumbs and melted butter in a bowl and stir until the crumbs resemble coarse sand.
2. Line the base of a 9-inch (23 cm) springform pan with parchment paper, folding the excess paper underneath the base to form a tighter seal along the edge of the pan and base. Grease the base and sides well.
3. Transfer the Oreo crumb mixture to the base and press down along the edges using a metal measuring cup. Set aside while preparing the ice cream filling.
4. Mix together the ice cream and espresso on medium speed using the paddle attachment of a stand or hand-held mixer until completely combined. Scrape down the sides of the bowl often.
5. Do not allow ice cream to melt too far; it should retain a "soft serve" consistency, still thick, smooth and heavy.
6. Transfer into the pan with the prepared Oreo crumb base. Smooth out the top using an offset spatula and cover with plastic wrap. Freeze overnight.
7. To create clean slices, use a hot knife and clean the knife before each slice. Serve each slice drizzled with mocha Kahlua sauce.

MOCHA KAHLUA SAUCE

You can substitute extra coffee instead of Kahlua if you prefer this without alcohol. Frangelico or Grand Marnier can also be substituted for the Kahlua.

MAKES 2 CUPS (500 mL)

12 oz (350 g) dark or semi-sweet chocolate

⅓ cup (80 mL) heavy cream

¼ cup (60 mL) coffee

3 tbsp (45 mL) Kahlua

1. Melt the chocolate in a metal bowl over a pot of simmering water (or use a double boiler).
2. Add the cream, coffee and Kahlua. Stir very well. The mixture should be smooth and syrupy, and all the chocolate should be melted. Continue to heat if some chocolate remains unmelted.
3. Allow to cool completely. The sauce can be stored refrigerated for up to 5 days.

This cake needs to chill overnight in the freezer, so plan ahead. You can make a double batch of the mocha Kahlua sauce, as it keeps for a long time in the fridge and is perfect for drizzling on top of sundaes, s'mores or even pancakes!

PECAN PIE

Americans recognize this dish as being a product of the South, but can't agree on where precisely it came from or when—and surprisingly there's no written record of it until the 1940s. Canadians, of course, know that it's just a regional variation of our unofficial national dish, the butter tart. Larry elevated our version with a higher proportion of pecans than guests were accustomed to finding, and also liked to sneak in a bit of dark Belgian chocolate from Calgary-based chocolatier Callebaut.

1980s 1990s 2000s 2010s

MAKES ONE 9-INCH (23 CM) PIE
OR TART

1 recipe parbaked all-purpose pie dough
   (recipe follows)

4 eggs

¾ cup (180 mL) sugar

½ tsp (2.5 mL) fine salt

3 oz (85 g or ⅓ cup + 1 tbsp/95 mL)
   melted unsalted butter

⅔ cup (160 mL) corn syrup

3 cups (750 mL) pecan halves

1. Prepare parbaked pie crust as directed in the all-purpose pie dough recipe.
2. Preheat the oven to 375°F (190°C).
3. Combine the eggs, sugar and salt until thoroughly incorporated. Add the melted butter and corn syrup, stirring well.
4. Spread out the pecan halves in an even layer of the parbaked pie crust. Pour the filling mixture over the pecans, and using a rubber spatula, push the nuts down so that they remain submerged as much as possible.
5. Place the pecan pie in the preheated oven, on the lowest rack. Bake for approximately 40 minutes or until the pie is puffy and firm. When the pie is tapped, the filling should "shift" but not "jiggle."
6. Remove from the oven and allow to cool completely before serving.

Toasting the pecans before baking really adds an element of butteriness to the final pie. Either a 9-inch (23 cm) glass pie pan or a metal tart pan can be used for this recipe.

ALL-PURPOSE PIE DOUGH

MAKES ENOUGH PIE DOUGH FOR 2 SINGLE CRUSTS OR 1 DOUBLE CRUST

2 cups (500 mL) all-purpose flour

2 tsp (10 mL) sugar (if using for a sweet pie)

1 tsp (5 mL) fine salt

8 oz (225 g or 1 cup/250 mL) unsalted butter (cold)

½ cup (125 mL) sour cream (full fat, not light sour cream)

1. Combine the flour, sugar and salt in a large mixing bowl. Whisk very well to mix.
2. Cut the butter into ½-inch (1 cm) cubes and toss into the flour mixture.
3. Using clean, dry hands, squeeze the flour and butter together with your thumbs and fingers. Incorporate the butter into the dough until you have pea-sized crumbs of flour-coated butter.
4. Add the sour cream to the bowl and use a fork or rubber spatula to fully combine the dough. If the dough feels too dry and does not fully come together after being mixed well, then add 1 teaspoon (5 mL) of cold water. Do not add any more than what is absolutely necessary or you will end up with tough dough.
5. Shape the dough into a ball and use a knife to cut it in half. Form into 1-inch- (2.5 cm) thick discs and coat with a thin layer of flour. Wrap each disc in plastic wrap and refrigerate for at least 1 hour before rolling out. Dough can also be frozen for future use at this point if wrapped tightly in foil.
6. If the pie dough has been in the refrigerator for more than 2 hours, allow to come to room temperature for 10 minutes or so, otherwise the pastry will be too hard to roll out evenly.
7. Sprinkle your countertop or flat surface with a light coating of flour. Also coat your rolling pin with some flour.
8. Roll the pie dough from the centre outward, turning the dough after two or three rolls to make sure the bottom is not sticking. You can also flip the dough and roll the underside to ensure even thickness throughout. You should aim for a thickness of ⅛ to ¼ inch (3 mm to ½ cm).
9. Transfer to the baking pan by rolling the dough over the rolling pin and unrolling it onto the pan. Gently lift up the edges of the pie crust and settle it into the bottom of the pan without pressing or stretching too much as this may cause the dough to shrink when baked. Trim the edges to within ¼ inch (½ cm) with a knife and fold the short overhang underneath the top edge of the pie plate to create a scalloped edge using your fingers.
10. Poke holes all over the bottom of the pie dough and refrigerate for at least 30 minutes.
11. To blind bake (or parbake) the pie crust, line the cold pie dough with foil and weigh down with dry beans or pie weights. Bake at 350°F (180°C) for 20 to 25 minutes. Carefully remove the foil and weights, return to the oven and bake for another 10 to 12 minutes or until golden.
12. Use as directed in the recipe.

CHEESECAKE WITH STRAWBERRY RHUBARB COMPOTE

1980s 1990s 2000s 2010s

MAKES ONE 9-INCH (23 CM) CHEESECAKE

2 lb (1 kg or four 8 oz/250 g packages) softened cream cheese

1 cup (250 mL) sugar

1¾ cups (435 mL) sour cream

6 eggs

1 tsp (5 mL) vanilla extract

1 tsp (5 mL) orange zest

1 tsp (5 mL) lemon zest

Graham cracker crust (recipe follows)

Strawberry rhubarb compote (recipe follows)

Use only full-fat cream cheese and sour cream for this recipe. Lower-fat versions contain too much water and will affect the final texture of the cheesecake.

The world went mad for cheesecake in the 1980s, and Larry didn't mind playing along. What was notable about ours was the inclusion of rhubarb, which during an era when most better restaurants had their eyes on exotica, had the reputation of being something that grew in old people's gardens. Now, of course, it's a locavore darling, not just because it's local, but because its extreme tartness renders it the ultimate fruit for cooking—even if it does happen to be a vegetable.

1. Preheat the oven to 225°F (105°C).
2. Mix the cream cheese on medium speed using the paddle attachment of a stand or hand-held mixer until completely lump free. Add the sugar and continue beating until sugar is completely combined. Scrape down the sides of the bowl often.
3. Mix in the sour cream and blend well. Add the eggs one at a time, mixing in each egg completely before adding another.
4. Add the vanilla and orange and lemon zest.
5. Mix for an additional minute until all ingredients are completely homogeneous. The mixing time from start to finish should take no longer than 8 minutes.
6. Transfer the mixture into the cooled graham crust, trying to retain as smooth a surface as possible once all the batter has been poured in. Tap the cheesecake several times on the counter to remove any large air bubbles trapped in the batter.
7. Bake on the lower third of the oven for 2 hours and 40 minutes. Place a pan of boiling water on the lowest rack to keep the oven moist. This will decrease the likelihood of cracks in your cheesecake. The cheesecake should jiggle only in the centre inch; otherwise, bake for additional 10-minute intervals until it is done.
8. Turn the oven heat off and open the door slightly, allowing the cheesecake to cool in the warm oven for an hour—this reduces the chances of the cheesecake forming cracks.
9. Remove from the oven and cool to room temperature before refrigerating. Chill at least 8 hours or overnight before serving.
10. To create clean slices, use a hot knife and clean the knife before each slice. Serve with strawberry rhubarb compote.

GRAHAM CRACKER CRUST

1 cup (250 mL) graham cracker crumbs

2 tbsp (30 mL) sugar

2.67 oz (75 g or ⅓ cup/80 mL) melted salted butter

1. Preheat the oven to 350°F (180°C).
2. Combine the graham crumbs, sugar and melted butter in a bowl and stir until the crumbs resemble coarse sand.
3. Line the base of a 9-inch (23 cm) springform pan with parchment paper, folding the excess paper underneath the base to form a tighter seal along the edge of the pan and base. Grease the base and sides well.
4. Transfer the graham mixture to the base and press down along the bottom and edges using a metal measuring cup.
5. Bake for 10 minutes or until golden brown and fragrant. Allow to cool completely.

STRAWBERRY RHUBARB COMPOTE

¾ cup (180 mL) port wine

½ cup (125 mL) red wine

¼ cup (60 mL) orange juice

2 tbsp (30 mL) raspberry vinegar

¼ cup (60 mL) dark-brown sugar

1 lb (450 g) frozen ½-inch-cut (1 cm) rhubarb

8 oz (225 g) fresh quartered strawberries

1. Reduce the port, red wine, orange juice, raspberry vinegar and sugar in a non-aluminum saucepan until syrupy and very thick, almost like caramel, approximately 10 minutes.
2. Immediately add the rhubarb and strawberries to the reduction. Cover with a lid and simmer for approximately 10 minutes or until the rhubarb pieces are tender and the strawberries have softened to a sauce-like consistency.
3. Allow to cool completely. The compote can be stored refrigerated for up to 5 days.

APPLE COBBLER

Do you really need a big-shot chef to come up with your recipe for one of the most down-home desserts? As it happens, we didn't. Chuck wasn't super interested when the manager of Calgary's Tin Palace location, Ron Sachkiw, mentioned that his mom made some pretty hot desserts, so Ron called up Mom for some recipes and baked them himself for Stan to try. Later, a food columnist described one of them as sexy, which proves, says Ron, that they really were hot.

1980s 1990s 2000s 2010s

**MAKES ONE 8- × 8-INCH
(20 × 20 CM) COBBLER**

1½ lb (680 g) peeled and cored Granny Smith apples (about 2 lb/1 kg whole apples)

¾ cup (180 mL) brown sugar

¼ cup (60 mL) heavy cream

2 tbsp (30 mL) cornstarch

1 tsp (5 mL) lemon juice

1 tsp (5 mL) cinnamon

Pie crust (recipe follows)

Pie topping (recipe follows)

Vanilla ice cream (optional)

Maple syrup or butterscotch sauce, for garnish (optional)

1. Peel, core and cut apples into quarters, then slice crosswise into ¼-inch (½ cm) triangular slices. Toss with the brown sugar and allow to macerate for at least 30 minutes.
2. Preheat the oven to 350°F (180°C).
3. After 30 minutes, strain the juices from the apples into a glass measuring cup. You should have ½ to ⅔ cup (125 to 160 mL) of liquid. To this, add the cream, cornstarch, lemon juice and cinnamon. Stir well.
4. Transfer the apples to a microwave-safe bowl. Microwave on high for 2 minutes, stirring well so that the apples cook evenly. Return to the microwave and heat for an additional 2 minutes. The apples should be soft but not mushy. Strain out the liquid and add it to the cornstarch mixture.
5. Microwave the cornstarch mixture until it thickens to a custard-like consistency, 2 to 3 minutes depending on the power of your microwave.
6. While still hot, mix together with the apples. The mixture should coat each apple slice evenly. Allow to cool slightly.
7. Prepare the pie crust and top with the apples, patting the mixture down so that the surface is flat.
8. Spread the pie topping evenly over the entire pan.
9. Bake for 30 minutes or until the topping is golden brown and the liquid inside is bubbling.
10. Remove from the oven and allow to cool completely before cutting into portions.
11. Serve with vanilla ice cream and a drizzle of maple syrup or butterscotch sauce for extra decadence.

You can use any combination of Granny Smith, Fuji or Gala apples, depending on your preference—as long as the total weight of the peeled and cored apples equals 1½ pounds (680 g).

PIE CRUST

3 oz (85 g or ⅓ cup/80 mL) unsalted butter (cold)

1⅛ cups (280 mL) all-purpose flour

¼ cup (60 mL) powdered sugar

¼ tsp (1.25 mL) fine salt

1 egg yolk

1. Cut the butter into ½-inch (1 cm) dice.
2. Combine the flour, powdered sugar and salt in a food processor. Add the butter and pulse until butter is incorporated into the flour as chunks about the size of peas.
3. Add the egg yolk and continue pulsing until a rough dough comes together but has not yet formed a ball.
4. Alternatively, use a pastry cutter to incorporate the butter into the flour. Add the egg yolk and mix well until the dough begins to come together and turns a light yellow.
5. Coat an 8- × 8-inch (20 × 20 cm) pan with cooking spray or butter. Turn out the pie crust onto the pan and gently pat it onto the bottom of the pan. Press down lightly around the edges and centre so the surface is as even as possible.
6. Bake in a 350°F (180°C) oven for 15 to 20 minutes or until the edges begin to turn golden brown.

PIE TOPPING

¾ cup (180 mL) slivered almonds

1 cup (250 mL) rolled oats

¾ cup (180 mL) all-purpose flour

½ cup (125 mL) brown sugar

½ tsp (2.5 mL) cinnamon

4 oz (115 g or ½ cup/125 mL) melted salted butter

1. Using a food processor or knife, chop the almonds into ¼-inch (½ cm) pieces, approximately the same size as the rolled oats.
2. Combine the almonds, oats, flour, brown sugar and cinnamon until well mixed.
3. Add the melted butter and stir until all ingredients are moistened.
4. Can be stored refrigerated for up to 2 days.

TRIPLE CHOCOLATE MOUSSE CAKE

1980s 1990s 2000s 2010s

MAKES ONE 9-INCH (23 CM) CAKE

Given the decade this cake comes from, we probably don't need to tell you that Larry's original version had a dollop of bourbon in it. In the spirit of the current decade, we should point out that the cake is gluten-free, and so a great option for those with dietary restrictions that involve wheat.

CHOCOLATE FUDGE LAYER

8 oz (225 g) semi-sweet chocolate

2.67 oz (75 g or ⅓ cup/80 mL) melted salted butter

⅓ cup (80 mL) sugar

1 tbsp (15 mL) cocoa

1 tsp (5 mL) instant coffee granules

½ tsp (2.5 mL) fine salt

2 eggs

1 egg yolk

¼ tsp (1.25 mL) vanilla extract

1. Preheat the oven to 350°F (180°C). Line the base of a 9-inch (23 cm) springform pan with a large piece of parchment paper, folding the edges underneath the base to create a seal around the edge of the pan. Grease the sides and base very well.
2. Melt the chocolate in a metal bowl over a pot of simmering water (or use a double boiler). Add the butter and stir well. Remove from heat once all the chocolate is completely melted and glossy.
3. Add the sugar, cocoa, coffee granules and fine salt to the melted chocolate, stirring well to combine. Allow to cool slightly.
4. In a separate bowl, mix the eggs, egg yolk and vanilla. Fold this gently into the chocolate mixture.
5. Pour into the springform pan. Bake for 12 to 15 minutes or until the middle of the fudge looks puffy and the edges are set.

CHOCOLATE MOUSSE LAYER

10 oz (285 g) semi-sweet chocolate

2¼ cups (560 mL) heavy cream, divided

3½ tsp (17.5 mL) powdered gelatin (approximately 1½ packages)

3 eggs, separated

1 tsp (5 mL) vanilla extract

1. Melt the chocolate in a metal bowl over a pot of simmering water (or use a double boiler).
2. Using a stand or hand-held mixer, whip 2 cups (500 mL) of the cream until soft peaks form. Chill in the refrigerator while preparing the rest of the steps. If using the stand mixer, transfer the whipped cream to a different bowl and wash the mixer bowl very well, as any trace of fat will affect the egg whites later on.
3. Sprinkle the gelatin over 2 tablespoons (30 mL) of cold water and allow it to bloom, approximately 10 minutes.
4. Heat the remaining ¼ cup (60 mL) of the cream in the microwave until it begins to bubble. Pour it into the bloomed gelatin and stir very well with a whisk. Make sure all the gelatin has melted and that no clumps remain. While still warm, add the cream mixture to the 3 reserved egg yolks. Add the vanilla and stir all ingredients well.
5. Pour this egg yolk and cream mixture into the melted chocolate. Mix very well again. Set aside.
6. In a very clean bowl, beat the egg whites until stiff but not dry peaks form. Do not overbeat.
7. Add the egg whites to the chocolate mixture and fold together to lighten the chocolate base.
8. Once the egg whites are mixed in, fold in the chilled whipped cream gently but thoroughly. There should be no visible specks of white in the resulting mousse.
9. Pour the mousse over the cooled chocolate fudge base. Use an offset spatula to smooth out the top.
10. Chill for at least 2 hours.

WHITE CHOCOLATE
MOUSSE LAYER

8 oz (225 g) white chocolate

1 cup (250 mL) heavy cream, divided

1 tsp (5 mL) powdered gelatin (approximately ½ package)

2 eggs, separated

1 tsp (5 mL) vanilla extract

2 cups (500 mL) mixed berries or chocolate shavings,
   for garnish (optional)

**Plan ahead when making this cake, as it needs
6 hours to set up properly. This is a stunning end to
a meal for a special occasion!**

1. Melt the white chocolate in a metal bowl over a pot of simmering water (or use a double boiler).

2. Using a stand or hand-held mixer, whip ¾ of the cream until soft peaks form. Chill in the refrigerator while preparing the rest of the steps. If using the stand mixer, transfer the whipped cream to a different bowl and wash the mixer bowl very well as any trace of fat will affect the egg whites later on.

3. Sprinkle the gelatin over 1 tablespoon (15 mL) of cold water and allow it to bloom, approximately 10 minutes.

4. Heat the remaining ¼ of the cream in the microwave until it begins to bubble. Pour it into the bloomed gelatin and stir very well with a whisk. Make sure all the gelatin has melted and that no clumps remain. While still warm, add the cream mixture to the 2 separated egg yolks. Add the vanilla and stir all ingredients well.

5. Pour this egg yolk and cream mixture into the melted white chocolate. Mix very well again. Set aside.

6. In a very clean bowl, beat the egg whites until stiff but not dry peaks form. Do not overbeat.

7. Add the egg whites to the chocolate mixture and fold together to lighten the chocolate base.

8. Once the egg whites are all mixed in, fold in the chilled whipped cream gently but thoroughly. Make sure the mousse is completely mixed.

9. Pour the mousse over the cooled chocolate mousse layer, using an offset spatula to smooth out the top if necessary. Allow to set for at least 6 hours or overnight.

10. To serve, use a paring knife to release the edges of the mousse cake from the pan. Remove the sides of the springform pan, being careful not to damage the sides of the cake.

11. Have a container of hot water and a cloth ready for your knife, as you will need to clean and dry the knife before each slice.

12. Make a clean cut down the middle of the cake and clean your knife well. Proceed to make cuts down the cake as you continuously clean the knife before each slice.

13. Serve with mixed berries or chocolate shavings if desired.

Triple Chocolate Mousse Cake

WARM GINGERBREAD CAKE

Larry's use of shredded fresh ginger set our version apart from many others when it debuted back in the 1990s. Unchanged to this day, the dessert is a beloved comfort-food staple, found on fall and winter menus chain-wide, served with Mario's vanilla gelato, roasted apples and a salted caramel sauce. It's a giant of a cake, and because of that denseness it needs to be turned at least once while baking. Give it about an hour to settle down, then carefully open the door and gently turn it about halfway round.

1980s **1990s** 2000s 2010s

MAKES ONE 9-INCH (23 CM) CAKE

1¼ cups (310 mL) hot water

1⅛ cups (280 mL) fancy molasses

2 tbsp (30 mL) finely grated ginger (microplaned)

5 oz (140 g or ⅔ cup/160 mL) room-temperature butter

1½ cups (375 mL) brown sugar

2 eggs

4 cups (1 L) all-purpose flour

1 tbsp (15 mL) baking powder

1¼ tsp (6.25 mL) ground cinnamon

¾ tsp (3.75 mL) fine salt

¼ tsp (1.25 mL) ground cloves

Vanilla ice cream

Roasted apples (recipe follows)

Salted caramel sauce (page 209)

1. Bring the hot water, molasses and grated ginger to a simmer in a small saucepan. Cover and simmer for 5 minutes. Cool to room temperature before proceeding with the remaining steps.
2. Preheat the oven to 300°F (150°C).
3. In the bowl of a stand mixer or using a hand-held blender, cream the butter until fluffy and light coloured. Add the brown sugar and continue creaming until the sugar has dissolved into the butter and the mixture is very soft. Scrape down the bowl several times during this step.
4. Add the eggs, one at a time, mixing after each addition.
5. Mix together the flour, baking powder, cinnamon, salt and cloves. Make sure the mixture is well incorporated.
6. Add a quarter of the dry ingredients to the butter and sugar mixture. Mix until all dry ingredients are incorporated. Add a third of the cooled ginger and molasses mixture and mix slowly until combined into the batter. Repeat, adding another quarter of the dry ingredients, followed by another third of the ginger liquid. Repeat these steps, ending with the dry mixture. The mixing time between each addition should be 1 to 1½ minutes long. Scrape down the sides of the bowl extremely well during the whole process.
7. Line the base of a 9-inch (23 cm) springform pan with parchment paper, folding the excess paper underneath the base to form a tighter seal along the edge of the pan and base. Grease the base and sides well.
8. Transfer the gingerbread batter to the prepared pan and bake in a preheated 300°F (150°C) oven for 2 hours. A skewer inserted in the middle should come out clean with a few moist crumbs sticking to it.
9. Serve with vanilla ice cream, roasted apples and salted caramel sauce.

ROASTED APPLES

1 lb (450 g) peeled and cored Granny Smith apples

¼ cup (60 mL) brown sugar

1 oz (28 g or 2 tbsp/30 mL) melted salted butter

1. Preheat the oven to 450°F (230°C).
2. Quarter each apple and slice each quarter into 4 lengthwise to make 16 wedges.
3. Toss with the brown sugar and butter until evenly coated.
4. Transfer the apples to a parchment-lined rimmed baking tray.
5. Bake for 5 minutes. Immediately remove from the oven and allow to cool completely. The apples can be stored refrigerated for up to 2 days.

CHOCOLATE HAZELNUT BAR

This extraordinary dessert from Hamid Salimian might have some ingredients that sound unfamiliar. True, magical, mystical feuilletine is found mostly in pro kitchens, but it's certainly available online and at gourmet shops, and gianduia is merely the original Italian hazelnut and milk chocolate blend, which shouldn't be too hard to find. In a pinch, corn flakes can be subbed for the feuilletine, but the result won't be as refined.

1980s 1990s 2000s **2010s**

SERVES 4–6

3.5 oz (100 g) solid gianduia (hazelnut milk chocolate)

1.6 oz (45 g) feuilletine

2½ tbsp (37.5 mL) corn syrup

½ cup (125 mL) heavy cream

8.8 oz (250 g) dark chocolate (65 percent)

1.3 oz (37 g or 2½ tbsp/37.5 mL) ½-inch (1 cm) diced cold butter

Salted caramel sauce (recipe follows)

Orange segments (recipe follows)

Vanilla ice cream (optional)

1. Prepare a double boiler by bringing a pot of water to a simmer.
2. Place the gianduia in a large bowl and set it over the simmering water. Make sure the bowl does not touch the water. Whisk until the chocolate is melted.
3. Prepare a 6-inch (15 cm) square pan by lining it with overlapping layers of parchment paper. The bottom and sides must be completely lined with parchment paper so that the chocolate bar releases easily. Do this by laying two long strips of parchment one perpendicular to the other in the pan. Leave the overhang to act as handles to help lift out the chocolate bar once it is formed.
4. Combine the fully melted gianduia with the feuilletine and corn syrup, folding together gently. Pour the mixture into the prepared pan and use an offset spatula to spread it evenly to the edges. Freeze for 20 minutes.
5. In a small pot, bring the cream to a bare simmer. Remove from heat and add the dark chocolate and butter. Use a rubber spatula to stir until the chocolate and butter have melted into a smooth ganache. Do not whip air into the ganache, as this will ruin the final texture.
6. Immediately pour the ganache over the frozen chocolate base. Shake the pan a few times to even out the surface and release any large air bubbles that may have formed.
7. Freeze for another hour.
8. Remove from the freezer and release from the pan by lifting the "handles" of parchment paper.
9. Evenly drizzle ¼ cup (60 mL) of salted caramel sauce over the entire top of the dessert. Spread evenly from edge to edge using an offset spatula. Avoid scraping the ganache.
10. Using a very hot knife, cut into 6 equal strips. Once you make a cut, pull the knife toward you without lifting up. This keeps the milk chocolate from streaking through the ganache. Clean and dip the knife after every cut.
11. Spread some salted caramel sauce on each serving plate and spread with an offset spatula to create a decorative swipe. Place a serving of the chocolate bar over the caramel and garnish with some orange segments. Serve with some vanilla ice cream if desired.

SALTED CARAMEL SAUCE

¾ cup (180 mL) sugar

2 tbsp (30 mL) water

½ cup (125 mL) heavy cream

2 oz (57 g or ¼ cup/60 mL) 1-inch (2.5 cm) diced cold salted butter

Pinch fine salt

1. In a medium-sized pot over medium heat, bring the sugar and water to a boil until it reaches the golden caramel stage, approximately 7 to 10 minutes depending on the size of your pot. Do not stir this mixture or the sugar will crystallize.
2. Be very careful not to leave the caramel at any point as the mixture can go from the perfect shade of amber to burned in less than 30 seconds. Swirl the pot if necessary to even out the caramelization process.
3. Once you reach the amber caramel stage, reduce heat to low and very carefully add the cream in a slow stream. The cream will bubble ferociously, so use extra care during this step.
4. Return the heat to a simmer, and then remove from heat and whisk in the butter and salt. The butter should melt into the sauce and thicken it slightly.
5. Allow to cool completely before transferring to an airtight container. The salted caramel sauce can be stored refrigerated for 5 days.

ORANGE SEGMENTS

1 orange

1. Use a paring knife to remove the peel and all the pith from an orange. Follow the orange shape as much as possible to reduce waste.
2. Slip the knife between one of the segments and the connective membrane, trying to retain as much of the flesh as possible to produce beautifully shaped large orange segments.
3. Cut until you reach the centre of the orange, but do not cut through the membrane.
4. Continue cutting around the entire orange until you have removed all the pulpy flesh.
5. Discard the membrane and use the segments in the desired recipe.

BERRIES AND CREAM SHORTCAKE

1980s 1990s 2000s **2010s**

MAKES 4 SHORTCAKES

8 shortcakes (recipe follows)

Vanilla cream cheese mousse (recipe follows)

2 cups (500 mL) mixed seasonal berries (quartered strawberries, blueberries, raspberries and blackberries)

Graham almond topping (page 212)

Icing sugar

Mint leaves (optional)

Fay Duong was looking for a lighter, more summery dessert to replace a cheesecake that had reached retirement age. She balanced layers of very airy shortcake inspired by New York City's Momofuku Milk Bar with a cream cheese mousse that pays tribute to the dish's superannuated predecessor, and finished it with seasonal berries.

1. Place 1 shortcake on the bottom of a dessert bowl.
2. Top with 2 tablespoons (30 mL) of vanilla cream cheese mousse, slightly off-centre. Arrange ¼ cup (60 mL) of berries on the other side of the mousse, allowing the berries to scatter randomly around the bowl.
3. Top with a second shortcake, followed by another 2 tablespoons (30 mL) of vanilla cream cheese mousse and ending with another ¼ cup (60 mL) of berries.
4. Crumble 2 tbsp (30 mL) of graham almond topping over the berries, allowing some of the larger crumbs to fall naturally. Using a sifter, sprinkle the entire dessert with icing sugar. Garnish with mint leaves if desired.
5. Repeat with the remaining dessert bowls. Serve immediately.

SHORTCAKES

MAKES 24 SHORTCAKE BISCUITS

2 eggs

¼ cup (60 mL) heavy cream

2⅔ cups (660 mL) cake flour

½ cup (125 mL) sugar

⅓ cup (80 mL) brown sugar

1½ tsp (7.5 mL) baking powder

1 tsp (5 mL) fine salt

6 oz (170 g or ¾ cup/180 mL) 1 inch
   (2.5 cm) diced cold butter

Icing sugar

1. Combine the eggs and cream until well mixed. Refrigerate while you prepare the rest of the ingredients.
2. Measure the cake flour, sugar, brown sugar, baking powder and salt into the bowl of a food processor and pulse several times to blend the ingredients.
3. Add the diced butter and pulse until the mixture resembles bread crumbs. Scrape down the sides several times during this process to make sure no pockets of dry flour remain. There should be no visible lumps of butter in the mixture.
4. Add the reserved cream and egg mixture and blend until the liquid is absorbed and the dough begins to form.
5. Transfer the dough to a mixing bowl and form into a solid ball. Do not overwork the dough, or your shortcakes will be tough. It's okay if the dough is quite wet and sticky at this point.
6. Cover the dough with plastic wrap and refrigerate for at least 3 hours or overnight.
7. Prepare a shallow container of icing sugar. This will be used for dredging the shortcake dough. Preheat the oven to 350°F (180°C).
8. Using a large tablespoon or soup spoon, scoop out 1-ounce-sized balls (30 g; about 4 teaspoons/ 20 mL of dough or a #40 scoop). Transfer to the icing sugar and using your hands, roll until it is thickly coated.
9. Place onto parchment-lined rimmed baking trays and bake for 7 to 8 minutes or until the edges turn golden brown and the centre is soft but dry to the touch.
10. Remove from the oven and allow to come to room temperature. Use the same day or within 6 hours.

VANILLA CREAM CHEESE MOUSSE

12 oz (350 g) room-temperature cream cheese (1½ 8 oz/
   225 g packages)

½ cup (125 mL) icing sugar

1 tsp (5 mL) lemon zest (microplaned)

½ tsp (2.5 mL) vanilla extract

½ vanilla bean (seeds only)

1. Place the cream cheese into the bowl of a stand mixer and whip with the paddle attachment on low speed for 3 minutes. Scrape down the sides with a rubber spatula and turn the speed to medium. Mix until smooth and creamy, an extra 2 minutes, scraping down the sides of the bowl as necessary.
2. Add the icing sugar, lemon zest, vanilla extract and vanilla seeds and mix until all the ingredients are evenly distributed.
3. Transfer to an airtight container. The cream cheese mousse can be stored refrigerated for 5 days.

KEY LIME PIE

Nowadays, before we open a new location, we scout out favourite local dishes to add to the menu. Sometimes they stay there, other times they travel easily throughout the chain, as was the case with this dessert, which Hamid Salimian and Dawn Doucette prepared for our Miami launch. To make sure this ends up as tasty where you live as it did in Miami, cautions Dawn, pick out the freshest of limes, since they don't keep as well as retailers seem to believe.

1980s 1990s 2000s **2010s**

MAKES ONE 9-INCH (23 CM) PIE OR TART

1 tsp (5 mL) powdered gelatin (approximately ½ package)

¾ cup (180 mL) key lime juice

4 eggs

1 cup (250 mL) sugar

1 tsp (5 mL) lime zest (microplaned)

4 oz (115 g or ½ cup/125 mL) ½-inch (1 cm) diced cold butter

Graham cracker crust (recipe follows)

Whipped cream

Graham almond topping (recipe follows)

1. Prepare a double boiler by bringing a pot of water to a simmer.
2. Sprinkle the gelatin over 2 tablespoons (30 mL) of cold water. Allow to fully bloom.
3. Place the key lime juice, eggs, sugar and lime zest in a large bowl and place over the pot of simmering water.
4. Whisk constantly over medium heat. When the mixture is thick enough to coat the back of a spoon, add one piece of butter at a time, whisking until each piece of butter is completely mixed in before adding another piece.
5. Add the bloomed gelatin and whisk again until it has dissolved into the lime curd. At this point, the lime curd will be quite thick.
6. Strain the curd into the prepared graham cracker crust shell.
7. Refrigerate for at least 6 hours or overnight before serving to allow the curd to set.
8. Garnish with whipped cream and graham almond topping.

GRAHAM CRACKER CRUST

1 cup (250 mL) graham cracker crumbs

2 tbsp (30 mL) sugar

2.67 oz (75 g or ⅓ cup/80 mL) melted salted butter

1. Preheat the oven to 350°F (180°C).
2. Combine the graham crumbs, 2 tablespoons (30 mL) of the sugar, and melted butter in a bowl and stir until the crumbs resemble coarse sand.
3. Transfer the graham mixture to a glass or metal pie plate and press down along the bottom and sides using a metal measuring cup.
4. Bake for 10 minutes or until golden brown and fragrant. Allow to cool completely.

GRAHAM ALMOND TOPPING

⅓ cup (80 mL) graham cracker pieces

⅓ cup (80 mL) toasted slivered almonds

¼ cup (60 mL) sugar

1 tbsp (15 mL) all-purpose flour

⅓ cup (80 mL) melted salted butter

1. Preheat the oven to 300°F (150°C).
2. Using a food processor, pulse the graham crackers and toasted almonds to 1/16-inch (2 mm) pieces.
3. Transfer to a large mixing bowl and add the sugar, flour and melted butter.
4. Mix very well and spread out over a parchment-lined baking tray.
5. Bake for 10 minutes, stirring occasionally while baking to ensure even cooking. The colour of the topping should be golden brown.
6. Remove from the oven and allow to cool completely. Break up any large clumps.
7. Transfer to an airtight container if made ahead. Store at room temperature if using within 2 days; refrigerate if storing for longer. Use within 5 days.

PEANUT BUTTER SKILLET COOKIE

1980s 1990s 2000s **2010s**

MAKES 4 COOKIES

4 peanut butter cookies (recipe follows)

Vanilla ice cream

Salted caramel sauce (page 209)

½ cup (125 mL) roasted peanuts

¼ cup (60 mL) icing sugar

It's said that a person cannot truly understand their country of birth until they move away from it. So what did Brian Skinner come to realize about Canada during his years cooking in London and Copenhagen? Mostly, that as a nation we are utterly obsessed with peanut butter. Accordingly, this dish is his tribute to Canada—and to the kind of campfire summer vibes that so many Canadians have enjoyed as part of their birthright.

1. Preheat the oven to 400°F (200°C).
2. Place each cookie in an individual skillet, or if necessary, use an oven-safe plate or shallow bowl.
3. Bake in the oven until warm throughout, approximately 5 minutes.
4. Remove from the oven and top each warm cookie with a scoop of vanilla ice cream.
5. Drizzle with salted caramel sauce and top with 2 tablespoons (30 mL) of roasted peanuts and a dusting of icing sugar. Repeat with the remaining cookies.
6. Serve immediately while still warm.

PEANUT BUTTER COOKIES

2.67 oz (75 g or ⅓ cup/80 mL) room-temperature butter

1 cup (250 mL) smooth peanut butter

¾ cup (180 mL) sugar

⅓ cup (80 mL) brown sugar

¼ tsp (1.25 mL) fine salt

2 eggs

1 tsp (5 mL) vanilla extract

1 cup (250 mL) all-purpose flour

1 tsp (5 mL) baking powder

½ cup (125 mL) chocolate chips

1. Combine the butter and peanut butter in the bowl of a stand mixer and, using a paddle attachment, mix on medium speed until smooth and creamy.

2. Slowly incorporate the sugar, brown sugar, fine salt, eggs and vanilla into the mixer. Turn speed up to medium-high and mix for 5 minutes until light and fluffy.

3. Combine the flour, baking powder and chocolate chips in a separate bowl. Slowly add this to the liquid mixture, mixing on low speed until just incorporated.

4. Chill the cookie dough for 30 minutes before portioning and baking.

5. Preheat the oven to 325°F (165°C).

6. Portion ½ cup (125 mL) scoops of cookie dough onto a parchment-lined rimmed baking tray, leaving 4 inches (10 cm) between each cookie.

7. Bake for 15 to 17 minutes or until the edges are lightly toasted. Allow to cool in the pans and transfer to wire racks once cool to the touch.

brunch

Judging from some of the ones we've seen over the years, there is no meal that attracts a more diverse crowd than the weekend brunch. At this table: the happy extended family with a couple of tagalong friends, all dressed up and on their way home from church. At the next one: the gaggle of buddies, some of whom slept on a couch the night before, loading up on carbs, coffee and bacon, wondering if it's possible to will away a headache in time to get back to the bar to watch the big hockey or football game.

The other odd thing about brunch is that it seems to flit in and out of style as fast as you can poach an egg. Why, we can't say, but what we can say is that brunch must have been very much in style in 1988, the year it was launched at Calgary's Tin Palace.

Larry lived mostly in Edmonton during his decade sharing top chef duties with Chuck, so he was camping out at a hotel for a week before the grand launch. He thought he had things so perfectly in order that he could afford to duck out the back door to buy a tube of toothpaste. He returned five minutes after opening time to find the restaurant packed, the kitchen slammed, and a long line out the front door. In a panic, he advised the manager at the doors to close and lock them. "Well, Larry," said the manager, "would you like me to lock the people inside the doors in, or would you like to help me push them out?"

Larry didn't have to think about that for very long, so he went back into the kitchen and resigned himself to spending the next several hours standing over a hot grill.

HUEVOS RANCHEROS

For a guy who knows his way around the fanciest of French dishes, Larry wasn't one to put on airs. When we asked him how and why he decided to pull together this Tex-Mex standard for our Tin Palace brunches, he explained that he was already doing salsas and quesadillas, so why not?

1980s 1990s 2000s 2010s

SERVES 4

1 lb (450 g) Yukon gold potatoes

8 oz (225 g) pork sausage

12 eggs

1½ tsp (7.5 mL) fine salt, divided

1 tsp (5 mL) ground black pepper, divided

½ cup (125 mL) milk

2 cups (500 mL) shredded cheese blend (Monterey Jack, cheddar)

4 flour tortillas (10 inches/25 cm)

Vegetable oil for frying

¼ tsp (1.25 mL) smoked paprika

¼ tsp (1.25 mL) ground cayenne

2 tbsp (30 mL) butter, divided

¼ cup (60 mL) coarsely chopped green onions

1 cup (250 mL) salsa (page 241)

½ cup (125 mL) sour cream

1. Dice the potatoes into ½-inch (1 cm) pieces. Rinse in cold water several times until the water runs clear. Allow to drain for 20 minutes.
2. While the potatoes are draining, remove the pork sausage from its casing and break into 1-inch (2.5 cm) chunks.
3. Combine the eggs, 1 teaspoon (5 mL) of salt, ½ teaspoon (2.5 mL) of pepper and milk until well mixed. Set aside.
4. Assemble the cheese quesadillas by spreading a quarter of the cheese blend into one half of each flour tortilla. Fold in half. You should end up with 4 half moons of cheese-filled tortillas. Cook the quesadillas over a griddle or large skillet on medium heat until the tortillas are golden brown and the cheese is well melted. Keep warm in a low oven.
5. Simultaneously, heat the oil in a deep fryer or large Dutch oven to 350°F (180°C). Cook the potatoes for 3½ minutes. The potatoes should be fully cooked and golden brown.
6. Remove from the fryer and transfer to a stainless steel bowl. Season with the salt, pepper, smoked paprika and cayenne. Keep warm in a low oven along with the quesadillas.
7. Heat a nonstick skillet over medium heat and cook the sausage until browned, stirring often, approximately 6 to 8 minutes. Remove from the pan and transfer to a plate.
8. Heat the same nonstick skillet over medium heat and melt 1 tablespoon (15 mL) of the butter. Pour half the egg mixture into the skillet and stir it around with a spatula. Swirl it around until it begins to set, about 3 minutes. Add half the sausage and half the green onions, spreading them evenly over the eggs. Cook for 2 minutes, using the spatula to loosen the edges as necessary. Carefully fold the omelette in half using the spatula and cook for 1 minute more. Carefully slide the omelette onto a serving plate, flipping it over as you do; keep warm in a low oven.
9. Repeat the process with the remaining 1 tablespoon butter and the remaining egg mixture, sausage and green onion.
10. Cut the quesadillas in half, then in half again to produce 4 wedges. Arrange on one end of the plate.
11. Plate half an omelette next to the quesadilla, then some home fries next to the omelette. Repeat with the remaining three plates.
12. Serve with some salsa and sour cream for the quesadillas.

HONEY BUTTERMILK BISCUITS

Brunch was going through one of its cyclical popularity spurts when Stew Fuller and Karen Lyons took our original biscuit recipe and simplified it a touch. Easy to make: check. Melts in the mouth: check. Delicious: check.

1980s **1990s** 2000s 2010s

MAKES 8–10 BISCUITS

2¾ cups (660 mL) all-purpose flour

2½ tbsp (37.5 mL) baking powder

2 tsp (10 mL) fine salt

⅔ cup (160 mL) frozen butter

1½ cups (375 mL) buttermilk (full fat)

¼ cup (60 mL) honey

2 tbsp (30 mL) melted salted butter

1. Preheat the oven to 375°F (190°C).
2. Combine the flour, baking powder and salt into a large bowl.
3. Using a coarse hand grater, push the butter through quickly to make small grated pieces that are about the size of peas. Toss into the flour mixture and break up any large clumps of butter so that the flour coats the butter evenly.
4. Combine the buttermilk and the honey. Add to the bowl and mix gently with a spatula until all the liquid is absorbed.
5. Turn out onto a floured counter and fold gently until a soft, sticky dough forms. Use a bench scraper to help pick up the dough and fold over itself.
6. Pat the dough into a rectangle that is approximately 1 inch (2.5 cm) thick. Use a very sharp knife and cut into approximately 2-inch (5 cm) squares.
7. Brush the tops of the biscuits with melted butter and transfer to parchment-lined rimmed baking trays, leaving ample space between each biscuit, as they tend to rise and expand during baking.
8. Bake for 16 to 18 minutes depending on the heat of your oven. The tops should be golden brown and the biscuits should have puffed up nicely.
9. Allow to cool slightly. Serve immediately

PARMESAN GOAT CHEESE FRITTATA

1980s 1990s 2000s **2010s**

SERVES 4–6

8 eggs

1 oz (28 g or 2 tbsp/30 mL) butter

¼ cup (60 mL) medium-diced roasted red peppers (page 243)

¼ cup (60 mL) oven-dried grape tomatoes (page 48)

2 tbsp (30 mL) grated Parmesan cheese

2 tbsp (30 mL) pesto (page 242)

2 oz (57 g or ¼ cup/60 mL) goat cheese

2 tbsp (30 mL) finely minced Sicilian olives

1 tbsp (15 mL) toasted pine nuts

1 cup (250 mL) baby arugula

¼ cup (60 mL) finely shaved fennel

¼ cup (60 mL) chopped chives

Preserved lemon dressing (recipe follows)

Pinch fine salt

There was a time when the vegetable kingdom wasn't represented in a North American breakfast, or even generally a brunch. This delicious frittata from David Wong has echoes of the Middle East, with its goat cheese and preserved lemon, but maybe its most notable aspect is the arugula. Brunch? Lunch? Dinner?

1. Preheat the oven to 400°F (200°C). Heat a large nonstick frying pan over medium heat.
2. Break the eggs into a small bowl and mix well; the yolks and whites must be fully incorporated and fluffy.
3. Heat the butter in the pan until foamy but not brown. Add the eggs, roasted peppers, dried tomatoes and Parmesan cheese.
4. Using a small rubber spatula, stir the bottom and edges of the pan to encourage even cooking. Stir for 30 seconds or until the mixture begins to form curds.
5. Place in the preheated oven and cook for approximately 8 minutes or until the eggs are just set.
6. Remove immediately from the heat and transfer to a platter. Top with the pesto, goat cheese, Sicilian olives and pine nuts.
7. Toss the arugula, fennel and chives with a drizzle of the preserved lemon dressing. Season lightly with salt.
8. Arrange the salad over the frittata and serve immediately.

PRESERVED LEMON DRESSING

½ cup (125 mL) vegetable oil

¼ cup (60 mL) lemon juice

¼ cup (60 mL) finely chopped preserved lemons (page 244)

2 tsp (10 mL) sugar

1 tsp (5 mL) champagne vinegar

1. Combine all ingredients into a deep container and using a hand-held blender, purée all ingredients until they are emulsified and the lemon rind is finely chopped. Alternatively, use a food processor to achieve a smooth dressing.
2. Transfer to an airtight container and refrigerate. The dressing can be stored refrigerated for 10 days. Mix well before use.

FRENCH TOAST WITH BERRIES

It's the little things that Dawn Doucette does to transform this: the thick sourdough, the orange zest, the ground cinnamon. And of course the maple syrup (we use Quebec's Cosman & Webb Single Forest Organic Maple Syrup), which is one of the best foods on earth, instead of pancake syrup, which is one of the worst.

1980s 1990s 2000s **2010s**

MAKES 8 PIECES

8 slices sourdough bread (1 inch/2.5 cm thick), day-old or slightly stale

French toast egg mix (recipe follows)

1 oz (28 g or 2 tbsp/30 mL) butter

Maple syrup

Whipped cream

Mixed berry compote (recipe follows)

Icing sugar

1. Heat a griddle or large nonstick pan over medium heat.
2. Dip the bread slices one at a time into the French toast egg mix, submerging for 15 seconds. Gently press your fingers up and down the bread to maximize absorption of the egg mix. Make sure both sides are well soaked. Repeat with the remaining slices.
3. Simultaneously, place the butter onto the preheated griddle or pan and allow it to melt and foam but do not brown! Cook the bread slices as soon as you finish dipping them, transferring the soaked bread one at a time onto the griddle.
4. Cook the first side for 4 minutes or until golden brown, and then flip and cook for another 3 to 4 minutes or until golden brown as well.
5. Transfer to a plate and serve with maple syrup, whipped cream, berry compote and icing sugar as desired.

FRENCH TOAST EGG MIX

4 eggs

½ cup (125 mL) whole milk

2 tbsp (30 mL) heavy cream

1 tsp (5 mL) vanilla extract

½ tsp (2.5 mL) orange zest

1. In a large bowl, mix the eggs until they are well scrambled.
2. Add the milk, cream, vanilla extract and orange zest. Use immediately.

MIXED BERRY COMPOTE

10 oz (285 g) frozen mixed berries such as blackberries, raspberries or strawberries

½ cup (125 mL) sugar

3 tbsp (45 mL) water

¼ tsp (1.25 mL) ground cinnamon

8 oz (225 g) frozen blueberries

1½ tsp (7.5 mL) lemon juice

1. Combine the frozen mixed berries, sugar, water and cinnamon in a medium-sized pot and bring to a simmer, stirring occasionally.
2. Reduce the heat to low and cook for 20 to 30 minutes or until slightly thickened. The berries should be broken down into a thick jam-like consistency.
3. Add the frozen blueberries and simmer for an additional 5 minutes.
4. Remove from heat and add the lemon juice.
5. Serve slightly warm, or if made ahead, cool completely and transfer to an airtight container. Refrigerate for 3 days maximum.

CROQUE MADAME

Another case of elevating the potentially ordinary, again from Dawn Doucette. Check out the roasted serrano sauce!

1980s 1990s 2000s **2010s**

MAKES 4 SANDWICHES

12 oz (350 g) thinly shaved Virginia ham

8 slices sourdough bread

1 oz (28 g or 2 tbsp/30 mL) room-temperature butter

4 oz (115 g) white cheddar, shredded

4 poached eggs

Roasted serrano cream sauce (recipe follows)

1 tbsp (15 mL) finely chopped chives

1. Heat the ham in the microwave for 45 seconds or until just warm. This will ensure a thoroughly hot sandwich and cheese that melts nicely.
2. Spread the butter over one side of the sourdough bread. Flip the bread so that the buttered side is facing down.
3. Arrange the bread so that you have two rows.
4. Evenly distribute the shredded cheese over the sandwich bottoms and top with the heated ham, making sure there is even coverage. Close the sandwiches.
5. Place the sandwiches on a preheated griddle or nonstick pan. Cook until golden brown on the first side, approximately 3 minutes.
6. Flip and continue cooking until the second side is also golden brown and the cheese is fully melted.
7. Transfer each sandwich to a plate and top with a poached egg. Pour about ½ cup (125 mL) of roasted serrano cream sauce over the egg and the sandwich.
8. Garnish with some chives. Serve immediately.

ROASTED SERRANO CREAM SAUCE

1 serrano pepper, whole

2½ cups (600 mL) heavy cream

2 oz (57 g) grated Parmesan cheese

2 oz (57 g) shredded white cheddar

½ tsp (2.5 mL) fine salt

1. Place the whole serrano pepper on a foil-lined tray and roast under a broiler until the outside is charred and the pepper is soft. This will take approximately 10 minutes.
2. Immediately place in a sealed container to allow the skin to loosen from the flesh. Once the pepper is cool enough to handle, peel off the skin and remove the stem and seeds. Chop the flesh roughly and place in a pot along with the cream.
3. Bring to a low simmer and continue simmering until reduced to about 2 cups (500 mL). Strain through a sieve and discard the peppers.
4. Return the reduced cream to the same pot and bring back to a simmer. Add the Parmesan and white cheddar, stirring constantly until the cheeses are fully melted, approximately 3 minutes.
5. Sir in the salt and remove from heat. Strain through the sieve again to ensure a smooth consistency.
6. Keep warm before serving.

BREAKFAST SANDWICH

Proof again, this time from Chef Ryan Stone, that aioli ranks with the most magical of kitchen ingredients. Here it adds that little bit of zing that would be absent from a sandwich like this if it contained only the conventional elements, however complementary they may be.

1980s 1990s 2000s **2010s**

MAKES 4 SANDWICHES

8 slices dry-cured bacon

1 oz (28 g or 2 tbsp/30 mL) butter

8 slices sourdough bread

Caramelized lemon aioli (recipe follows)

4 oz (115 g) thinly sliced Gouda cheese

2 tbsp (30 mL) vegetable oil

8 eggs

½ tsp (2.5 mL) fine salt

½ tsp (2.5 mL) ground black pepper

4 green lettuce leaves

8 slices tomato

1. In a large nonstick skillet, cook the bacon to your preferred level of doneness, but don't make it overly crisp.
2. Spread the butter over one side of the bread.
3. Once the bacon is cooked, drain it on paper towels and wipe down the pan. Use the same skillet to cook the buttered sides of the sourdough bread. The bread should be golden brown and toasted on the buttered side. Remove from heat.
4. Arrange the bread so that you have two rows.
5. Spread 1 tablespoon (15 mL) caramelized lemon aioli on the non-griddled side of each slice (making a total of 2 tablespoons (30 mL) of caramelized lemon aioli for each sandwich).
6. Evenly distribute the sliced cheese over the heels.
7. In a separate nonstick skillet, heat 1 tablespoon (15 mL) of vegetable oil until it ripples. Carefully break 4 eggs into the pan, spacing them around 1 inch (2.5 cm) apart. Keep the yolks soft if you prefer and cook to your desired temperature. Season with salt and pepper. Immediately transfer the cooked eggs over the cheese so that it melts slightly.
8. Cook the remaining 4 eggs and place them over the cheese.
9. Arrange the lettuce over the crown followed by 2 slices of tomatoes, topped by the bacon. Repeat with the remaining sandwiches.
10. Put the sandwiches together and cut each sandwich in half neatly.
11. Transfer each sandwich to a plate and serve immediately.

CARAMELIZED LEMON AIOLI

1 lemon

½ tsp (2.5 mL) vegetable oil

½ cup (125 mL) mayonnaise

2 tsp (10 mL) confit garlic (page 242)

1. Cut the lemon in half crosswise.
2. Heat the vegetable oil in a small skillet over medium heat until it ripples.
3. Place the lemon halves cut side down on the pan and caramelize until golden brown, approximately 3 to 5 minutes.
4. Press the lemon halves through a citrus press and collect the juice in a medium-sized bowl. Strain the juice through a fine mesh strainer to remove any seeds or flesh that may have gotten through.
5. Combine the mayonnaise and confit garlic with the lemon juice. Whisk together until all ingredients are homogeneous.
6. If made ahead, transfer to an airtight container and refrigerate. The aioli can be stored refrigerated for 5 days maximum.

RICOTTA PANCAKES
WITH ROASTED PEARS

1980s 1990s 2000s **2010s**

SERVES 4–6

1 tsp (5 mL) vegetable oil

Ricotta pancake batter (recipe follows)

1 cup (250 mL) ricotta, divided

Roasted pears (recipe follows)

1 cup (250 mL) orange segments
(page 209)

Maple butter (page 97)

Maple syrup

Brian Skinner says that within the Chef Collective he has the reputation of "cooking for the ladies," and sure enough, when he first unveiled this ricotta pancake dish with berries and lemon, female tasters were suitably impressed. But that dish was for the summertime. This alternative for the other three seasons takes advantage of pears' status as good keepers, and appeals equally to the gents.

1. Heat the vegetable oil in a griddle or large nonstick pan over medium heat until it ripples.
2. Scoop ¼ cup (60 mL) of batter for each pancake and allow to cook. You can cook as many as you can fit in your pan.
3. Divide 2 teaspoons (10 mL) of ricotta in small pieces on top of the cooking batter.
4. After approximately 2 minutes, once the surface bubbles of the pancake begin to pop, flip the pancake and cook for another 1 to 2 minutes.
5. Arrange the pancakes ricotta side up on each plate. Top with some warm roasted pears, orange segments and 1 tablespoon (15 mL) of maple butter.
6. Garnish with 2 teaspoons (10 mL) of ricotta in several small pieces around the pancakes.
7. Repeat with the remaining plates and serve with maple syrup on the side.

ROASTED PEARS

1 lb (450 g) peeled and cored Bosc or
Anjou pears

1 oz (28 g or 2 tbsp/30 mL) melted salted
butter

1. Preheat the oven to 400°F (200°C).
2. Peel and core each pear and slice into ½-inch- (1 cm) thick lengthwise slices.
3. Toss together with the butter until evenly coated.
4. Transfer the pears to a parchment-lined rimmed baking tray.
5. Bake for 6 minutes. Immediately remove from the oven and allow to cool completely.
6. The pears can be stored refrigerated for up to 2 days.

RICOTTA PANCAKE BATTER

2 cups (500 mL) all-purpose flour

⅓ cup (80 mL) sugar

1 tsp (5 mL) baking powder

1 tsp (5 mL) baking soda

¾ tsp (3.75 mL) fine salt

3 eggs + 1 egg yolk, separated

1 cup (250 mL) buttermilk

¼ cup (60 mL) melted salted butter

1 tsp (5 mL) vanilla extract

2 tbsp (30 mL) minced preserved lemon
(page 244)

1. Sift the flour into a large mixing bowl. Add the sugar, baking powder, baking soda and fine salt.
2. Using a hand mixer, whisk the egg whites in a separate bowl until medium-sized peaks form. Add the buttermilk and mix on medium speed until well combined, approximately 15 seconds.
3. Add the egg yolks, melted butter and vanilla to the egg white mixture, and mix on medium speed until combined, approximately 15 seconds.
4. Add the flour mixture and preserved lemon to the egg mixture and mix on the lowest speed for 15 to 20 seconds. There will still be pockets of flour in the batter—this is what you want.
5. Fold the batter by hand until it is just mixed.

AVOCADO CHORIZO HASH

What is it about eggs Benedict that makes it such a classic? The eggs, the ham, the English muffin? Of course not. It's the hollandaise. Meanwhile, there's another breakfast classic—one that suggests hitting the trail rather than tucking in the napkin—the breakfast hash. As it happens, Reuben Major had long been in the habit of adding a little hollandaise to his own morning hashes, and he wondered if that would translate to a restaurant brunch. Answer: Yes!

1980s 1990s 2000s **2010s**

SERVES 4

1 lb (450 g) chorizo sausage meat

1 cup (250 mL) medium-diced white onion

Vegetable oil for deep-frying

1 lb (450 g) medium-diced red potatoes

2 tsp (10 mL) olive oil

1½ cups (375 mL) halved cremini, oyster or portobello mushrooms (or a mixture of each), chopped into 1-inch (2.5 cm) pieces

8 poached eggs

1 cup (250 mL) hollandaise sauce (recipe follows)

1 medium-diced avocado

1 tbsp (15 mL) finely chopped chives

1. Remove the casing from the chorizo sausage and break into ½-inch (1 cm) chunks.
2. Heat a nonstick skillet over medium heat and add the chorizo and onion, allowing the fat to render out and encouraging caramelization on all sides, approximately 5 minutes. Transfer to a platter.
3. Preheat a deep fryer or a large Dutch oven half full of vegetable oil over medium-high heat.
4. Once the oil has reached 300°F (150°C), carefully fry the diced potatoes until golden brown, approximately 4 to 5 minutes. Stir several times to ensure the pieces do not stick together.
5. Drain from the oil and transfer to a paper towel–lined bowl. Keep warm.
6. Using the same nonstick skillet used for the sausage, heat the olive oil until it ripples, and cook the mushrooms, caramelizing well and allowing all the liquid to evaporate. This step will take approximately 6 to 7 minutes.
7. Add the chorizo and onions and toss well.
8. Divide the potatoes evenly between each plate. Top with some of the chorizo mushroom mixture and add 2 poached eggs in the middle of the bowl.
9. Nap ¼ cup (60 mL) hollandaise sauce over the poached eggs.
10. Garnish each serving of hash with some avocado and chives.

HOLLANDAISE SAUCE

⅓ cup (80 mL) white wine vinegar

3 tbsp (45 mL) minced shallots

3 egg yolks

⅔ cup (160 mL) melted clarified butter

¾ tsp (3.75 mL) lemon juice

½ tsp (2.5 mL) Dijon mustard

Pinch cayenne

1. In a small pot, reduce the white wine vinegar and shallots until 2 tablespoons (30 mL) remains.
2. Place the egg yolks in a metal bowl over a pot of simmering water (or use a double boiler).
3. While whisking continuously, slowly stream in the vinegar shallot reduction until fully incorporated.
4. Continue whisking over the heat until the egg yolks turn pale yellow and thicken to the ribbon stage. Be careful to control your heat at this stage, as the eggs can overcook and scramble in seconds!
5. Using an immersion blender, keep the speed on medium as you slowly stream in the butter.
6. Slowly blend in the lemon juice, mustard and cayenne until fully combined.
7. Place in a very gentle steam bath to keep warm (approximately 100°F/38°C).

Ribbon stage is when you can lift the whisk out of the egg yolks and move it across the bowl and the trail of egg yolks dripping off of the whisk will momentarily hold its shape when it hits the surface of the yolks.

BLOODY CAESAR

It's always five o'clock somewhere. That's the philosophy of a surprising proportion of our brunch guests, and their drink of choice happens to be a concoction that ranks with insulin as Canada's most important gift to the world (whether the world knows it or not). So it's entirely appropriate that our beverage director, Cameron Bogue, has devoted more energy to the Caesar than to any other cocktail.

We'll get to Cameron's epic Caesar quest shortly, but first let's have a quick recap of the Caesar story. The year is 1969, and charged with inventing a signature drink for the opening of a Calgary hotel's Italian restaurant, the restaurant's manager, Walter Chell, casts his mind to Spaghetti Vongole and reasons that tomatoes and clams seem to go well together. Thus inspired, he mashes up some clams to extract their "nectar," and adds this to vodka, tomato juice and a blend of spices and Worcestershire sauce, and then serves the world's first Caesar, to instant acclaim. Coincidentally, around the same time, Mott's is in the process of introducing their proprietary Clamato. Canadians put two and two together, and the drink soon spreads from sea to sea to sea, so that in a typical year 350 million Caesars are consumed in Canada.

So, as Canadians know, a Caesar is always good—but how often is it great? Cameron Bogue happens to be a native of Portland, Oregon, and although much of his bartending career has played out in Canada, he nevertheless brought something of an outsider's skepticism to the task of perfecting the Caesar. Recognizing that the drink contains all five flavour constituents—sweet, sour, bitter, salty and umami—he gathered a large tasting panel and served them deconstructed Caesar after deconstructed Caesar, attempting to determine which spices and seasonings were ideal.

Then he took the preferred choices, blended them together, and further tweaked the seasoning mix with the help of additional tasters. The Caesar that we now serve our brunch customers contains 12 constituent parts within the drink itself and another 4 on the rim. In the

recipe reproduced here, we've provided the complete formula for rim spices but simplified the drink a little, because—sheesh—go to the work we do in putting together our seasonings and it will be five o'clock before you're drinking it. One further note from the Department of Don't Try This at Home: Cameron specifies that every Caesar be served with a pepperoni stick custom made using exactly the same spice mix.

EARLS SIGNATURE CAESAR

While we have had a classic Caesar on the menu for almost thirty years, this signature Caesar was created by Cameron Bogue in 2010.

1. Rim a Mason glass with Caesar rim spice and pack the glass with ice.
2. Add the vodka, followed by the Clamato juice and then the Caesar spice mix (according to your desired heat level).
3. Garnish with a lime wedge, pickle spear and jerky or landjäger sausage.
4. Serve with a straw.

1980s 1990s 2000s 2010s

MAKES 1 CAESAR

Caesar rim spice (recipe follows)

1.5 fl oz (45 mL) premium vodka

4 fl oz (120 mL) Mott's Clamato juice

1 to 2 tbsp (15 to 30 mL) Caesar spice mix (recipe follows)

Lime wedge

Pickle spear

Beef jerky or landjäger sausage (see note)

Earls has a Vancouver butcher make the jerky we serve at our Canadian locations using the same dry spice mix we use for the rim.

CAESAR RIM SPICE

MAKES 1 CUP

½ cup (125 mL) roasted garlic pepper spice

⅓ cup (80 mL) celery salt

1 tbsp (15 mL) coarsely ground black pepper

1. Combine all ingredients in a lidded container and shake thoroughly to mix everything together well.
2. Store at room temperature in a tightly sealed container for up to 2 weeks.

CAESAR SPICE MIX

MAKES 1 CUP

1½ tsp (7.5 mL) Montreal steak spice

1 tsp (5 mL) prepared horseradish

¼ tsp (1.25 mL) onion powder

¼ cup + 1 tbsp (75 mL) HP sauce

¼ cup (60 mL) Worcestershire sauce

3 tbsp (45 mL) pickle brine

1 tbsp (15 mL) soy sauce

1½ tbsp (22.5 mL) green Tabasco

½ tsp (2.5 mL) red Tabasco

1. Combine all ingredients and whisk thoroughly to distribute everything evenly.
2. Refrigerate in a sealed container until needed and shake well before use. This mix can be stored for up to 9 days in a sealed container. Exposure to air will decrease the potency of the spices.

earls fall chicken feastival featuring

CHICKEN HUNAN

KUNG POW!

and other favourite chicken dishes

FIG.1

FIG.3

FIG.

FIG.3

FIG.1   FIG.2   FIG.3

pantry items

In theory this chapter is devoted to the basics: the routine, low-stress building blocks that even a small child can easily master. And if you believe that, let us tell you about our tomato sauce.

Chuck spent his first twelve years at Earls trying and failing to come up with a decent tomato sauce, and not even because he really wanted to, but because Stan Fuller—his boss, remember—asked him to. Every couple of years he'd go back to the drawing board, if that's what you call a test kitchen, and every couple of years he'd come up with something that didn't completely nail it.

Chuck's experience may have been maddening, but it was also instructive, and ultimately he came to several realizations. First, he was cooking his sauce too long. A shorter cooking time makes for fresher flavours. Second, and somewhat conversely, fresh tomatoes aren't necessarily best. For one thing, most are picked green or grown in greenhouses in artificial media and with middling exposure to the sun. During tomato season, yes, fresh may be the way to go, but otherwise, canned tomatoes and tomato pastes and purées are often better, since the tomatoes were probably picked ripe and from a field. Third, there is one particular variety of tomato that makes the very best sauce, and one particular processor, in North America at least, that cans them in the best possible way.

That variety is the San Marzano, which originated in a town of the same name near Naples. San Marzanos are stronger-tasting, sweeter and less acidic than more popular Romas (which were in fact bred from San Marzanos). As for the supplier, it is California-based Stanislaus Food Products, which does indeed use only tomatoes picked fresh from the fields.

One final, vexing detail: Stanislaus sells its products only to restaurants. Sorry about this, but the only way to be sure you're going to taste the perfect tomato sauce tonight is by eating at Earls.

VEGETABLE STOCK

Over the past few years we've reformulated all of our basics to remove meat products where not absolutely necessary, which allows us to assure vegetarians that the meal they've asked for truly is vegetarian. Here's a vegetarian stock that can be subbed for chicken or other stocks in recipes of many kinds.

MAKES 4 CUPS (1L)

1 cup (250 mL) red onion trim

½ cup (125 mL) carrot trim

½ cup (125 mL) celery trim

1 tbsp (15 mL) vegetable oil

5 cups (1.25 L) water

½ cup (125 mL) tomato trim

1 tbsp (15 mL) confit garlic (page 242)

¼ cup (60 mL) parsley stems

2 thyme sprigs

1 bay leaf

1. Preheat the oven to 425°F (220°C).
2. Roughly chop the onion, carrot and celery. Toss with the vegetable oil and transfer to a parchment-lined rimmed baking tray.
3. Bake in the preheated oven for 18 to 20 minutes or until the vegetables are caramelized.
4. Remove the vegetables from the oven and place in a large pot along with the water, tomato trim, confit garlic, parsley stems, thyme and bay leaf.
5. Bring to a simmer over high heat, then reduce heat to low and continue simmering for approximately 45 minutes or until reduced to 4 cups (1L) after straining the solids.
6. Strain the liquid through a fine mesh strainer and discard the solids.
7. Transfer to an airtight container and refrigerate. The vegetable stock can be stored refrigerated for 9 days maximum or frozen for 2 months.

This recipe gives exact measurements, but in reality, you may have different combinations of leftover vegetables. You don't have to follow this recipe to the letter. Use what you have on hand, and as long as the total ratio of vegetables to liquid remains the same, you will end up with a flavourful stock that will provide great base notes of flavour to the recipes you use it in.

QUESADILLA SPICE

MAKES ⅔ CUP (160 mL)

3 tbsp (45 mL) ground black pepper

2 tbsp (30 mL) ground cumin

2 tbsp (30 mL) fine salt

2 tbsp (30 mL) chili powder

1 tbsp (15 mL) dried ground oregano

1. Combine all the spices until very well mixed. Store in a dry container, sealed well.

If you cannot find dried ground oregano, you can grind regular dried oregano in a spice grinder until it is the same consistency as the chili powder.

CAJUN BLACKENING SPICE

MAKES 1 CUP (225 mL)

2 tbsp (30 mL) dried oregano

1 tbsp (15 mL) dried thyme

1 tsp (5 mL) red pepper flakes

½ cup (125 mL) paprika

1 tbsp (15 mL) ground black pepper

1 tbsp (15 mL) ground white pepper

1 tbsp (15 mL) fine salt

1 tsp (5 mL) ground cayenne

1. Grind the dried oregano, thyme and red pepper flakes in a clean spice grinder until the mixture is the same texture as the paprika. Combine with the rest of the ingredients and mix very well until thoroughly distributed. Store in a dry container, sealed well.

Increase the cayenne if you like a spicier blend.

BRINED CHICKEN

Brining the chicken not only improves the flavour greatly, but also causes the protein strands in the chicken to retain water during and after cooking. This results in flavourful, moist chicken that makes all the difference compared to unbrined chicken. The same brine can be used for pork chops, turkey or any lean meat.

Chicken breasts/pieces (skin-on bone-in or boneless skinless depending on recipe)

Chicken brine (recipe follows)

1. Place the chicken pieces in a large lidded container, making sure there is ample space between each piece to have contact with the brine.
2. Cover with enough brine to submerge each piece of chicken completely. Seal well.
3. Refrigerate on the bottom shelf for 24 hours before using.
4. Once the time has elapsed, strain off the brine and discard it. Transfer the chicken to a clean rimmed baking tray.
5. Pat the chicken dry with paper towels. Use according to the recipe.

CHICKEN BRINE

MAKES 2 CUPS (500 mL)

2 cups (500 mL) water

¼ cup (60 mL) fine salt

½ cup (125 mL) parsley leaves and stems (tightly packed)

1 tbsp (15 mL) honey

1 tbsp (15 mL) black peppercorns

6 bay leaves

4 garlic cloves, smashed

2 thyme sprigs

1 lemon, halved

1. Combine all ingredients in an appropriately sized pot and bring to a boil over high heat. Boil for 1 minute.
2. Remove from heat and allow to cool to room temperature.
3. The brine can be stored refrigerated for up to 7 days.

STICKY TOFFEE SAUCE

MAKES 1 CUP (250 mL)

4 oz (115 g or ½ cup/125 mL) salted butter

½ cup (125 mL) tightly packed brown sugar

½ cup (125 mL) heavy cream

½ tsp (2.5 mL) vanilla extract

We have two sticky sauces we use on our desserts: a caramel sauce and a toffee sauce. The caramel sauce is best known as the gooey sauce we pour over our Warm Gingerbread Cake. It's pretty complicated—it requires a candy thermometer, quite a few ingredients, and careful watching as we slowly cook it. The toffee sauce on the other hand, which we use for our chocolate sticky toffee pudding and our ice cream sundae, is simple and dare we even say, foolproof. You might see us on TV cooking the gingerbread cake around the holidays, and when we do we substitute the toffee sauce instead because it has just four ingredients, cooks in about one minute and can sit in your fridge for week or so—and it's delicious.

1. In a medium-sized pot over medium heat, melt the butter and brown sugar together until completely melted and the butter begins to foam.
2. Slowly stream in the heavy cream, whisking well until fully incorporated.
3. Return the heat to a simmer, and then remove from heat and whisk in the vanilla extract.
4. Allow to cool completely before transferring to an airtight container. The sticky toffee sauce can be stored refrigerated for 9 days.

SAN MARZANO TOMATO SAUCE

MAKES 3½ CUPS (800 mL)

1 28 oz can (approximately 3½ cups/800 mL) whole San Marzano tomatoes

1 tbsp (15 mL) tightly packed fresh oregano leaves

1 tsp (5 mL) fine salt

1. Use your hands or a pair of scissors to break the tomatoes down to approximately ¼- to ½-inch (½ to 1 cm) pieces.
2. Finely julienne the oregano and add to the tomatoes along with the salt. Mix well.
3. Can be prepared ahead and held refrigerated up to 4 days ahead. Stir well before use.

SALSA

MAKES 2 CUPS (500 mL)

1 lb (450 g) Roma, beefsteak or hothouse tomatoes (see note)

1 oz (30 g) serrano peppers

2 tsp (10 mL) minced garlic

1 tsp (5 mL) fine salt

You can use Roma, beefsteak or hothouse tomatoes for this recipe, choosing whichever is the ripest and most flavourful during the season. Charring the tomatoes and serrano peppers is an important step to attaining the smoky flavour. Just make sure you turn your exhaust fan on high while broiling!

1. Place the tomatoes on a baking sheet (do not line with parchment as it will burn during the charring process). Broil in the oven for approximately 5 minutes or until the skin of the tomatoes is blackened and cracked, exposing the flesh of the tomatoes underneath.

2. Remove from the oven and, using tongs, flip the tomatoes to expose the parts underneath to the heat of the broiler. Repeat the charring for another 5 minutes. Remove from the oven and transfer to a deep bowl.

3. Remove the stems from the serranos and repeat the charring process on one side only of the chilies, approximately 4 to 5 minutes. Combine with the tomatoes in the deep bowl.

4. Add the garlic and salt and purée with an immersion blender. Alternatively, transfer all ingredients to a regular blender or processor and purée until smooth. Refrigerate until needed. Can be stored for 5 days.

PESTO

MAKES 1½ CUPS (375 mL)

2 cups (500 mL) fresh basil leaves (tightly packed)

⅓ cup (80 mL) toasted pine nuts

½ cup (125 mL) finely grated Parmesan cheese

3 finely minced garlic cloves (about 1 tbsp/15 mL)

½ tsp (2.5 mL) fine salt

½ tsp (2.5 mL) ground black pepper

½ cup (125 mL) olive oil

1. Place the basil and pine nuts in the bowl of a food processor. Pulse 3 or 4 times until the basil and pine nuts are finely chopped.
2. Add the Parmesan cheese, garlic, salt and pepper, pulsing a few more times until pasty.
3. With the food processor running, drizzle in the olive oil in a slow stream. Be patient with the process: adding the oil slowly will help emulsify the sauce and keep it from separating.
4. Can be prepared ahead and stored refrigerated for up to 4 days. Stir well before use.

This is the most basic version of pesto. You can substitute almonds, walnuts or pistachios for the pine nuts for interesting variations. The basil can also be combined or substituted with different soft herbs such as oregano, tarragon, arugula or spinach.

CONFIT GARLIC AND GARLIC OIL

MAKES 1⅓ CUPS (330 mL) PUREED GARLIC CONFIT
MAKES ¾ CUP (180 mL) CONFIT GARLIC OIL

1 lb (450 g or 2¾ cups/660 mL) peeled garlic cloves

½ cup (125 mL) olive oil

½ cup (125 mL) vegetable oil

1. In a medium-sized pot, bring all ingredients to a gentle simmer over medium-low heat.
2. Reduce heat to low and continue simmering until garlic cloves are golden brown and soft, approximately 1 hour. Stir occasionally to promote even cooking.
3. Remove from heat and drain the confit garlic, reserving the garlic oil in a separate container. Allow the oil to cool completely.
4. Purée the confit garlic using a hand-held blender or food processor. The garlic should form a smooth paste.
5. Transfer to an airtight container and refrigerate. The puréed garlic can be stored refrigerated for 2 weeks. The garlic oil can be stored refrigerated for 3 weeks.

This recipe keeps for weeks in the refrigerator, so make more than you need!

CONFIT GARLIC BUTTER

MAKES 1½ CUPS (375 mL)

8 oz (225 g or 1 cup/250 mL) room-temperature butter

⅓ cup (80 mL) confit garlic purée (page 242)

1 tbsp (15 mL) finely chopped parsley

½ tbsp (7.5 mL) Dijon mustard

½ tsp (2.5 mL) ground black pepper

½ tsp (2.5 mL) fine salt

1. In the bowl of a stand mixer or using a hand-held blender, whip the butter until light and fluffy. The butter will double in volume once properly whipped.
2. Add the rest of the ingredients and mix very well, scraping down the bowl several times to make sure everything is well mixed.
3. Transfer to an airtight container and refrigerate. The confit garlic butter can be stored refrigerated for two weeks or frozen up to a month.

A batch of confit garlic butter is handy to keep around in the freezer. It's great on top of steak, with steamed mussels or even with hot pasta!

ROASTED RED PEPPERS

MAKES ABOUT 2 CUPS (500 mL)

1½ lb (680 g) red peppers, whole

¾ cup (180 mL) balsamic vinegar

½ cup (125 mL) vegetable oil

¼ cup (60 mL) olive oil

1 tsp (5 mL) confit garlic (page 242)

½ tsp (2.5 mL) fine salt

½ tsp (2.5 mL) ground black pepper

1. Preheat the oven to 350°F (180°C).
2. Halve each red pepper, removing the stem and seeds. Place the pepper halves skin side up on a parchment-lined baking tray.
3. Bake for 18 to 25 minutes or until the skin side is slightly blackened and the peppers are soft. Place in a lidded container for 15 minutes to allow the skin to loosen from the flesh. Peel the skin off using your fingers, trying to keep the peppers as intact as possible.
4. Combine the balsamic vinegar, vegetable oil, olive oil, confit garlic, salt and pepper into a clean sealable container.
5. Submerge the peppers in the marinade overnight. Remove the peppers from the marinade.
6. Transfer to an airtight container and refrigerate. The roasted red peppers can be stored refrigerated for 5 days.

PRESERVED LEMONS

MAKES 8 PRESERVED LEMONS

8 lemons

½ cup (125 mL) coarse salt

2½ tsp (12.5 mL) coriander seed

1 cinnamon stick

2 bay leaves

⅔ cup (160 mL) lemon juice

1. Rinse and scrub the lemons. Cut off the stems, and then partially cut in half lengthwise, retaining 1 inch (2.5 cm) uncut from the base. Then make another lengthwise cut perpendicular to the first cut as if you are cutting an X into each lemon but not all the way through. The cuts will look like quartering a lemon.
2. Toss the lemons with the coarse salt, coriander seed, cinnamon stick and bay leaves. Use your hands to pack the salt into the lemons.
3. Transfer the lemons into a large lidded container. Press the lemons down firmly to encourage the juices to release.
4. Close the container and let sit at room temperature overnight.
5. The next day, press the lemons down firmly to encourage more juice to release. Repeat this step on the third day.
6. After the third day, add the lemon juice and seal the lid. Allow to sit at room temperature for 30 days before using.
7. After 30 days place in the refrigerator. Store for 5 months maximum.
8. To use preserved lemons in cooking, remove one from the container and rinse to remove the salt. Discard any seeds and pulp and use only the rind. Chop finely.

RED PEPPER RELISH

MAKES 2 CUPS (500 mL)

1 cup (250 mL) white wine vinegar

¾ cup (180 mL) ¼-inch (½ cm) diced white onion

1⅔ cup (400 mL) ¼-inch (½ cm) diced red peppers

1 tsp (5 mL) crushed red chili flakes

¼ cup (60 mL) sugar

1 tbsp (15 mL) grainy Dijon mustard

1. In a medium-sized pot, bring the white wine vinegar, onion, red peppers and chili flakes to a boil. Immediately reduce heat to low and simmer, stirring occasionally, until only ⅓ of the liquid remains. This will take 20 to 25 minutes.
2. Stir in the sugar and mustard. Continue to cook until the consistency turns syrupy, about 15 minutes.
3. Transfer to an airtight container and refrigerate. The relish can be stored refrigerated for 5 days.

JACK DANIEL'S BARBECUE SAUCE FOR RIBS

MAKES 2 CUPS (500 mL)

⅔ cup (160 mL) ketchup

½ cup (125 mL) tomato paste

⅓ cup (80 mL) Jack Daniel's Whiskey

3 tbsp (45 mL) apple cider vinegar

2 tbsp (30 mL) white vinegar

1 tbsp + 1 tsp (20 mL) Worcestershire sauce

1 tbsp (15 mL) molasses

1 tsp (5 mL) ground black pepper

½ tsp (2.5 mL) fine salt

½ tsp (2.5 mL) celery seeds

¼ tsp (1.25 mL) cayenne pepper

1. Bring all ingredients to a boil in a medium-sized pot. Allow to cool to room temperature.
2. Transfer to an airtight container and refrigerate. The barbecue sauce can be stored refrigerated for 5 days.

DEMI-GLACE

MAKES 2½ TO 3 CUPS (600 TO 750 mL), DEPENDING HOW MUCH IT IS REDUCED

1 oz (28 g or 2 tbsp/30 mL) butter

½ cup (125 mL) roughly chopped onion

½ cup (125 mL) roughly chopped celery

½ cup (125 mL) roughly chopped carrots

¼ cup (60 mL) all-purpose flour

5 cups (1.25 L) beef stock (canned or boxed)

1 bay leaf

2 large sprigs fresh thyme

8 stems fresh parsley

10 whole black peppercorns

2 tbsp (30 mL) red wine

1. Heat the butter over medium heat in a large Dutch oven. Once it has melted, add the onions, celery and carrots. Sauté until translucent and softened.
2. Sprinkle in the flour and stir to coat the vegetables. Cook the flour for approximately 3 minutes, stirring constantly. The flour should smell toasted and will turn light brown.
3. Slowly pour in a little beef stock, stirring constantly to avoid lumps.
4. Pour in the rest of the beef stock and the remaining ingredients, except the red wine.
5. Bring to a simmer and allow to reduce by half, approximately 40 minutes.
6. Strain the sauce through a fine mesh strainer or a layer of coarse cheesecloth and return to the pot. Discard the solids.
7. Add the red wine and return to a simmer.
8. Remove from the heat and allow to cool.
9. Transfer to an airtight container and refrigerate. The demi-glace can be stored refrigerated for 9 days or frozen for a month.

This demi-glace is a quick version because it uses already prepared beef stock but enriches it with sautéed vegetables—a more realistic sauce than making everything from scratch!

the next chapter

Back in the 1980s and 1990s, some guys with names like Bus, Stan, Chuck, Larry, Stew, George and David did an extraordinary thing. They invented a new kind of restaurant, and in fact an entire category of restaurants (generally called "premium casual") that's one of the fastest-growing segments in the industry, both in Canada and the US. Bus's view is that much of our history was a cosmic accident that just kind of happened, so here's a question: What if a bunch of younger people sat down and seriously strategized about remaking our restaurant so that it could shine just as brightly over the next couple of decades as the current Earls has until now? What would that look like?

Well, we're going to find out.

In the months before this book was published, that new Earls was slated to open its doors in Calgary. Called Earls 67, it takes over a prime location opened in time for the 1988 Winter Olympics and in need of buffing up. Except that it hasn't been buffed up, it's been taken apart like little Johnny did the alarm clock and put back together like Steve Jobs and company did the Macintosh.

Maybe because Earls president Mo Jessa is a Calgary boy, he's taken an extra-special interest in this project, although it's also true that a venture like this might be expected to have the president's attention. So let's put Mo on the spot as we explore the Restaurant of the Future Today.

Mo, why would anyone change something as perfect as an Earls?

Mo: The reality of young people is very different from that of boomers or Gen-Xers. They live in smaller spaces; their work lives involve long hours over a computer; they use and love social media but they also need to connect in person; they're more health-conscious but they're also up for some hedonism.

Right. But what does that have to do with altering the perfection that is an Earls?

Mo: So you do a place that says, hey, they understand me! You call up a few of Canada's most innovative design firms, say Craig Stanghetta's Ste Marie Design and Phoebe Glasfurd of Glasfurd & Walker and ask "If you were doing the first Earls ever—nothing off the shelf, no multiple locations, everything consciously sourced— what would it look like?" And the answer is, it looks pretty different. On one end you have a kind of beer hall/luncheonette with communal tables. On the other a glamorous cocktail lounge, with locally distilled spirits, all of that. In the middle a coffee bar, but not what you'd expect: the best coffee program in town, not from us, but from a local coffee spot that's already acknowledged as the best around. You put USB connections and charger plugs in the tables, and filter the local water so that no one needs to drink pop or bottled water. There will be areas that are used in three or four different ways, from morning, through lunch, during the afternoon, at dinner, and late at night.

That's great. Will there be food, by any chance?

Mo: Some items from the Earls menu, though not as you imagine them, and lots of new ones too, and many in a whole different style. More small plates for sharing. Robata grills so we can do those smaller servings—marinated beef skewers, say. A real sense of where the food comes from—the plants and animals, the ways things are cooked. Some extravagant dishes but, for example, a dish that matches champagne with a hot dog. You know, high/low. But that only works if the hot dog is

unbelievable, so that's been formulated by a local sausage maker, again the best around.

Thank you for doing this, Mo.

Mo: Wait, there's more. You didn't ask about the parrots.

The parrots? Aren't they a little, uh, jejune?

Mo: That's what some designers must have thought, so they were phased out a few years ago, but the team working on Earls 67 loves them all over again, so they're back.

And there you have it: parrots! Earls for a new generation.

Mo Jessa, Earls President

index

acknowledgements

Our sincere thanks goes to Chef Fay Duong, who not only spent countless hours re-testing and re-measuring hundreds of old recipes, but did them all in her own home kitchen to make sure they would work in your kitchen and who, along with Chef Dawn Doucette, prepared and styled each of the dishes we photographed for the book.

This book wouldn't exist without Cate Simpson, who project managed by wrangling chefs, writers, photographers and the Fuller family to produce, not just a cookbook, but a historic record of one of Canada's most successful family owned restaurants.

And lastly, thanks to John Sherlock, David Strongman and Clinton Hussey for their wonderful photography; Jim Sutherland for his writing expertise; Becky Paris Turner for her cover styling; Clay Fuller and Mo Jessa for their countless hours of research; Robert McCullough of Appetite by Random House for holding our hand so gently; and the team at Penguin Random House: Lindsay Paterson, Paige Farrell and Bhavna Chauhan.

Menu

Traditionally brewed pale ale only at Earls

ple keep asking "What is my secret?" Great food, fresh, and a no frills approach, is the honest answer. ls, eat a little, eat a lot philosophy means you are eating the best for less. Garnishes, bread & butter & omitted so that fresh, daily prepared meats, chicken, fish & vegetables are served deliciously at unbelievable.

a lot · Fun to Share

lack pepper	4.95	French Style Onion Rings	2.95
o Skins	4.95	Thinly cut, crisp, lightly seasoned	
y smoked bacon		Fresh Herbed Italian Pan Bread	1.50
	4.95	w/extra virgin olive oil	
ortilla Chips	3.50	Grilled Garlic Italian Pan Bread	1.95
	6.95	Cheese Bread	2.95
cucumbers & cilantro		Homecut Fries	1.95
	6.95	- with gravy	2.25
es & cumin seed		- with peppercorn sauce	2.50
	6.95	Fresh Herbed Crust Pizza	4.95
	4.50		

Fresh Made Soups & Salads

Earl's House Salad — 3.95
Seasonal greens, romaine lettuce, tomato and cucumber tossed with Earl's personally selected balsamic vinegar and virgin olive oil

Thai Chicken Salad — 7.95
Thai dressing, chopped mint & cilantro over romaine, fresh steamed noodles & peanuts, with herbed lime chicken

Acapulco Chicken Salad — 6.95
w/sour cream & cilantro salsa

Caesar Salad — 3.95
w/Italian Grana Padano Parmesan
Entrée Size w/garlic bread — 6.95

Hot Chicken Caesar — 6.95
Blackened Chicken Caesar — 6.95
Lots of Clams Chowder — 3.50
Classic French Onion Soup — 3.50

We Make Our Soups From Scratch

Fresh West Coast Salmon

t - fresh fish, a variety of great salads. to tell you about today's fresh features.

Earl has this philosophy

Earl wanted to make Earl's different so he did. Earl's simple philosophy of great food, served fresh, without a lot of frills has never been compromised. In this fast-pace time of short cuts, Earl has never changed his high standard of delicious, wholesome food prepared fresh daily.

That's the difference at Earl's.

Eat a little Eat a lot

DRY RIBS	4.95	**GUACAMOLE & SALSA**
Fried until crispy and seasoned with coarse salt and pepper		**NACHOS** 6.95
		CHICKEN BURRITO 3.95
CHEDDAR AND BACON		**CHICKEN FINGERS** 4.95
POTATO SKINS	4.95	Fresh chicken breast, crunchy breading served
Aged cheddar and hickory smoked bacon		with a sweet plum sauce
MONTEREY BAY		**THUMBS UP** 4.50
CALAMARI	4.95	Crispy breading, jalapeno jack cheese
Monterey bay baby squid, tender and delicious with fresh yogurt, sour cream, cucumber, sweet onion and parsley.		served with Earl's super plum sauce
		CHICKEN
SALSA AND		**WINGS** 5.50
TORTILLA CHIPS 3.50		Fresh chicken wings. Crispy fried and seasoned hot.
SALSA NACHOS 6.95		
tortilla chips, cooked fresh. Italy freshly grated aged cheddar and jalapeno jack cheeses and jalapeno peppers. Earl makes his own salsa from sweet onions, cucumbers and tomatoes.		**FRENCH STYLE**
		ONION RINGS 2.95
		Thinly cut, crisp, lightly seasoned
GUACAMOLE		**ITALIAN PAN BREAD** 1.50
NACHOS 6.95		**GARLIC BREAD** 1.95
Earl's guacamole is made from two ripe avocados, limes and cumin seed.		**CHEESE BREAD** 2.95
		FRESH HOMECUT FRIES 1.75
		with gravy 1.95

Soups and Salads

Earl also uses his acclaimed soups, and made fresh daily in our kitchen. Earl adds fresh Grade A beef or chicken, fresh vegetables and a selection of herbs and spices. Earl's salads and dressings set a new standard for freshness and flavour.

That's the difference at Earl's.

THAI CHICKEN SALAD — 7.95
Thai dressing, chopped mint & cilantro over romaine, fresh steamed noodles and peanuts, herbed lime chicken.

ACAPULCO CHICKEN SALAD — 6.95
Sliced breast of grilled quesadilla chicken over crispy greens tossed with Italian parmesan dressing in a tortilla shell with fresh salsa and sour cream.

CAESAR SALAD — 3.95
Freshly grated parmesan, from Parma, Italy, chopped garlic, anchovies and crispy tomato have made this the "Earl" of salads.
Entrée size — 6.95

EARL'S HOUSE SALAD — 3.95
Seasonal greens, romaine lettuce, tomato and cucumber tossed with Earl's personally selected balsamic vinegar and virgin olive oil

BLACKENED CHICKEN CAESAR — 6.95
Chicken sauteed with Earl's blackening spices over our Caesar Salad.

CALAMARI CAESAR

CLAM CHOWDER
Lots of clams with clam, it's outstanding

FRENCH ONION
Slowly simmered stock, natural broth, sweet and sherry

GARLIC BREAD
CHEESE BREAD

Earl's Tips the Vine Fine Bit
Buy the Glass
Buy the Bottle

Made Fresh Daily Desserts

Mocha Kahlua Pie	3.95	
Nºodle Kahlua		
Double Decadent Custard		
Chocolate Mousse	3.95	
Fresh Hot Granny Smith Apple Pie	3.50	
with frozen yogurt	3.95	

Fresh Made From Our Own Kitchen

Fresh Baked Pecan Flan	3.50
Guittard Chocolate Pecan Flan	3.95
Frozen Yogurt Shakes	2.95
blackberry, raspberry, strawberry, chocolate, or vanilla	

The difference at Earls...

Earl's Favourites

FUZZY NAVEL			2.75
FROSTY VINE			3.75
STRAWBERRY	3.75	EARLS FRESH WATERMELON	
RASPBERRY	3.75	CHAMPAGNE COOLER	3.75
BLACKBERRY	3.75		
WATERMELON	3.75	COCKTAILS	3.75
		FESTIVALS	2.75
LONG ISLAND ICE TEA	3.75	PREMIUM COCKTAILS	3.95
		SPECIALS	2.95
CAESAR	3.75	LIQUEURS	2.95 3.95

Draught Beer

Pilsner	1.95	12 oz glass	2.25
	DOMESTIC		2.75
	AMERICAN		2.75
	IMPORTED	from	3.25

Eat a little · Eat a lot

SZECHWAN CHICKEN	4.95	SALSA AND TORTILLA CHIPS	2.50
DRY RIBS	3.95	THUMBS UP	4.50
CHEDDAR AND BACON POTATO SKINS	3.50	CHICKEN FINGERS	
MONTEREY BAY CALAMARI	4.95	CHICKEN WINGS	
		GARLIC BREAD	
CHEESE NACHOS WITH SALSA	5.25	CHEESE BREAD	
		FRESH HOMECUT	1.75
GUACAMOLE NACHOS	6.25	HOMECUT FRIES WITH GRAVY	
		HOMECUT FRIES WITH PEPPERCORN SAUCE	
		SAUTÉED VEGETABLE	

Summer Salads

HOT CHICKEN CAESAR	5.95	CAESAR SALAD	
TERIYAKI CHICKEN	5.95		

Fresh Herbed Crust Pizza

Earl uses ripe roma tomatoes, fresh basil, and aged Parmesan and Fontina Cheeses on his thin crispy herbed crust pizza — 4.95

Made Right Here With Pride

Entrées

Choice Grain Fed Lean, 28-day Aged Beef	
Fresh West Coast Salmon	Market Price
Top Sirloin Steak w/garlic bread	
Steak & Prawns	13.95
New York Steak	12.95
New York	13.95
w/Madagascar peppercorn sauce	
Blackened New York	13.95
Above items served with sauteed mushrooms & your choice of fresh pasta, homecut fries or baked potato (after 5 p.m.)	
Grilled Teriyaki Chicken Breast	
Teriyaki Chicken & Prawns	13.95
Blackened Cajun Chicken	9.95
Charbroiled Chicken	9.95
w/hickory B.B.Q. sauce	
Rack of B.B.Q. Pork Ribs	14.95
1/2 Rack of B.B.Q. Pork Ribs	10.95
B.B.Q. Chicken & Ribs	14.95
Above items served with your choice of fresh pasta, homecut fries or baked potato (after 5 p.m.)	

Bigger, Better Burgers

Bigger Better Burger	5.95
w/ripe beefsteak tomato, lettuce, onion, mayonnaise, mustard & pickle	
Cheddar Burger	6.50
Bacon Cheddar Burger	6.95
Jack Burger	6.50
Bacon Jack Burger	6.95
Mushroom Burger	6.95
Cheddar Chicken Sandwich	6.50
Earl's Uniquely Great Clubhouse	6.95
Charbroiled fresh chicken breast, hickory smoked bacon, lettuce, tomato & mayonnaise	
B.C.L.T.	
Earl's way with cheddar cheese	
Above items served w/homecut fries or side house salad.	
Chicken Quesadilla	6.95
w/cheddar & jalapeno jack cheese (& salad)	

guini	7.95	
n chopped basil and shallots, in a sun-ripened tomato sauce		
with Half Breast of Chicken	9.95	
with Spicy Calabrese Sausage	9.95	
tucini Alfredo	6.95	
h cream & Grana Padano Parmesan		
Earl's Size	9.95	
tucini Chicken Stirfry	8.95	
vegetables in a fresh grated ginger oyster sauce		
wn Stirfry	9.95	
wn & Chicken Stirfry	9.95	
etarian Stirfry	7.95	
Swiss chard, broccoli, sweet peppers and shiitake mushrooms served over steamed ese noodles with a ginger oyster sauce		

Menu

Traditionally brewed pale ale only at Earls

ple keep asking "What is my secret?" Great food, fresh, and a no frills approach, is the honest answer. ls, eat a little, eat a lot philosophy means you are eating the best for less. Garnishes, bread & butter & omitted so that fresh, daily prepared meats, chicken, fish & vegetables are served deliciously at unbelievable.

Gourmet Blend Cappuccinos & Lattes

zen Yogurt — 2.95
blackberry, raspberry, wberry or chocolate sauce
zen Yogurt — 3.95
pure clover honey
mocha kahlua sauce